X-Ways Forensics
Practitioner's Guide

X-Ways Forensics Practitioner's Guide

Brett Shavers

Eric Zimmerman

Jimmy Weg, Technical Editor

ELSEVIER

AMSTERDAM • BOSTON • HEIDELBERG • LONDON
NEW YORK • OXFORD • PARIS • SAN DIEGO
SAN FRANCISCO • SINGAPORE • SYDNEY • TOKYO

Syngress is an imprint of Elsevier

Acquiring Editor: *Chris Katsaropoulos*
Editorial Project Manager: *Benjamin Rearick*
Project Manager: *Punithavathy Govindaradjane*
Designer: *Matthew Limbert*

Syngress is an imprint of Elsevier
225 Wyman Street, Waltham, MA 02451, USA

Library of Congress Cataloging-in-Publication Data
Shavers, Brett.
  X-Ways Forensics practitioner's guide / Brett Shavers, Eric Zimmerman.
    pages cm
  Includes bibliographical references and index.
  ISBN 978-0-12-411605-4 (alk. paper)
1. X-Ways Forensics (Computer program) 2. Forensic sciences. 3. Criminal investigations.
I. Zimmerman, Eric, 1974- II. Title.
  HV8073.S4228 2014
  363.250285'53–dc23

                                                                                    2013022602

British Library Cataloguing-in-Publication Data
A catalogue record for this book is available from the British Library

ISBN: 978-0-12-411605-4

Printed and bound in the United States of America
Transferred to Digital Printing in 2013

www.elsevier.com • www.bookaid.org

For information on all Syngress publications, visit our website at *store.elsevier.com/Syngress*

Introduction

INTRODUCTION

The need for this book arose because some examiners did not want to try X-Ways Forensics (XWF) since it looked different from other forensic suites. Some considered it harder to use or were under the impression that XWF was just a hex editor. For those who have not tried XWF, the authors hope to enlighten those potential users of the powerful capabilities of XWF. The authors also hope to explain the inner workings of XWF so that current users will find it even more helpful in nearly every analysis.

Much like anyone else, when you find something that works, you stick with it. Excuses for not trying a different forensic suite may sound reasonable at first, but in reality, they are not. Just because an examiner attended a course about software Brand A should not result in only using Brand A, nor should it preclude learning to use another tool. In addition, holding a certification in Brand B shouldn't preclude the use of other tools. It is the underlying forensic skill that has been developed during one's studies that should be leveraged across a wide variety of software programs.

Most new tasks are difficult, at least at first. Activities like riding a bicycle, driving a car, and cooking dinner are examples of difficult tasks that become easier with effort and time until finally they become second nature. Working with XWF (both through this book and in casework) is not different from learning any new skill, and over time, XWF will become as easy to use as riding a bicycle. XWF is remarkably intuitive, perhaps not seemingly at first, but its straightforward nature actually makes it easier to master than many other tools.

Intended audience

We developed this book for every user of XWF including those who have been using XWF for years as well as those that have yet to take the first step to use XWF in their examinations. As this book details using a forensic software application using real life examples, it is intended for users who have an intermediate to advanced level of understanding about computers, operating systems, and file systems. While various sections and chapters touch on certain aspects of operating systems, software, and hardware, they do not contain detailed information on these topics, nor does this book contain detailed information on file systems such as FAT, NTFS, HFS, or EXT. These topics are better described apart from the use of XWF in this book. In other words, this is not a book on learning how to do forensics. Rather, it is a book on how to use XWF.

Our hope is to give the reader a solid reference for using XWF in any forensic examination as either a compliment to current forensic tools or the primary forensic tool in any examination. We will present real-world case studies so that readers can see firsthand how capable XWF is as a forensics application. We expect readers of this book to be demanding of their current tools and assume that they are using their current tools to the highest potential. With that said, this book will show how to exploit the capabilities of XWF in order to examine electronic media quickly and accurately.

Brief history of X-Ways Forensics

Before delving into an overview of how XWF has improved since its creation, it would be helpful to have a better understanding of the origins of XWF. In 2002, Stefan Fleischmann started a software development company while he was a student at the University of Münster in Germany. Upon graduation, Stefan worked in the private sector where he specialized in training others in Systems Applications and Products (SAP). In 2002, Stefan started X-Ways Corporation.

Based on feature requests from users, XWF released the "computer forensics version of WinHex" on May 17, 2004. It was not until June 21, 2004, that the first version of XWF was released. The following year, Stefan hosted the first training course in Seattle, Washington. Since then, XWF has seen many releases that have added hundreds of new features. To date, XWF has over 35,000 users worldwide ranging from state, local, and federal law enforcement agencies to Fortune 500 companies and everything in between.

As the reader will soon see, XWF is a full featured and extremely powerful program with hundreds of features and capabilities not found in other forensic programs. The ingenuity of XWF lies in the multitude of features and capabilities behind a seemingly simple user interface. To put it in Stefan's words, with XWF, there is any number, or "X," ways of doing things. To view the many updates and added features, the reader can find a constantly updated list at http://www.x-ways.net/winhex/mailings/.

This book's primary goal is to explain how to best use the capabilities of XWF in a wide variety of situations. Throughout the following chapters, we take an incremental or building block approach, so the reader can become thoroughly familiar and competent with each function and feature of the program.

One of the most significant design points of XWF is its ability to allow an examiner to choose only the operations necessary to accomplish a task. In other words, XWF does not require every single option to be run on every single forensic image before the review process can begin. In fact, the evidence review process can be initiated as soon as a piece of media or an image is opened in XWF, either as a preview or to triage the evidence using some of the more advanced capabilities of XWF.

In certain types of cases, an examiner may never need to use the advanced capabilities of XWF at all. Contrast this with other tools that require a lengthy amount of time to preprocess a case before even conducting a basic review.

A constant theme throughout the book is an emphasis on case workflow. We describe various methods for workflow that can reduce the time of analysis and result in a better product, without taking any shortcuts. Whereas some tools may require a large block of time and machine-intensive preprocessing, we show case flow options with real life examples to define case preparation, with the granularity based on the needs of the case. Many of these options exist only with XWF, and, by knowing the options, you can control the time spent on analysis to reach key objectives in your cases.

Finally, we suggest you check the XWF forums often. Enhancements and updates can occur literally by the hour, and the forums are the best place to find such information.

Comparisons to "other" forensic suites

A single, all-encompassing digital forensic suite does not exist, as any given forensic suite may do a single task better than another forensic suite. In fact, in most cases, a specifically developed application that does only one task might be the better tool to use than a suite. An example could be software designed solely for Internet analysis or parsing certain Windows artifacts.

In addition, one forensic tool simply cannot do everything by itself. The examiners that rely solely upon one tool may be doing a disservice to themselves because most examinations require a multitude of different software applications for a comprehensive examination. Of course, some tools are more comprehensive than others and provide more value for the price, but these variables fluctuate depending on the requirements of examiners, usage policy and procedures, and so forth. It is important not to equate value with price, as they are often at odds.

Keep in mind that you can consider your forensic software and hardware as tools in a toolbox, each with a specific purpose. Our goal in this book is not to disparage any forensic application nor place any application in a negative light. In most cases, you need more than one forensic application to examine a particular case thoroughly, just as you need more than one hammer and a single pair of pliers in your toolbox.

While reading this book, you may choose to implement XWF into your toolbox, perhaps as a validation tool initially, but most likely it will become your primary tool as you gain a better understanding of its capabilities and efficiencies. Either way, you still need more than one tool to be effective in your job. This book will also show how the integration of other forensic applications can work well with XWF to fully exploit capabilities or fill any gaps that might exist in other tools.

ORGANIZATION OF THIS BOOK

Each chapter builds upon the preceding chapter, and each chapter stands on its own for the topics presented in that chapter. With that said, we recommend that you read each chapter in order so that you gain and reinforce a solid foundation and understanding of XWF.

By the time you read this book, there will have been one or more updates to XWF. Certain features as outlined in this book may have been changed or improved in addition to adding new features. Keep in mind that WinHex and XWF have had a steady growth of updates and improvements. In fact, there is an average of 41 days between new versions! With this in mind, this guide to using XWF is not out of date as the vast majority of information contained herein still applies, but to make sure you are aware of the latest updates, check out the XWF Web site on a regular basis. Rest assured that there will be an update anywhere between a week and 41 days between each version or service release.

We are confident that you are holding in your hands the definitive guide to the most frequently updated and powerful tool in the digital forensics field.

Chapter 1: Installation and configuration of X-Ways Forensics

We have to start somewhere, so starting with the installation, setup, and configuring of XWF is a good place to begin. Chapter 1 begins with a broad overview of features and a brief explanation of the graphical user interface used by XWF. It will conclude with a walkthrough of the initial configuration steps required to give XWF the basic information it needs to function.

Chapter 2: Case management and imaging

XWF handles just about all types of electronic evidence: hard drives, physical memory, compact discs, and even remotely acquired evidence. Each of these items represents that media XWF can forensically image and process. Chapter 2 describes how to capture electronic evidence with methods that are flexible and efficient, depending upon the needs of the examiner.

Chapter 3: Navigating the X-Ways Forensics interface

A key element in using any software is being able to efficiently and effectively navigate through the myriad of buttons and options the program exposes. Chapter 3 shows succinct methods of navigation that will serve well with every use of XWF.

Chapter 4: Refine volume Snapshot

Volume Snapshots are unique to XWF and are one of the most powerful features that exist within the program. A Snapshot is an instrumental feature in XWF and is used for data carving, indexing data, and preprocessing evidence for analysis. Chapter 4 shows the many choices available when creating and refining a Snapshot of evidence with examples to maximize your choices based on the needs of that particular case or item of evidence.

Chapter 5: The XWF internal hash database and registry viewer

Chapter 5 explains in detail how to create and import hash data sets to use as hash comparisons of files. Hash comparisons are one of the most commonly used methods of identifying known and notable files by their hash value.

A section describing the Registry Viewer is also in Chapter 5. Although this section does not teach registry forensics, it does show how to use the XWF Registry Viewer as part of an analysis of the registry.

Chapter 6: Searching in X-Ways Forensics

Searching for data with XWF is unrivaled. No other forensic utility has the granularity, configurability, accuracy, and speed as does XWF. Chapter 6 shows XWF users how to effectively search and export hits efficiently and effectively by using indexed searches, GREP searches, and searches in hex.

Chapter 7: Advanced use of XWF

The advanced use of XWF covers processes of detailed analysis techniques and uncommon situations. Chapter 7 shows how to maneuver in hex, gather free and slack spaces, examining physical memory, template editing, and the use of scripts and the X-Tensions API. With that said, advanced use of XWF does not necessarily mean that it is any more difficult or essential to the successful use of the program. It merely means using features and methods that may not be used regularly.

Chapter 8: X-Ways Forensics reporting

An analysis is not completely finished until you generate a report. In Chapter 8, you will see how to create and customize a report best suited for your examination using built-in features of XWF as well as adding information from other sources resulting in a complete and thorough report.

Chapter 9: X-Ways Forensics and electronic discovery

Chapter 9 describes a unique use of XWF, in the field of electronic discovery. Although XWF is a digital forensics application, the same features that make it a superior forensic application also make it a superior choice in electronic discovery cases.

Chapter 10: X-Ways Forensics and Criminal Investigations

Situations occur where examiners or first responders are confronted with computer systems to search, yet may not have enough information to justify a seizure of those systems. In these instances, such as a consent to search or monitoring a parolee, XWF enables a high-level triage or preview of electronic media and, when required, provides extreme granularity in analysis in the field with no reduction in capabilities. Chapter 10 presents several methods of conducting searches of these types using XWF.

SUMMARY

We are confident that after you read this book you will dog-ear pages, highlight sentences, write notations in the margins, and place it on the desk right next to a small stack of your other well-worn and well-used reference books.

With your XWF dongle and this guide, you will have the tools and knowledge to not only conduct in-depth forensic analysis in the lab and the field but also further develop into someone who knows his or her job as well as the science behind computer forensics. Beware the forensic examiners who are proficient in XWF as they most likely know their stuff regardless of the tools they choose to use.

Finally, we believe that after reading this book and spending some time using XWF, you will ask yourself one question: "Why did I wait so long before trying out X-Ways?"

Case Management and Imaging

INFORMATION IN THIS CHAPTER

- Introduction
- Creating a case file
- Creating/adding evidence files (forensic images)
- Creating forensic images with XWF
- Reverse imaging
- Skeleton imaging
- Cleansed imaging
- CD/DVD
- Physical memory imaging
- Container files
- Working with RAID arrays
- Augmenting with F-Response
- Shortcuts
- Summary

INTRODUCTION

Every forensic software suite needs a way to manage a related set of forensic images and XWF is no exception. After creating a new case, we will discuss how to image a wide variety of physical devices so that they can be added to our case.

Much like other forensic tools, XWF can create forensic images from almost every type of digital media. What distinguishes XWF is that it uses much more intelligence when imaging a device. For example, most other tools can compress an image file but do so blindly by compressing all of the data on a device. In contrast, XWF is smart enough to know when data are already compressed, and when it sees such data, it doesn't waste time trying to compress that data again. For example, why waste time trying to compress an AVI video? This results in a much more efficient imaging process. As we have discussed, the default values in XWF were chosen very carefully and the values used when imaging are no exception.

In addition to creating forensic images from source devices, XWF can create and manage container files that allow you to create subsets of data for many purposes. One example would be to provide a limited and focused set of data to another examiner with a particular specialty.

As you know, XWF is a Windows-based forensic tool but that does not limit its capabilities to deal with a wide range of file systems including Ext*, HFS, Reiser, etc. When used in conjunction with F-Response, XWF can interact with essentially any system you may encounter including Solaris, FreeBSD, AIX and of course, Windows.

In Chapter 1, we covered the basics of installing and initially configuring XWF. After reading this chapter, you will have the knowledge to work with, and add evidence to, an XWF case. Once you have one or more pieces of evidence in a case, the true power of XWF can be brought to bear on that evidence.

CREATING A CASE FILE

XWF allows an examiner to interact with various things such as hard disks, partitions, physical memory, and file systems without creating a case. However, we strongly recommend that a case be created as this is how *many* additional features of XWF are made available including automated logging, global collection and resolving of SIDs to usernames, and report file generation, to name a few.

To work with a case, it is necessary to display the **Case Data** window. By default, XWF displays this window on the left side of the interface as shown in Figure 2.1.

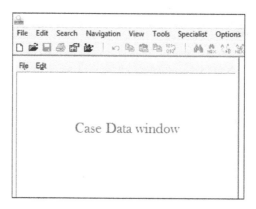

FIGURE 2.1

Case Data window.

If the **Case Data** window is not visible, it can be shown by selecting **View | Show** and checking the box next to **Case Data** as seen in Figure 2.2.

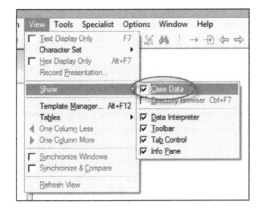

FIGURE 2.2

Toggling the **Case Data** window.

Initially, only two options will be available under the **File** menu: **Create New Case** and **Open case**.

Creating a new case

To create a new case, select **File | Create New Case** from the **Case Data** window and a dialog will be displayed allowing you to set various properties about the case. The case properties window is composed of four sections as seen in Figure 2.3.

FIGURE 2.3

Case property window.

For each of the sections, the fields are mostly self-explanatory, but some merit additional discussion.

General case information section

By default, XWF will create a subfolder in the path listed in the **Directory** property with the same name that we enter in the **Case title/number** property. As a reminder, the default value for **Directory** will be taken from whatever path is entered under the **Options | General** menu in the **Folder for cases and projects** text box.

A corresponding XWF case file (.xfc) and folder will be created in the path listed in the **Directory** property as well. For example, if the defaults were used to create a case as seen in Figure 2.3, the file and folder shown in Figure 2.4 would be created.

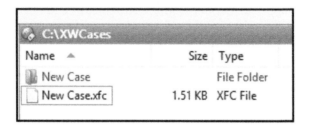

FIGURE 2.4

Directory layout for a new case.

As more cases are created, more directories and .xfc files will be created in a similar manner. It should be noted that Windows will not allow two cases with the same name to exist in the same directory. Should an existing case exist, XWF will tell you to correct the conflict. To avoid this, simply use a unique value for the **Case title/number** property. For example, using a unique case number may be more appropriate than using a subject name for the case title. For example, 2013_01_15_001 signifies the first case initiated on January 15, 2013. Using this method, you will not have a possibility of conflicting case numbers.

XWF TIPS AND TRICKS

Case Management and Directory Structure

As an alternative, a new subdirectory can be created in the **Directory** property by selecting the ... button to the right of the text box. By creating a new directory based on, for example, a case number, the .xfc and corresponding case directory can be more self-contained. Once the ... button is clicked, a new folder can be created by clicking the upper right most folder icon in the **Select Folder** dialog. This icon will display a tooltip of *Create New Folder* if you hover the mouse over it.

The **Description** and **Examiner** properties are optional, but we recommend that you include as much detail as possible as it will make working with older cases easier because you won't have to refer to additional notes if they are contained in the case. Use the **Description** property to include general case information and not information related to a particular piece of digital evidence. As images are added to a case, they will also have a place to enter detailed information about each image. In sum, fill out each section according to your policies.

Audit trail and activity logging section

Each of the check boxes in this section controls whether XWF will automatically add entries in its audit trail as you use the program. This is a fantastic feature because it self-documents the exam as you progress. When it comes time to generate a report, you can optionally include the audit trail information. The button next to the **Log Recover/Copy command** checkbox allows you to choose the fields that will be logged when you recover or copy items from evidence objects. In addition to enabling or disabling various pieces of the audit trail, you can also view the log via the corresponding buttons or delete the audit log if you wish. Finally, if **In case log subdir** is checked, XWF will create the log file in the _log subdirectory of the main case directory. If unchecked, the log file will be created in the same directory the items are recovered to.

If **Default to evidence object folders for output** is checked, XWF will initially select the folder that corresponds to the evidence object you are recovering files from in the **Recover/Copy** dialog. If unchecked, XWF will remember the last folder used for recovering files.

For complete details as to what is logged, see the **Case Log** section of the XWF manual.

Code pages section

The code pages section allows for up to two different code pages to be selected that will be used when processing certain files (such as e-mail subject lines and file names inside zip archives) in your case. Depending on the kinds of data in a particular case, adjust one or both of the code pages accordingly. In most circumstances, it is not necessary to change the defaults. However, when working with Linux, it may be helpful to keep the default ANSI code page and then select Unicode UTF-8 for the second. This will better enable XWF to do such things as convert file names inside archives and display the subject of e-mail messages properly.

Other options section

Finally, the last section includes options related to report generation (covered in Chapter 8), time zone information, auto-save interval, etc. Each will be discussed below.

The **Report (Options)** button brings up a dialog that allows for the customization of the report files XWF can generate. Since we have nothing in our case to report and reporting will be covered in detail in Chapter 8, this option will be skipped for now.

The **Display time zone** button allows for the selection of a time zone to be used by XWF when interpreting and displaying various date/time values in the program.

Check the **Individual time zones per evidence object** checkbox if you need to use a different time zone per evidence object, e.g., a forensic image. Exactly how to select a different time zone for each evidence object will be discussed after we have a few pieces of evidence in our case.

The **Auto save interval in min** value determines how long XWF will wait after a change is made before automatically saving the case file. XWF will NOT save every X minutes, but rather only after a change is made to the case and the specified number of minutes then passes. XWF will also save the case when closing a case or when you exit XWF.

The **No. of case file backups** option determines how many copies of previous versions of a case XWF will maintain. Depending on your backup policies, you can adjust this value for more or less protection should the main .xfc file become corrupt. Note that only the .xfc files are backed up and that no backups of the potentially much larger case subdirectory are automatically made.

The **Add disk partitions to the case automatically as well** option, if unchecked, will require relevant partitions found in a forensic image to be added to the case manually.

The **Protect case file against opening** has three options:

Fully checked: A password can be added to the case file that will prevent anyone without the password from opening the case file.
Half-checked: A password can be added to the case file that will allow the case to be opened in read-only mode. Clicking the **Password** button allows for the entering of a password in both the fully and half-checked states.
Unchecked: Anyone with the ability to open XWF can open a case file and modify it.

An example of each option type is shown in Figure 2.5.

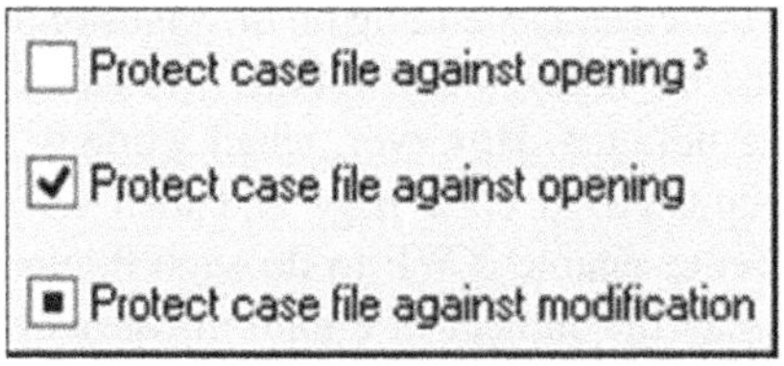

FIGURE 2.5

Unchecked, fully checked, and half-checked example.

The **RVS: Protect against duplicates of crasher files** option determines if XWF will track and prevent identical "bad" files from being processed or reprocessed. In XWF, RVS stands for Refine Volume Snapshot. Volume snapshots will be explored in detail in Chapter 4. For example, if this option is checked and hash values are calculated when performing a Refine Volume Snapshot operation, any duplicate (based on the hash value) files will also be omitted from processing should a file cause XWF to crash. Any files that meet this criterion are logged and added to a Report Table (reporting is fully discussed in Chapter 8) that allows for manual review of those files to determine whether any of them are relevant and warrant further manual processing.

The **SIDs** button, once an image of a Windows-based system is added to a case, will display the Security Identifier (SID) of various accounts along with the corresponding username. An SID is a unique identifier for a user or user group in Windows. XWF populates these values when an image is added to a case. All SIDs across all pieces of media in a case will be displayed.

Once you have the various options set, click the **OK** button to create the case. To view the case properties again, click the **Edit** menu in the **Case Data** window and then select **Properties**.

XWF TIPS AND TRICKS

Changing a Case Title/Number

After a case is created, XWF allows you to change the **Case title/number**. However, changing the **Case title/number** will NOT result in the case folder or the .xfc file being renamed.

Once back at the main **Case Data** window, you can interact with the new case in several ways by using the **File** and **Edit** menus and/or right-clicking on the root level of the case. The root level (in the **Case Data** window) will have a purple XWF icon next to it as well as the case title or number that you assigned.

CREATING/ADDING EVIDENCE FILES

After a new case is created or an existing one is opened, we can add various pieces of evidence to it, such as forensic images (e01 and dd files for example), that most examiners are familiar with. An e01 file is a propriety file format that contains a bit-for-bit copy of a medium. In addition to the data found on the medium, an e01 file contains a cyclic redundancy check (CRC) for certain 32k chunks of data as well as the ability to store the hash of the entire stream of data inside the e01. By comparing both the overall hash and the CRCs of the various chunks of data, it is possible to tell whether any data have changed (because the overall hash fails to match) as well as exactly those parts of the data have been corrupted (because one or more CRCs fails to match).

dd images are similar to e01 files in that they contain a bit-for-bit copy of a medium, but dd files do not contain additional verification data within them. As such, you must validate a dd image against a hash of the entire medium. In both cases, you would know something has changed if the source hash doesn't match the image hash. In addition to full support for these commonly used image types, XWF understands Mode 1 and Mode 2 Form 1 ISO CD images with 2352 bytes per sector (if they are not spanned) as well as VMware's Virtual Machine Disk images (VMDK) and dynamic Virtual PC VHD images. XWF also allows for individual directories and/or files to be added to a case. While we haven't covered container files yet, it is often better to add individual files and/or directories to a container file rather than directly to a case. This will be covered in the section on container files below.

One very powerful and unique capability of XWF is the ability to image a hard disk in reverse. This is useful if there is a damaged section of the hard disk that cannot be read by other imaging tools or through conventional imaging (beginning to end or forward imaging). By creating an image in a traditional manner to the point of damage and then continuing the process in reverse starting at the last sector, XWF can generate a nearly complete image with a small gap that corresponds with the physically damaged section of the disk.

XWF TIPS AND TRICKS

The File System Matters!

When creating reverse images, be sure to save such images to an NTFS formatted partition. FAT32 is not supported.

In addition to forensic images of hard drives, CDROMs, etc., you can add images of physical memory.

XWF is fully capable of working with a hard drive or other storage device without taking a forensic image of the device, but we recommend using a forensic copy of a device as opposed to working with the actual piece of evidence. You can also employ a write blocker should you want to examine an original device. In some instances, working on a live system cannot be avoided (when encryption is detected, when working on a business server that cannot be taken down, working with exotic RAID setups, etc.). Should you run into such a case, XWF is fully capable of working with a running system with minimal impact.

CREATING FORENSIC IMAGES WITH XWF

The most common type of imaging you will encounter is the imaging of hard disks from a "dead box" system. All "dead box" means is that a computer is powered off as opposed to being powered on with the operating system running, i.e., a "live box."

Once you have one or more hard drives, we will need to make them available to the computer system on which XWF is running. To do this, we will employ a forensic write blocker that will prevent any changes from being made to the hard drive during the imaging process. In short, Windows needs to "see" at least a physical device on the computer regardless of whether it has a drive letter under My Computer.

Once the hard drive is connected to the write blocker, the write blocker is powered on and Windows detects the drive, we are ready to image the disk.

For most imaging jobs, XWF will be used without creating a case. That is, XWF will be opened and only used to create a forensic image of one or more pieces of

FIGURE 2.6

View Disk dialog.

digital media. To create an image, press **F9** or use the **Tools | Open Disk** menu to bring up the **View Disk** dialog as shown in Figure 2.6.

If you are running WinHex instead of X-Ways Forensics (and not in read-only mode), then the same dialog window is entitled **Edit Disk** instead.

Unless you have a need to image an individual partition, we recommend that you select a device under the **Physical Media** section. Simply select the physical device you want to open in XWF. In Figure 2.6, HD0 is selected. XWF will open the disk and display some basic information about the disk, including any partitions XWF was able to discover, the start sectors, unpartitionable space, and so on.

XWF can now fully interact with the hard drive we have just opened. Double-clicking on a partition will open that partition and XWF will begin traversing all the sectors in the partition. This is the initial volume snapshot process that consists of parsing various file system metadata such as the Master File Table (MFT). At this point, we are not interested in working directly against a running hard drive, so we will avoid opening an individual partition.

XWF is now ready to create a forensic image of the hard disk. To begin the process, select **File | Create Disk Image**, or press **Alt-C** as shown in Figure 2.7.

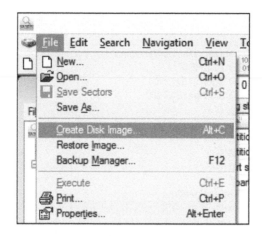

FIGURE 2.7

Beginning the imaging process.

XWF TIPS AND TRICKS

Imaging via Command Line

XWF supports creating image files via the command line as well as via its graphical user interface. The XWF manual contains the syntax for command line imaging.

While XWF has everything it needs at this point to make an image, several
optional changes are recommended as shown in Figure 2.8.

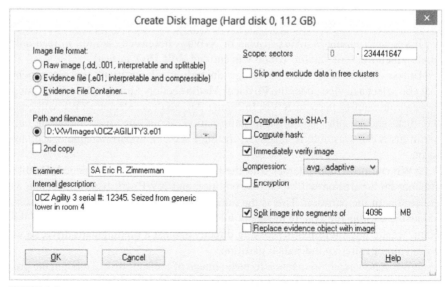

FIGURE 2.8

Create Disk Image dialog.

XWF TIPS AND TRICKS

From Fast to Faster!

By default, when creating e01 files, XWF uses a number of extra threads depending on the number of processor cores present. In the lower right corner is a small button that, when clicked, allows for increasing this number. To maximize performance, you may want to experiment and increase this value for even better performance.

The first two options under image file format are self-explanatory. The third, **Evidence file container**, allows you to create a disk image as an XWF container as opposed to an e01 or dd file. Several third-party tools can understand the basic information in XWF containers, so this is a viable option in some scenarios. Of course, XWF (and some other tools) can be used to create an e01 or dd image of an XWF evidence container that is usable by any tool capable of understanding either format, but this is not required to use the container in XWF.

The **Path**, by default, will reflect the directory as entered in **Options | General**. The **filename** will default to the model of the drive as determined by XWF's interrogation of the drive's information. This information can also be viewed via the **Specialist | Technical Details Report** menu item. To change the path or file name, select the . . . button to the right of the path. You can also optionally create a second image at the same time by checking the appropriate box. This is faster than creating a single image and then copying it later. It is best if the second image is created on a different physical device than the initial image in order to minimize the time it takes to create the image and additional copy.

Enter as many details as you wish about the selected hard drive in the **Internal description** box. This may include such things as the hard drive make, model, and serial number, the source of the drive (for example, where it was seized from, the client name, etc.), custodian or suspect name, etc. This information will be preserved in the image file in the case of an e01. For both e01 and dd images, this information will also be included in a text file (created in the same directory as the image itself) that contains details of the imaging process.

The **Scope** simply defines how much of the disk you wish to image. Typically, you will image the entire medium. You can also choose to exclude data in free clusters, but this option shouldn't be used for the vast majority of imaging projects.

Finally, you can determine whether to employ hash verification and select which hash algorithms to generate for this image. At a minimum, we recommend that you select SHA-1. While MD5 is a valid hash algorithm, particularly with respect to disk images, the SHA-1 algorithm is less susceptible to attack. We also suggest that you check the **Immediately verify image** box, so XWF will validate that the image is a forensic duplicate by generating and comparing the hash values for the source and image file. XWF will only validate the image by comparing the hash value for the topmost hash algorithm, not both (you can always generate the hash value of the second image and compare it to the primary image's hashes though). By default, XWF will split images into 4 GB chunks.

When creating a second image file, XWF will not allow the images to exist on the same drive letter, so be sure you have at least two destination drives available. Also, when creating a second image file, XWF will not automatically verify the hash of the second image.

The **Replace evidence object with image** option is only available when adding media directly to a case and then imaging that media (as opposed to using **F9** to select a device as discussed above). There are several ways to do this to include right-clicking the case root node and selecting **Add Medium** or clicking the **File** menu in the **Case Data** window and selecting **Add Medium**. Regardless of the method you choose, the **Open Disk** dialog will be displayed. **Replace evidence object with image** is a very handy option that can replace the physical device in the case with an image file once an image is created. Using this option works well for smaller medium such as thumb drives, etc., but for larger devices, we recommend another technique that is outlined in another section below.

XWF TIPS AND TRICKS

True AES Encryption for e01s

Should you have a hard drive that contains sensitive information, XWF can fully encrypt the data in the e01 image using 128- or 256-bit encryption. This is vastly different from simple password protection of e01s found in other tools that can easily be bypassed by simply opening an e01 and reimaging it. Secure the password for future use as the image will not be accessible without it.

You can also prevent people from making unencrypted copies (by reimaging an image after providing the password) by checking the **Prevent unencrypted copies** option.

Once you adjust the settings to your liking, click the **OK** button to start the imaging process. As XWF processes the media, various statistics will be generated and updated in real time as shown in Figure 2.9.

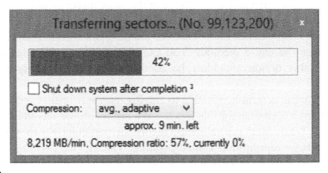

FIGURE 2.9

Imaging progress.

At the start of the imaging process, a text file is created that is updated as the imaging progresses. The text file will be saved to the same directory as the image file and will have the same filename as the image. In our example above, our image is named *OCZ-AGILITY3.e01*, so our text file would be named *OCZ-AGILITY3.txt*. This text file will contain various information about the hard drive including the number of sectors, where the image was saved, its capacity, partitions, etc. At the end of the imaging process, XWF will add the hash values to the file with an indication of whether the source and destination hashes matched.

If you cancel the imaging process before it completes, XWF will finalize the segment of the image file (when using e01 format) it is currently creating so that a consistent image file is generated. While you will end up with an incomplete image, it will be accurate to the point when the imaging process was canceled.

The process for imaging any other type of media is the same as imaging a hard disk. When this is not the case, it will be explained in the sections that follow.

Live response using XWF

In the previous section, we used a write blocker to connect a hard drive from a dead box to our computer. This is the traditional approach to creating forensic images and the one that you will use the most. However, as we have discussed, XWF can be used on a live system that cannot be shut down for whatever reason (such as a server at a business and a RAID array). To use XWF in a live environment, copy XWF to an external hard drive or other storage device and connect it to the computer to be imaged. If you have XWF on a thumb drive, connect an additional external hard drive to the computer if the thumb drive is not big enough to hold the image. Finally, connect your dongle (no drivers will be installed). Once the removable drives are recognized, open XWF. From this point forward, the imaging process in this scenario is exactly the same as we saw in the previous section.

Using XWF to review medium while imaging

In time-sensitive situations, it is often required to immediately begin reviewing a hard drive or other piece of media while an image is being created. To do this with XWF, begin the imaging process as we previously discussed. To begin the review process, open another instance of XWF, create a new case, and add the same device that you are imaging to the case.

Once the device is added to the case, you can start browsing its contents. Since you are working with a case, XWF will remember anything that you do against the device. Once the image is created in the other instance of XWF, right-click on the device in your case and select **Replace with new Image** from the **Case Data** context menu as shown in Figure 2.10.

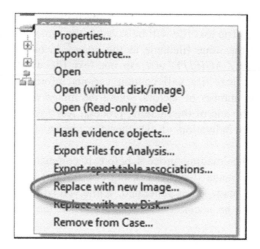

FIGURE 2.10

Replacing a device with an image.

Navigate to the directory where XWF created the image of the device and select the corresponding image file. XWF will then remove the device from your case and replace it with the image file. By using this technique, anything done against the volume snapshot of the device will be preserved such as report table associations, comments, viewed files, etc.

Basically, we let one instance of XWF image our drive while the second instance goes to work and examines the drive in a case. After the image is complete, we substitute the image for the disk and continue from where we left off. Using this technique enables you to get a head start by beginning an exam before the image was even complete!

This two-pronged approach allows you to start interacting immediately with your media rather than waiting for hours for the image to complete. This saves time and allows you to begin your examination immediately.

REVERSE IMAGING

XWF stands virtually alone in its ability to image a piece of media in reverse. This is particularly useful when dealing with a damaged hard drive that cannot be imaged using traditional means.

Reverse disk imaging is meant for hard disks with a severe physical defect that causes a computer to freeze or crash when reaching a certain area on the hard disk. Opposite of this is a disk with ordinary bad sectors that can cause a delay in the copy process but not necessarily a crash. Ordinary bad sectors do not keep you from getting to the end of the disk when copying in the traditional sense. The copying process will take longer when bad sectors are encountered, but it will eventually finish. With severely damaged drives, this is not the case and this is why reverse imaging was implemented in XWF.

Before discussing reverse imaging, we need to discuss XWF's disk cloning functionality. This feature is available via the **Tools | Disk Tools | Clone Disk** menu option. Alternatively, you can use the **CTRL-D** shortcut to bring up the **Clone Disk** dialog as shown in Figure 2.11.

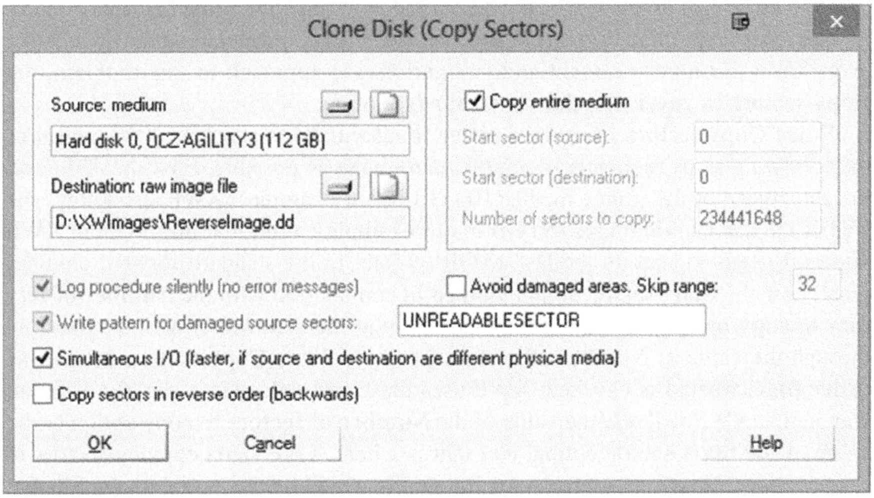

FIGURE 2.11

Clone Disk dialog.

After selecting a destination (either a hard drive or an unsegmented, raw image file), XWF is ready to clone the source device. By default, XWF will read from the beginning of the disk. Obviously, "cloning" implies that we are reproducing a medium, e.g., copy one hard drive to another. Perhaps you are wondering why imaging is involved here, particularly as we discussed it before. This will become clear as you read further.

The **Start sector (source)** option defines the scope of what sectors XWF will copy. The **Start sector** is simply the first (in the sense of left-most, or Sector 0) sector of the media that will be copied. By default, the entire range of sectors will be cloned. Unchecking the **Copy entire medium** box allows you to adjust the **Start sector** and/ or **Number of sectors to copy** properties.

In hard drives that somehow become physically or logically damaged, the damage tends to be located in contiguous sectors. Checking the **Avoid damaged areas** box tells XWF to, should it encounter an unreadable sector, skip the number of sectors as reflected in the **Skip range** option. This is desirable for reasons of speed during the copying process. If access to a single damaged sector causes a delay of 10 seconds (this value can be reduced when using one of the alternative disk access methods in **General Options**), then 1000 bad sectors will take 3 hours to overcome.

Creating the clone is now as simple as clicking the **OK** button.

Before we discuss the key options when reverse imaging, it would be helpful to work with a damaged media example. For instance, when employing the **Clone Disk** option to clone a disk or to create a single dd image of a 100 GB hard disk, the process fails after imaging 60 GB. At this point, you are left with a partial image that is 60 GB in size.

Before XWF, you would have no option to try to acquire the last 40 GB except by trial and error in guessing where the damage stops, then attempting to create another image from that point to the end of the drive and finally concatenating the files. However, XWF has a very elegant and straightforward approach to this problem, the **Copy sectors in reverse order (backwards)** option.

When **Copy sectors in reverse order (backwards)** is checked, XWF will take the following steps to create as complete an image as possible. First, XWF knows the actual size of the source media (100 GB in our example). XWF also knows the size of the destination image (60 GB in our example). With that information, XWF knows it needs to acquire the last 40 GB of data. In the standard forward cloning, recall how the **Start sector** option worked in conjunction with the **Number of sectors to copy** option in that XWF would begin at the start sector and copy sectors through the value of **Number of sectors to copy**. When **Copy sectors in reverse order (backwards)** is checked, XWF uses these two values in a slightly different way in that XWF will *add* the value of the **Number of sectors to copy** option to the value of the **Start sector** option, and that is where XWF starts copying sectors in reverse order. Your **Destination raw image file** would be the partial image file that XWF created initially.

If you choose your existing, partial image as the destination, XWF will ask if you want to overwrite the existing image. Click **Yes** at this point so XWF can reuse the existing image file later. Once you click **OK**, XWF will ask if you want to **Keep existing file and complete it from the intended rear end**. Click **Yes** to complete the reverse imaging process.

To summarize, XWF, as usual, is doing the thinking for us. If we start a single dd image or clone that then fails for any reason, we can start the cloning process over again without losing our partial image/clone. We need only leave all of the defaults alone with the exception of enabling the **Copy sectors in reverse order (backwards)** option. Since XWF knows what size the image should be and it can see what size the current partial image is, XWF appends the correct data to the back of the existing image that results in a near complete image! Magic!

SKELETON IMAGING

Another unique imaging feature of XWF is the ability to create images based on NTFS sparse file technology that only contains the exact bits of data (or more precisely, sectors) you choose to include in the image file.

Beyond containing the basic information about the file system (which is necessary for forensic software to be able to find such things as files and directories), these partial images can be used for anything from providing a snapshot of the file and directory names in an evidence object (without including any of the contents of the files or directories themselves) to including only registry hives. Since the images are based on raw image files, any tool that can understand a raw image (including the partitioning method as well as the corresponding file system of the original disk) can open and work with the skeleton image.

Before creating a skeleton image (SI), it is important to understand how the SI will be populated once it is open. After opening an SI, any read actions against an evidence object will be copied into the SI. As a result, we recommend opening the SI before interacting with a disk image or disk. By doing this, XWF will include the information from the initial volume snapshot in the SI (including file system information). In this scenario, we recommend opening an SI before opening a disk and adding it to your case.

Contrast the above scenario with a need to include just a portion of data from free space that you want someone else to be able to look at without providing the entire image. In this case, you would create an SI as outlined above, then select the data you wish to include, and hash it (selecting blocks of data and hashing it will be covered in Chapter 7). The benefit of using this approach over including the entire virtual "free space" file in an XWF container is that the original offsets of all data in the file system are preserved when using an SI.

To create an SI, select **File | Create Skeleton Image**. After entering a name for the SI, a dialog box is displayed as shown in Figure 2.12.

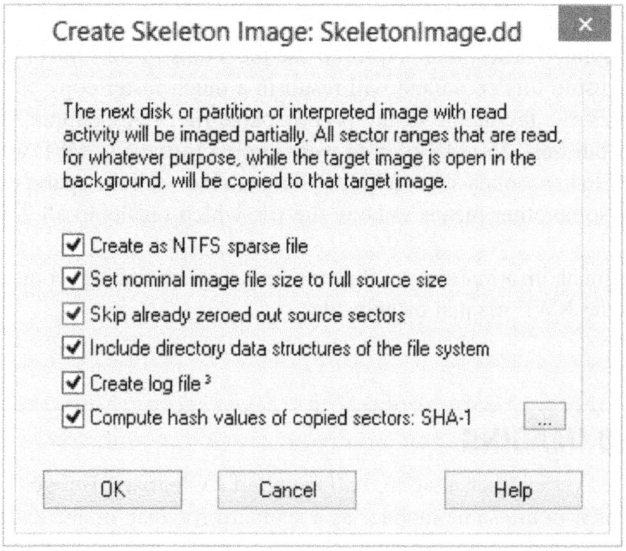

FIGURE 2.12

Skeleton image options.

Most of the options are self-explanatory.
Create log file has three options:

Fully checked: In addition to the log file created as described when half-checked, a secondary log file about the primary log file will be created. This log file is used to verify the integrity of the primary log file.
Half-checked: A log file will be created containing the hash values of the sectors that have been added to the SI.
Unchecked: No log file is created.

For example, if we name our SI *myskeletonimage.dd* and **Create log file** was half-checked, a log file named *myskeletonimage.log* is created that contains all of the sector ranges copied into the SI as well as the hash value for those sectors. If fully checked, an additional file, *myskeletonimage.log.log* will be created after *myskeletonimage.dd* is verified that contains the name of the log file, the date and time of its creation, the size of the log, and hash of *myskeletonimage.log*.

Once an SI is open, the menu option changes to **File | State** / **<Name of SI>** and selecting this option allows for changing the behavior of the SI. The default is **Reading any sector triggers acquisition**, but there are also options to pause acquisition via the **Idle** option or closing the SI. When **Close** is selected, the option to **Verify Skeleton Image** is available. Depending on your needs, you can use these options to start and stop the SI process.

The log file created when **Create log file** is fully or half-checked allows XWF to verify the integrity of the data contained in the SI, either manually or when the SI is closed.

We will cover how to add objects to the SI in Chapters 3 and 7.

When copying SI files, it is helpful to use the **Tools | File Tools | Copy Sparse** command as using this command will result in a much faster copy operation since XWF will preserve the nature of the NTFS sparse file. For example, if the SI was 2 TB in size but only 250 MB of data were copied to the SI, XWF would be able to copy this file in seconds since it knows how to deal with the sparse file. Contrast this to using some other means to copy the file which results in all 2 TB of the SI being copied.

For additional information on skeleton imaging, including both benefits and caveats, see the XWF manual or help file.

CLEANSED IMAGING

XWF provides yet another imaging option called a **Cleansed Image**. The cleansed image is created in the same manner as a standard forensic image except data you specify can be excluded from the acquisition. As detailed in Chapter 9 for eDiscovery cases, there are instances where specific data may need redaction due to privacy or privilege issues and a cleansed image meets this need.

Once the evidence media is added to XWF and the volume snapshot finishes, simply hide the data you wish to exclude before creating the image (we will cover how to hide items in Chapter 3). The hidden items will be excluded from acquisition and the sectors related to hidden items will be zeroed out or optionally watermarked with a value of your choosing. All other data are acquired as explained in the imaging section above. Since we have not covered such things as how to browse directories and hide items, a full discussion of this imaging option will be deferred until Chapter 9.

CD/DVD

When a CD or DVD drive is selected, an option to perform **Raw CD access** is available. This option is unchecked by default. When unchecked, XWF will process any file systems it sees on the CD/DVD drive in the same way as in the case of a hard drive. If the raw access option is checked, the contents of the drive will be displayed in hex without any interpretation of file systems, etc.

PHYSICAL MEMORY IMAGING

XWF by itself contains no way to capture the entirety of physical memory (except under Windows XP), but it can inspect memory on a per process basis. To do this, simply select **Tools | Open RAM**, expand a process, and select one of the sections of memory to examine. After clicking **OK**, the contents of the selected process will be displayed in a hex editor that can then be searched or reviewed as needed. XWF can access and image physical memory on a remote system when used with F-Response. This process will be explained in the F-Response section below.

In addition to accessing physical memory via F-Response, XWF can interpret memory dumps created by a wide variety of tools that can capture physical memory to a file, such as Helix (http://www.e-fense.com/), Moonsols Windows Memory toolkit (http://www.moonsols.com/windows-memory-toolkit/), and winpmem (https://code.google.com/p/volatility/downloads/list).

Once you have a physical memory dump, you can add it to your case via **File | Add Memory Dump** under the **Case Data** window or via the same option available in the context menu of the case root.

Once an image of memory has been added, XWF will traverse the raw memory similar to how it traversed the file systems on our hard drive. When XWF is finished with this step, you will be able to browse the contents of memory as shown in Figure 2.13. The memory layout of many, but not all, different Windows versions and service packs is supported.

Finally, should you add a disk image that contains a hiberfil.sys file to a case, XWF will automatically parse the file and add it to the case as shown at the top of Figure 2.13.

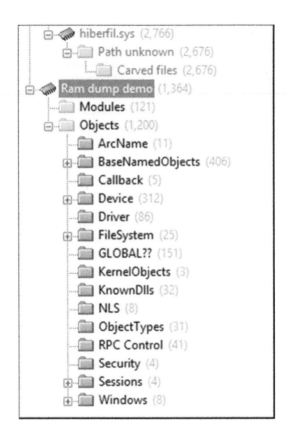

FIGURE 2.13

Memory dump in XWF.

CONTAINER FILES

XWF can create container files that are similar in function to container files used by other forensic suites (AD1 and L01 files for example). XWF container files use a special file system known as X-Ways File System Version 2 (XWFS2) that was designed to preserve as much metadata about files and directories as possible. XWF container files can easily handle up to one billion objects which make them very flexible.

XWF containers record both basic metadata that most third-party programs (EnCase from Version 5 onward and Mount Image Pro are two examples) can understand and advanced metadata that, as of the time of this writing, only products in the X-Ways family can understand.

To create a new container, select **Specialist | Evidence File Container | New** to bring up a dialog asking you to select a directory where you wish to save the container. By default, it will be the same directory where our hard drive image was saved. Enter a name for the container and click **Save**. XWF will append the extension for a container file, .ctr, to your file name. After clicking **Save**, a dialog with the configuration options shown in Figure 2.14 will be displayed.

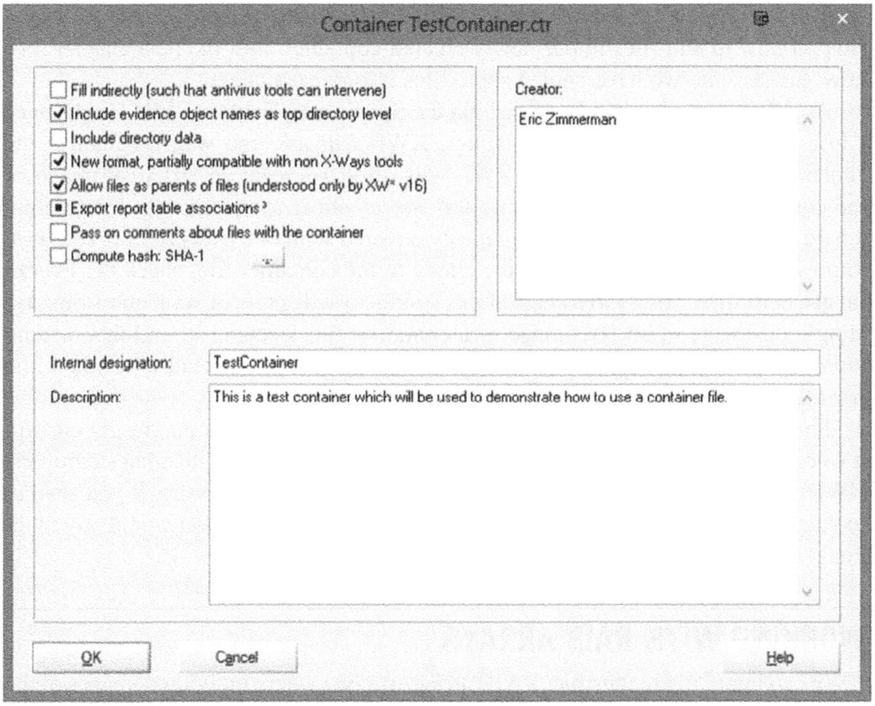

FIGURE 2.14

Container options.

While most of the options are self-explanatory, a few require a bit of elaboration. The **Fill indirectly** option, when checked, tells XWF to export any files that will be copied to the container to first be saved to a temporary directory on your computer in order for other programs such as a virus scanner to check them before they are then copied to the container. This ensures that no malware is copied into a container file. The **Include directory data** option, when checked, adds additional metadata about certain files (INDX buffers from directories in NTFS for example) to the container. These data often contains timestamps and other information advanced users sometimes require when looking at a set of directories and files. Finally, if you are exchanging a container file with other XWF users, or even for use in other tools, the **Export report table associations** and **Pass on comments about files with the container** options can be handy in that any report table associations and/or comments that have been assigned to files or directories will be maintained. The **Internal designation** acts as the volume label of the file system in the container.

When creating a new container, the defaults are reasonable for the vast majority of users.

After clicking **OK**, the container file is available to receive copies of files and directories from XWF. You can create as many XWF container files as you like, but XWF will only allow one container file to be open for writing at a time (and therefore only allow for copying of files into one container at a time).

Since we haven't covered general navigation in XWF, we will forego the discussion on how to add files to our newly created container until the next chapter. For now, just assume we have copied some files into our container.

An XWF container can be closed via the **Specialist | Evidence File Container | Close** menu. When closing a container, XWF will ask you want to finalize the container. If you elect to do so, XWF will offer to create an e01 disk image of the container. The options for doing this are identical to the process for creating a hard disk image that we have previously covered with one exception. If you wish to prevent any more files from being added to the container file, check the **Freeze target container file system** checkbox. Doing so will prevent someone from creating a dd image of an e01 image of a container file, opening it, and then adding more files to it. In effect, the container's file system becomes read-only when it is frozen.

Finalizing the container is not required and is usually done to compress or encrypt it when there is a need to share the information in the container with other examiners. XWF and other tools can view the container file as is in its raw state. If you need to look at what is inside a container file, add it to your case like you would any other image once you close the container.

WORKING WITH RAID ARRAYS

XWF can internally reconstruct RAID arrays in cases where individual images of the RAID disks have been acquired or where you have the physical disks that make up an array. XWF supports RAID level 0, 5, and 6 when reconstructing arrays. In addition to the images themselves, it is also critically important to know as much as possible about the RAID controller to which the disks were attached. Information such as the manufacturer of the controller, stripe size, parity information (backward, forward, delayed, dynamic, etc.) will be required by XWF to rebuild an array.

XWF TIPS AND TRICKS

Don't Image Individual Disks, Image the Array Itself

If possible, rather than image many hard disks in a RAID array, image the logical array itself. This can be done by imaging a computer in a live environment or via F-Response (this will be covered in a subsequent section). By imaging the logical array, you won't need to worry about any of the details as outlined in this section.

Before reassembling an array, the images that make up the array must be opened into XWF. This can be done via the **File | Open** option. You can designate an image in the **Files of type** dropdown box, but if you didn't, invoke the **Specialist | Interpret Image File As Disk** option to tell XWF to treat the individual image files as disks. Once the images are in the case, the process of putting them back in order can be started by using the **Specialist | Reconstruct RAID System** option as shown in Figure 2.15.

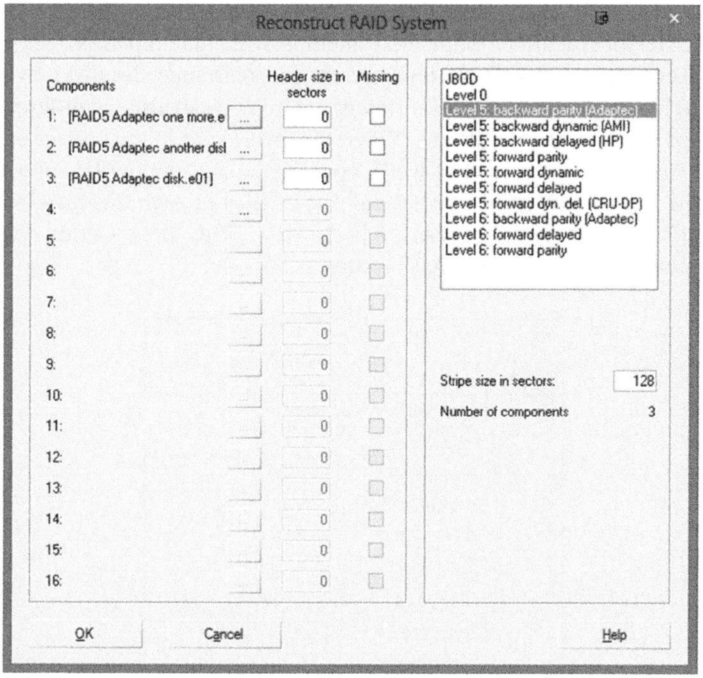

FIGURE 2.15

Reconstruct RAID System with images loaded—RAID 5 example.

Click the . . . button to load each of the images in the order that makes up the array. A bit of trial and error will most likely be necessary, but should you get the order wrong, no harm will be done to the images. If the order of the components is wrong, XWF may display a message, indicating that this and the **Directory Browser** may display random garbage, won't have a file count in directories, etc., as shown in Figure 2.16.

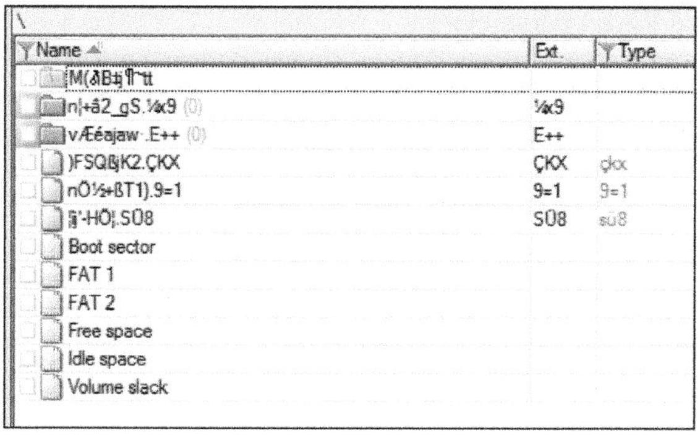

FIGURE 2.16

An incorrectly assembled RAID array.

To correct the situation, close the window that represents the incorrectly recon-structed RAID (or else after a while these attempts will clutter up the screen), go back into the **Reconstruct RAID System** option, and rearrange the disks by clicking the . . . and loading the images in a different order. You can also try different header sizes, stripe sizes, or parity patterns. When the images are in the correct order (and all other parameters are correct as well), opening the partition will display the con-tents of the file system including the number of files in each directory as seen in Figure 2.17. At this point, you can properly view JPEG files, Office documents, etc., that may be stored in the RAID system.

FIGURE 2.17

A properly reassembled RAID array.

Once correctly assembled, you should add the reassembled array to your case by right-clicking on the tab of the window that represents the reassembled array and choosing **Add to active case** as shown in Figure 2.18. Once the array is added to the case, it will show up in the **Case Data** window with a gold icon as opposed to the usual gray icon. After doing so, XWF will remember the correct component disks/images and RAID parameters.

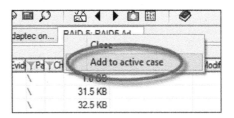

FIGURE 2.18

Adding the RAID array to a case.

In the case of RAID 5 arrays, XWF can reconstruct the array if it is missing one segment of the array. This is because parity is distributed across each segment of a RAID 5 array allowing one of its members to be absent. If you only have two of three segments, select one of the remaining two segments, add it twice, and check the **Missing** box on one of the duplicates and XWF will do the rest.

Finally, you can create a new forensic image of the reassembled, logical array by using the same options we discussed when imaging media in a previous section. Once the image is created, it can be added to the case and the individual images of disks in the array are no longer needed to be open in XWF.

XWF can also handle dynamic disk configurations in much the same way as above, but rather than choosing a flavor of RAID, you would choose the Just A Bunch Of Disks (JBOD) option and load each disk as we saw above. Once the dynamic disk is displayed as a single volume, it can be imaged like any other device.

More advanced capabilities and options are available and are thoroughly explained in the XWF manual in the **Reconstructing RAID Systems** section.

AUGMENTING WITH F-RESPONSE

It would be hard to describe F-Response any better than its creators, so here is a quote from the Web site:

> F-Response is an easy to use, vendor neutral, patented software utility that enables an investigator to conduct live forensics, Data Recovery, and eDiscovery over an IP network using their tool(s) of choice. F-Response is not another analysis tool. F-Response is a utility that allows you to make better use of the tools and training that you already have.
>
> F-Response software uses a patented process to provide read-only access to the full physical disk(s) of virtually any networked computer, plus the physical memory (RAM) of most Microsoft Windows® systems. Designed to be completely vendor neutral, if your analysis software reads a hard drive, it will work with F-Response.[1]

What does this mean to us, the forensics professional? Basically it means F-Response can expose physical drives, logical partitions, and memory from just about any operating system you are likely to encounter as well as things such as e-mail stores (i.e., Gmail, Yahoo, or any IMAP mail store), SharePoint databases, exotic raid setups, cloud storage, etc., as a device on your local machine. For a full list of supported operating systems and other supported targets, visit the F-Response Web site at http://www.f-response.com.

F-Response comes in several editions, but the core functionality in all of them is the same. The higher end editions allow such things as unlimited connections, the ability to programmatically interact with F-Response, and so on. For many forensic examiners, F-Response TACTICAL edition is the recommended edition to use.

TACTICAL edition comes in the form of two USB thumb drives: one for the subject computer and one for the examiner computer. To begin, insert the examiner thumb drive into your computer and start the software. Before the examiner machine can find the subject machine, F-Response needs to be started on the subject machine.

---

[1]http://www.f-response.com/.

Insert the subject thumb drive in the machine whose resources you wish to expose over a network and start the F-Response software. The subject machine is now beaconing out on the network looking for the examiner side of F-Response that is shown in Figure 2.19.

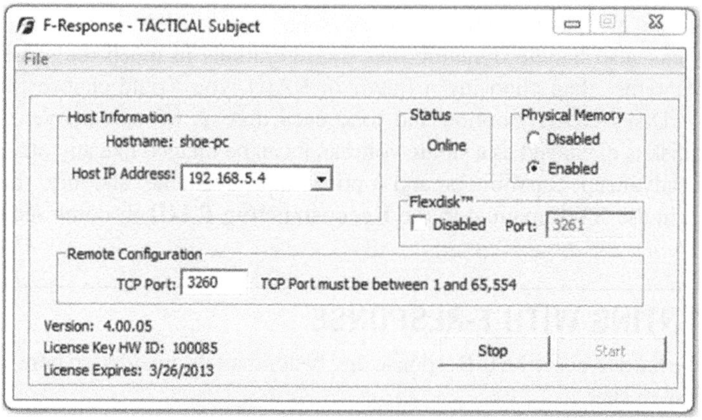

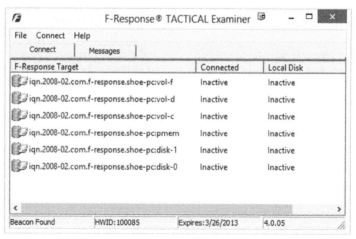

FIGURE 2.19

F-Response TACTICAL subject waiting for a connection.

Once the subject software is started, **select File | Auto Connect** on the examiner instance of F-Response. F-Response will find the subject computer[2] and display a list of resources that can be mapped to the examiner machine. In Figure 2.20, two physical disks containing three partitions have been exposed, as has physical memory.

F-Response Target	Connected	Local Disk
iqn.2008-02.com.f-response.shoe-pc:vol-f	Inactive	Inactive
iqn.2008-02.com.f-response.shoe-pc:vol-d	Inactive	Inactive
iqn.2008-02.com.f-response.shoe-pc:vol-c	Inactive	Inactive
iqn.2008-02.com.f-response.shoe-pc:pmem	Inactive	Inactive
iqn.2008-02.com.f-response.shoe-pc:disk-1	Inactive	Inactive
iqn.2008-02.com.f-response.shoe-pc:disk-0	Inactive	Inactive

Beacon Found   HWID: 100085   Expires: 3/26/2013   4.0.05

FIGURE 2.20

F-Response TACTICAL examiner after connecting.

---

[2]**Auto Connect** works best if both examiner and subject are on the same subnet, if this isn't the case, use the **Manual Connect** option from the **File** menu.

The next step is to select one or more devices for F-Response to make available on the examiner machine. Right-clicking on a device and selecting **Login to F-Response Disk** will map the remote disk as a local, physical disk on the examiner machine. In Figure 2.21, physical memory and both physical disks have been mapped to the examiner machine.

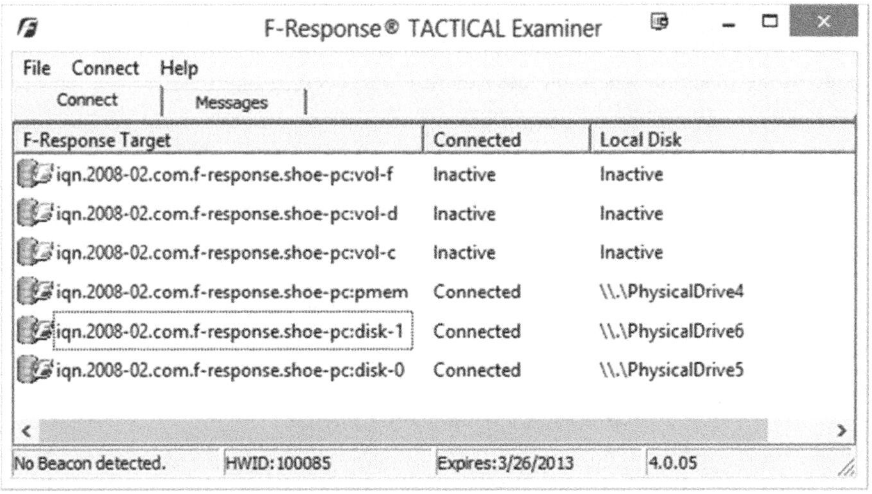

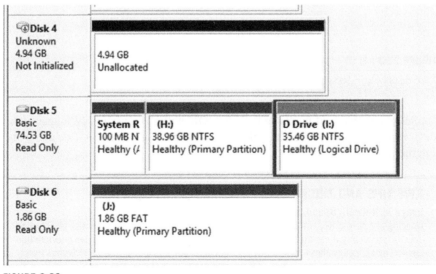

FIGURE 2.21

Devices mapped to local machine.

Using the Disk Management tool in Windows, we can see the newly connected devices as shown in Figure 2.22.

FIGURE 2.22

Windows Disk Management view of new devices.

If the physical disks contain file systems Windows understands, they will be mounted on a drive letter and can be accessed via My Computer. You can also use tools like Mount Image Pro to manage non-Windows file systems and assign a drive letter as Mount Image Pro contains file system drivers for HFS file systems.

You can now interact with each of the newly connected physical devices using XWF or any other tool. In XWF, you can image any of the devices exactly as outlined in the preceding section on imaging a hard drive. One thing you will notice is that any devices mapped by F-Response will have a manufacturer of "FRES" along with the name of the machine where the devices reside as seen in Figure 2.23.

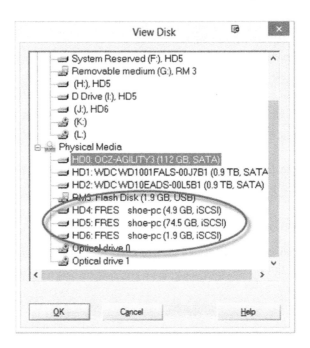

FIGURE 2.23

XWF displaying F-Response disks.

Selecting a piece of media and clicking **OK** will allow use of XWF against the device being opened in a read-only manner, across any network (including the Internet)!

XWF TIPS AND TRICKS

Image at Network Speed, not USB Speed!

Imaging to a hard drive connected via USB can be very time consuming because USB2 write speeds top out anywhere from 15 to 30 MB/second. USB3 and eSATA ports can alleviate this issue to a degree, but these ports are not very widespread, especially in server class machines.

After imaging the remote machine and/or memory, use the F-Response software on the examiner machine to disconnect the devices. Right-clicking on a connected local disk and selecting **Logout of F-Response Disk** will remove the device from the local computer. When all devices are removed, stop F-Response on both the subject and examiner machines and retrieve the thumb drives.

SHORTCUTS

F9: Bring up the View Disk interface
Alt-C: Bring up the Create Disk Image interface
CTRL-D: Bring up the Clone Disk interface

SUMMARY

This chapter covered how to start a new case in XWF in order to begin making use of the more powerful aspects of XWF. You learned how case data are organized and how to manage the files contained in a case.

Once a case was created, you learned how to create forensic images using techniques that can be used to image any piece of electronic media that you have physical access to, including RAID arrays. In addition, you saw how to leverage the power of F-Response in order to access storage devices and memory over a network via XWF.

Finally, you learned about reconstructing RAID arrays as well as container files including how to create them and the options XWF makes available when using container files.

Now that the necessary groundwork has been covered related to case management and adding evidence to a case, we can move on to an in-depth discussion of the XWF interface and how to efficiently and effectively navigate in XWF.

Before continuing to the next chapter, be sure to add at least one image of a hard disk to your case as we will need some evidence to interact with.

Contents

Navigating the X-Ways Forensics Interface

INFORMATION IN THIS CHAPTER

- Introduction
- **Case Data directory tree**
- Toolbar, **tab control**, and **Directory Browser options/filters**
- **Directory Browser**
- **Mode** buttons and **Details** pane
- **Status bar**
- Main menu
- **General Options** continued
- Volume Snapshot options
- **Viewer Programs** options continued
- **Security Options**
- Shortcuts
- Summary

INTRODUCTION

As previously mentioned, the X-Ways Forensics (XWF) interface looks and feels a lot like Windows Explorer but with many more options. In order to become proficient and efficient with XWF, it is necessary to understand how to interact with XWF to accomplish a given set of tasks as they relate to reviewing digital media. This chapter covers both basic and advanced navigation features of the XWF interface including working with the **Case Data** window and its **directory tree**, selecting and working with files and directories in the **Directory Browser**, and understanding the **Mode** buttons when looking at a particular file or group of files. After reading this chapter, you will have the knowledge necessary to effectively navigate the XWF user interface and you will use this knowledge throughout the remainder of the book.

CASE DATA DIRECTORY TREE

We will begin our coverage of the XWF interface with the **Case Data** window that we have previously seen. However, now that we have imaged one or more hard disks (or other media) and added them to a case, more options become available.

Underneath the case title is a virtual directory named **Case Root** followed by a number inside parentheses. The number represents the total number of items, both files and directories, in the case. This number will increment as new images are added, and various other functionalities of XWF are applied to the images.

After adding an image to XWF, it will appear under the **Case Root** of the **Case Data** window as shown in Figure 3.1. For illustration purposes, the partitions available in the image have been expanded to show the top-level directory structure in each partition.

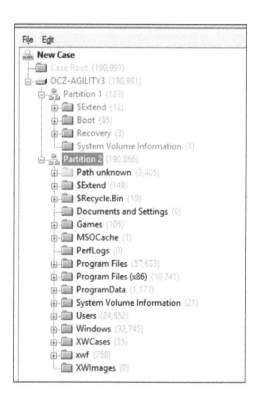

FIGURE 3.1

Case Data directory tree.

Navigating around the **directory tree** is exactly like using Windows Explorer. You can also double click a directory name to toggle whether the directory is expanded. For keyboard warriors, you can use keyboard shortcuts to interact with the **directory tree**. The left/right arrows or the +/− keys on the numeric keypad will expand and contract directories one at a time. The * key on the numeric keypad will recursively expand the selected directory.

Different options become available depending on what object you interact with in the **directory tree**. While a left click of the mouse selects the item you clicked on and sometimes opens an object in the **Directory Browser**, right-clicking objects in the **directory tree** will do different things. Starting from the top of the **Case Data** window, let's look at what right clicking each object in the **directory tree** does.

We already covered right clicking the case title in Chapter 2, so we will not discuss it here.

Right click behaviors

Right clicking on the **Case Root** object will bring up a dialog asking what evidence objects you want to include when generating a recursive view of the data in your case. This dialog is shown in Figure 3.2. In other words, rather than having to drill down into various directories looking for pictures, you could use the **Case Root** window to display every file regardless of what evidence object and directory may contain the files. From there, filtering for the items you are looking for becomes much easier. This concept will be covered in a later chapter, so we won't discuss it further at this point.

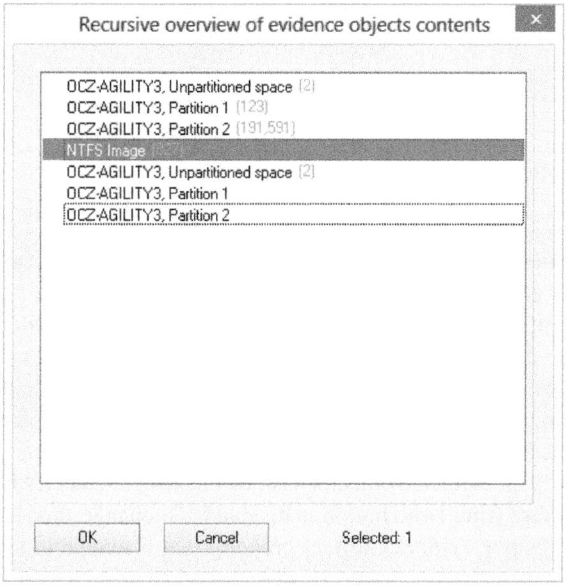

FIGURE 3.2

Recursive overview dialog.

Before we move on, let's take a closer look at what happens when you *left click* the **Case Root** node. Left clicking the **Case Root** node will open a tab that will display all of the physical devices and partitions in the current case. As you work with your evidence, if a particular device or partition is especially important, it can be marked as important by selecting the object, then either pressing the **SPACE** key or right clicking and choosing **Tag** from the context menu. Doing either of these will add a yellow flag to both the **Case Root** window and the **directory tree**.

Right clicking on an **evidence object** (a hard disk image, for example) will bring up a context menu with options similar to those that were available when right clicking the case title object as shown in Figure 3.3.

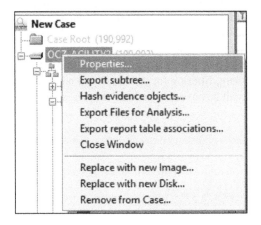

FIGURE 3.3

Evidence object context menu.

The **Properties** menu will bring up a dialog that lets you edit the name of the evidence object, add comments to the evidence object, etc.

The **Comments** field in the **Properties** dialog can be used to add such details as the primary user of a computer, where the computer came from, contact info, etc. On the right side of the window is a **Description** box that contains information related to the image file. Scrolling down to the bottom of the window will show you details related to the hashing and rehashing of the image file.

You can verify an evidence object's hash by clicking the **Verify hash** button. By default, the **Display time zone** button is disabled. To change this, enable the **Individual time zones per evidence object** property that is available in the case properties dialog.

One final thing to note in the evidence object window is the two arrows in the upper left corner. These arrows allow you to change the order of evidence objects in the case should you wish to reorder them. Of course, this option requires at least two evidence objects be in a case. An example of an evidence object property window is shown in Figure 3.4.

Evidence Object No. 1

Object title/number: OCZ-AGILITY3   Date added: 01/27/2013
Internal designation: [D:\XWImages\OCZ-AGILITY3.e01]   Size: 112 GB

Comments: Description:

This is a comment about this evidence object.   Model: OCZ-AGILITY3
                                                  Serial No.: ?
                                                  Firmware Rev.: 2.25
                                                  Bus: SATA

                                                  Total capacity: 120,034,123,776 bytes = 112 GB

                                                  Bytes per sector: 512
                                                  Sector count: 234,441,648
                                                  Windows disk signature: 964022CA
                                                  Unpartitionable space: 2,992 Sectors
                                                  SMART health status: OK

Hash: SHA-1   4F5E116C1F9A07A158C7DE2A6ADE241B089FA63E   Verify hash

                                                  Display time zone...

    OK   Cancel   Help

FIGURE 3.4

Evidence object properties.

The **Export subtree** menu allows you to export an ASCII representation of the **directory tree** to a file. For example, an export of the **directory tree** in Figure 3.1 results in what is shown in Figure 3.5. This can be used to add directory structure to a report or otherwise explain how a particular file system was laid out.

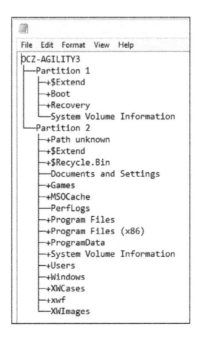

```
File   Edit   Format   View   Help
OCZ-AGILITY3
    ├─Partition 1
    │    ├─+$Extend
    │    ├─+Boot
    │    ├─+Recovery
    │    └─System Volume Information
    └─Partition 2
         ├─+Path unknown
         ├─+$Extend
         ├─+$Recycle.Bin
         ├─Documents and Settings
         ├─+Games
         ├─+MSOCache
         ├─PerfLogs
         ├─+Program Files
         ├─+Program Files (x86)
         ├─+ProgramData
         ├─+System Volume Information
         ├─+Users
         ├─+Windows
         ├─+XWCases
         ├─+xwf
         └─XWImages
```

FIGURE 3.5

Export subtree example.

The **Hash evidence objects** menu allows for the regeneration and comparison of hash values across several evidence objects. While you can verify the hash values of evidence objects individually, this is a much easier option should you need to verify several images at once (at the beginning of or end of a case, for example).

The **Export Files for Analysis** menu allows XWF to export a subset of files so they can be processed by an external program. Once the external program is done processing the files, XWF can import the results and display those results in the XWF interface. One such example of this is DoublePics (http://www.dotnetfabrik.de/de/doublepics) that is used to categorize and deduplicate images. For XWF to be able to interact with external programs, certain rules must be followed by the program. This will be covered in more detail in Chapter 7.

The **Remove from Case** menu item will delete an evidence object from the case in its entirety. If you remove an evidence object from a case, its volume snapshot and any associated items such as comments and report table associations will be removed as well.

Right clicking on a **partition** in an evidence object will bring up a context menu with options similar to what was available when right clicking an evidence object. In addition to the options we have already discussed, two new options are available: **Explore recursively** and **Collapse All**. **Explore recursively** behaves just as it did at the **Case Root** level, except that only the directories and files in the partition will be listed. **Collapse All** will simply contract every expanded directory in all partitions under the active evidence object.

Right clicking on a directory in a partition will immediately result in a recursive listing being displayed in the **Directory Browser** for the selected directory. Note that the directory icon is replaced with a blue arrow when a directory is viewed recursively (as opposed to its normal yellow icon). Holding the **CTRL** key while right clicking will bring up a menu that contains an **Export subtree** menu. This behaves exactly as we have seen before, except that the export will start from the selected directory as opposed to the entire **directory tree**.

Middle-click behaviors

Just as right clicking various objects resulted in certain behaviors, middle-clicking objects also invoke certain behavior. Middle clicking a partition will recursively toggle the tagging and untagging of all files and directories in the partition. Middle clicking a directory will recursively toggle the tagging and untagging of all files and directories in that directory. This is useful if you have tagged files in several different directories and want to untag everything in a given evidence object. This will become clearer after we discuss tagging later.

Now that you have a solid understanding of how to interact with the **directory tree**, expand one or more of the partitions in your image and then expand a few directories in the partition. Doing so will allow the following sections to make more sense.

TOOLBAR, TAB CONTROL, AND DIRECTORY BROWSER OPTIONS, FILTERS

The toolbar is no different in XWF than it is in any other program. A few items on the toolbar that deserve some detail are the forward and backward buttons that are the light-blue arrows in the middle of the toolbar. Clicking these buttons allows you to retrace and restore your path through evidence as you use XWF. These buttons are shown in Figure 3.6.

FIGURE 3.6

Backward and forward buttons.

XWF TIPS AND TRICKS

Use the Mouse!

Rather than moving the mouse to the forward or backward button and clicking on it, you can use the forward and backward buttons on your mouse which will save a considerable amount of time when navigating in XWF. This assumes that your mouse has more than three buttons!

Below the toolbar is the **tab control**. Directly below the **tab control** is the **caption line** of the **Directory Browser**. In Figure 3.7, the **tab control** contains three tabs, one for each object that is open (the physical device itself and two partitions in the example). Below the tabs, the currently selected directory is displayed in the **Directory Browser** caption. In the example below, the root directory (represented by a backslash character) is selected. If a directory is explored recursively, the selected directory will be displayed in italics with *and subdirectories* appended to the directory name. On the right side of the **Directory Browser** caption is a summary of the number of files and directories displayed in the **Directory Browser** (the **Directory Browser** will be covered below in the **Directory Browser** section).

In Figure 3.7, the summary is listed as *15+0+4=19 files, 16+0+1=17 dir*. Both the file and directory summary break down as follows:

$$\text{Existing} + \text{previously existing} + \text{virtual} = \text{total objects}$$

FIGURE 3.7

Tab control and **Directory Browser caption line**.

If no virtual files are listed, then no number for virtual files will be shown. Additionally, if no previously-existing files are listed, then no number for previously-existing files will be shown.

XWF TIPS AND TRICKS

Closing Evidence Objects

As you interact with evidence objects, more and more tabs will be created on the **tab control**. To close a tab, right click and choose close, middle click on a tab, or press **CTRL-W**. Should you wish to close all open tabs, press **CTRL-Q** and XWF will close every open tab at once.

The last thing to discuss in this section is the **Directory Browser Options, Filters** dialog that is shown in Figure 3.8. To open **Directory Browser Options, Filters**, left click anywhere on the **caption line** of the **Directory Browser**, use the shortcut **CTRL + F5**, the **Directory Browser** icon, or select menu option **Options | Directory Browser**.

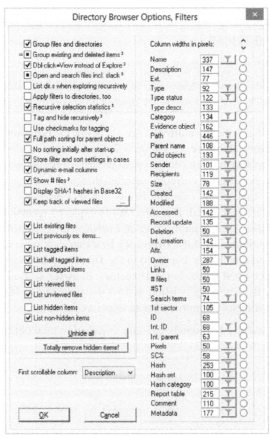

FIGURE 3.8

Directory Browser Options, **Filters** dialog.

The **Directory Browser Options**, **Filters** dialog contains three groups of options: General Options, item listing options, and **Directory Browser** column and filter options.

General Options

The General Options are in the upper left section of the dialog. As we have seen in Chapter 1, some of the options are tristate checkboxes.

If **Group files and directories** is checked, directories will be grouped together and displayed at the top of the **Directory Browser** and files will be grouped together below directories. If unchecked, directories and files will be listed in alphabetical order in the **Directory Browser**.

Group existing and deleted items has three options:

Fully checked: XWF creates two groups in the **Directory Browser**: the first consisting of existing files and directories at the top of the **Directory Browser** and the second containing all other types of files and directories below that.

Half-checked: XWF creates three groups where the first two are exactly the same as when fully checked. The third group will contain all the files and directories that are not recoverable. That is, the first cluster is no longer available.

Unchecked: No grouping will take place at all.

In both the fully and half-checked cases, the sorting is done *inside each group*, not as a whole.

When **Group existing and deleted items** is fully or half-checked, an additional symbol will be added to the column currently being sorted as a reminder that the extra groups exist. A single, horizontal line indicates that another group has been created in the **Directory Browser**. Two horizontal lines indicate that two additional groups have been created in the **Directory Browser**. Figure 3.9 shows an example of this option when in the half-checked state.

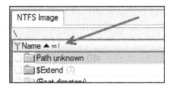

FIGURE 3.9

Symbol example with **Group existing and deleted items** half-checked.

We recommend half-checked or fully checked as it keeps known unrecoverable files out of the way which reduces "noise."

XWF TIPS AND TRICKS
Possible Gotcha!

Using the **Group existing and deleted items** option (either fully or half-checked) introduces some caveats you must be aware of. As outlined above, when this option is enabled, XWF creates additional groups in the **Directory Browser** that are not present when the option is unchecked. As such, you must check *all* groups to see whether what you are looking for is present. For example, when sorting by the **Name** column, if you are interested in a file starting with the letter *C*, you may expect it to be between the letters *B* and *D* at the top of the **Directory Browser** window. With this option on, you may not see it where you expect it to be and may think the file is not present at all. In reality, it may very well be present in one of the other groups that XWF creates as a result of enabling this option. When using this option, be sure to check each group for the presence of the file in which you have an interest.

You can configure XWF to view either a file's contents or its "children" when you double click the file. **Dbl-click=View instead of Explore** has three options:

Fully checked: The file will be viewed when double clicked.
Half-checked: You will be prompted to either view or explore a file when opening a file with child objects.
Unchecked: The file will be explored when double clicked.

You can always choose either the **View** or **Explore** option by right clicking a file in the **Directory Browser** as well.

Open and search files incl. slack has three options:

Fully checked: Slack contents will be searched regardless of whether files have been hidden or marked as irrelevant.
Half-checked: The slack space of files marked as irrelevant by hash comparison and/or hash database matching as well as files that have been hidden or filtered out *will not* be searched. Put another way, the slack of nonhidden or otherwise nonexcluded files *will* be searched.
Unchecked: File slack is never searched. Additionally, file slack will NOT be displayed when opening a file via the context menu or when viewing the file in **File** mode.

The takeaway from this option is that it allows you the ability to avoid searching "useless" objects, e.g., videos, while being able to search their slack areas. This is an exceptionally powerful way to maximize search efficiency. There are times when a video isn't worth looking at and as such the video itself can be hidden. Using this option in its fully checked state still allows for its slack space to be searched, and this is important because slack may contain part of a text file, for example. In other words, if you are looking for a snippet of text, rather than searching through 200 MB of binary data in a video, search a few kilobytes of that video's slack space instead.

If this option is half or fully checked, file slack will be shown in green when in **File** mode. The recommended setting is fully checked which ensures slack space is always searched.

If **List dirs when exploring recursively** is checked, a full listing of directory names will be included when exploring recursively. When unchecked, only files will be listed when exploring recursively. If you are interested in the directory structure or timestamps on directories, it is helpful to have them included with files when exploring recursively.

If **Apply filters to directories, too** is unchecked, directories will always be shown when filtering on the **Name** column. If checked, any directories whose name does not match one of the entered filter criteria will be hidden.

Recursive selection statistics has three options:

Fully checked: All files including child objects are taken into account when determining how many files and the size of files are calculated.

Half-checked: Child objects of files are not taken into account and only the parent files in a given directory are used in the calculation.

Unchecked: Only the items selected in the **Directory Browser** are taken into account when calculating statistics.

Tag and hide recursively has three options:

Fully checked: When tagging a directory, all files in the directory will be tagged, including any child objects of said files. When tagging a file, the file itself and any child objects will be tagged.

Half-checked: When tagging a directory, only the directory itself is tagged. When tagging a file, only the parent file itself will be tagged. Additionally, any child objects contained in a file will inherit the tagged state of its parent when new child objects are added to the volume snapshot via a Refine Volume Snapshot (RVS) operation. The RVS operation will be covered in detail in Chapter 4.

Unchecked: Only the file or directory itself will be tagged.

This option can also be controlled by holding the **SHIFT** key when tagging. If **SHIFT** is pressed when tagging, the opposite of the selected value of this option will be used. Tagging files will be discussed in more depth in the section on the **"Directory Browser."**

If **Use checkmarks for tagging** is checked, XWF will use a checkmark when tagging objects as opposed to filling in the box with a blue square.

If **Full path sorting for parent objects** is checked, any file with child objects will have their child objects listed directly after the parent file. If unchecked, all child objects will be grouped together after all parents have been listed for a given path.

If **No sorting initially after start-up** is checked, XWF will forget the last sorting criteria used upon start-up. In other words, columns in the **Directory Browser** will not be sorted when XWF is initially loaded which can save time if many objects were listed in the **Directory Browser**. Sorting will also be disabled when disabling filters when the **Directory Browser** is in recursive mode with this option checked.

If **Store filter and sort settings in cases** is checked, XWF will remember the filter and column sorting criteria on a case-by-case basis. When a case is opened, XWF will reload the saved settings. When unchecked, XWF uses the same filter and sorting criteria regardless of which case is open.

If **Dynamic email columns** is checked, XWF will add and remove e-mail-specific columns to the **Directory Browser**. If at least one e-mail message is visible in the **Directory Browser** and that e-mail contains a sender and recipient, the e-mail-specific columns will be shown. Otherwise, they will be hidden in order to make more room for other columns. Sender and recipient information is extracted via an RVS operation.

Show # files has three options:

Fully checked: XWF will calculate the total number of files in a directory or, in the case of a file, the number of child objects inside the file. This total is then displayed in both the **directory tree** and the **Directory Browser** in the **# files** column.

Half-checked: The total number of files will not be displayed in the **directory tree**, but will be displayed in the **Directory Browser** in the **# files** column.

Unchecked: The total number of files will only be displayed in the **Directory Browser** in the **# files** column.

When either fully and half-checked, the total number of files will be shown in parenthesis after the directory or file name.

If **Display SHA-1 hashes in Base32** is checked, SHA-1 values will be displayed in Base32 format in the **Directory Browser**. This is useful if working with peer-to-peer networks that use SHA-1 Base32 hashes, like Gnutella. If SHA-1 hash values are 40 characters/bytes in length, they are in Base16 (hex) format. If they are 32 characters/bytes long, they are in Base32 format.

If **Keep track of viewed files** is checked, XWF will track the activities that can be selected by clicking the ... button next to this option. If unchecked, XWF will not track whether files have been viewed. Viewed files will be discussed in more depth in the section on the "**Directory Browser**."

The **When identifying duplicates based on hash** suboption of **Keep track of viewed files** has three options:

Fully checked: Files in the same volume are marked as viewed when a duplicate is viewed (duplicate according to hashing or hard-linked file) or, if a file has been viewed already and duplicates are found via hash value, the duplicate files will also be marked as viewed.

Half-checked: Nothing happens to duplicates when *viewing* files, only when identifying said duplicates via hash value. Put another way, any duplicates found via hash value will inherit the view state of the original file.

Unchecked: Files are never marked as viewed at all based on hash duplicates.

When viewed in gallery (pictures only), when checked, will mark pictures as viewed when they are displayed in the gallery. This is useful when having to review many pictures in that you can uncheck the **List viewed items** option and retain a subset of pictures that you haven't viewed. The **When viewed in gallery (pictures only)** option is unchecked by default, so be sure to enable this if your investigation can benefit from it.

Item listing options

The item listing options are in the lower left section of the **Directory Browser Options, Filters** dialog. Most are self-explanatory. A unique property of some of these checkboxes is that checking them will result in another dialog being displayed that allows for the selection of related items. These will be pointed out below along with any options that require a bit more explanation.

The **List previously ex. items** checkbox, when clicked, will bring up another dialog that allows you to choose the types of previously existing files to show. If all items in the secondary dialog are unchecked, **List previously ex. items** will be unchecked as well. If one or more of the items in the secondary dialog are checked, **List previously ex. items** will be half-checked.

List half tagged items, when checked, will display files and directories who have at least one child object tagged. In other words, if you had a directory with four files in it and tagged two of the files, the parent directory of the tagged files would be half tagged. A directory or file is considered fully tagged when all of its child objects are tagged.

XWF allows you to hide files and/or directories in the **Directory Browser** via its context menu. Hiding files will be fully explained in the section on the "Directory Browser." The last two checkboxes, **List hidden items** and **List non-hidden items**, control whether hidden and/or nonhidden items are displayed in the **Directory Browser**. Any hidden files can always be viewed again by checking the **List hidden items** option. Use the **Unhide all** button to make all previously hidden files visible again. Should you wish to remove hidden files from the volume snapshot permanently, use the **Totally remove hidden items!** button. We recommend working with a copy of your case when using this option should you wish to reverse the process. A copy of a case can be created via the **Case Data | File | Save As** menu item.

Below the item listing options is the **First scrollable column** option. By selecting a column here, any columns to the left of the selected column will be pinned to the left side of the **Directory Browser** and will not be moved when scrolling to the right to see other columns. For example, if the column order starts with **Name** followed by **Description** and the first scrollable column is **Description**, the **Name** column will remain stationary when scrolling to the right.

Directory Browser column and filter options

The **Directory Browser** column and filter options are on the right side of the dialog.

The left side of the dialog contains the column name (**Description**, for example). The middle option allows for entering a number that corresponds to the width of the column in pixels. A zero indicates that the column will not be shown in the **Directory Browser**. You can also use the mouse to resize columns in the **Directory Browser** by clicking the separator between columns and dragging left or right.

Some of the columns will have a gray icon that looks like a funnel. Clicking this button will bring up a dialog that allows you to enter criteria for that filter. If a filter is active, the icon will appear as a blue funnel. Clicking an active filter will disable it. We will cover filters in the section on the "**Directory Browser**" and will forego a discussion on filters at this time.

Finally, to the far right of each column name is a radio button. This radio button is used to rearrange the order of the columns as they are displayed in the **Directory Browser**. To move a column, click the corresponding radio button. The first time a radio button is selected, the up and down arrows above all the radio buttons will flash. This indicates that you can use the up and down arrows to move the selected column up or down to whatever position in the list you desire. This is the only way to move columns around. You cannot drag and drop columns to a new position directly in the **Directory Browser**. If you wish to reset the columns to their default values, right click the arrows and confirm the reset action.

Directory Browser columns

While most of the columns listed have descriptions that are self-explanatory, a few require a bit more detail or emphasis.

The **Ext.** column is the extension of a file name as it exists in the file system, whereas the **Type** column is the actual file type (its typical extension or other designation) based on the results of the file type verification step (file signature) when RVS is executed.

The **Type status** column is related to the **Ext.** and **Type** options in that the **Type status** column will reflect whether the file type has been confirmed, is irrelevant, not in the file type list, etc. The **Type status** column has very powerful filtering options as it allows you to choose various status categories and the rank of a particular status. You can eliminate a lot of noise by assigning certain file extensions to lower valued ranks and then viewing files with a certain rank or higher. This will be covered in more detail in Chapter 7.

The **Child objects** column will display a list of comma-separated file names for any child objects found in the selected file.

The **Record update** column contains the last modified date and time of the file or directory's FILE record (on NTFS) or inode (on Linux files systems).

The **Deletion** column will reflect, when available, the date and time an object was deleted. This information is gathered by XWF when looking at various artifacts related to journaling file systems or when analyzing file systems that store these timestamps regularly.

The **Int. creation** (internal creation) column will contain dates and times XWF extracts from the metadata available in certain kinds of files during the RVS process. As described in the XWF help file and manual, internal timestamps are usually less volatile and more difficult to manipulate than file system-level timestamps. As such, they are useful for corroboration.

The **Attr.** column contains details (such as, but not limited to, Windows attributes) about an object such as its encryption status, if it was found in a volume shadow copy (VSC), contains an alternate data stream, etc.

The **Owner** column will display the user name of the owner of an object, if known. If unknown, the SID of the owner of the object is displayed.

The **Links** column contains a count of the number of hard links that exist for a file or a directory.

The **# files** column contains the total number of child objects contained in a file or a directory. This number corresponds to the number in parenthesis after a file or a directory name.

The **#ST** column is the number of search terms that have been found in an object. The **Search terms** column is related to **#ST** in that **Search terms** will contain a comma-separated list of all the search terms that were found in a given object. Searching and reviewing search hits will be covered in depth in Chapter 6.

The **ID** column is assigned either by the file system or by XWF. It is not guaranteed to be unique. In contrast, the **Int. ID**, or Internal ID, column is a unique value generated by XWF for each object in a volume snapshot. The higher the **Int. ID**, the more recently it has been added to the volume snapshot.

The **Int. parent** column contains the **Int. ID** value of the parent object.

The **Pixels** column reflects the size of graphics files in either thousands of pixels (KP) or megapixels. This column is populated as a by-product of the skin color percentage calculation or viewing a picture in either full screen, **Preview** mode, or the gallery.

The **SC%** column, or skin color percentage, reflects the percentage of skin tones present in a given graphic file. The higher the percentage, the more skin tones are present in a graphic file. This is useful for cases involving child pornography/child exploitation material in that sorting by this column allows for quickly locating such material. Black and white images can also be easily located in a similar manner.

The **Hash** column will contain the file's hash value if computed as part of the RVS process. The **Hash set** column reflects the internal hash database that a file's hash was found in, if any. Should a hash be found in more than one hash set, this column will reflect all the hash set names that contained the hash. The **Hash category** contains the category a particular hash set was assigned to, either irrelevant/harmless or notable/malicious.

XWF TIPS AND TRICKS

Houston, We've Got a Problem!

If a given hash is in two different hash sets and the categories are different for the hash sets, XWF will detect this and inform you of the inconsistency by adding an entry to the **Messages** window. In addition, as with any file whose hash value is found in the "notable" category, the icon and hash category will also turn red.

The **Report table** column contains any associated report table categories that have been created by an examiner. If more than one report table is associated with a file or a directory, they will be comma separated.

The **Comment** column contains anything the examiner wishes to annotate about a given file or directory. A single comment can be applied to multiple files by first selecting the files to which you wish to apply the same comment.

The **Metadata** column will contain any internal data that XWF has extracted as part of the RVS process. This includes such things as EXIF data, Word document authors, etc.

As you use XWF and become more familiar with these columns and their usage, you will show and hide different columns depending on the type of case you are working. In general, it is recommended to keep the number of visible columns as minimal as possible as opposed to displaying every column and having to scroll excessively to find the information you need.

DIRECTORY BROWSER

The **Directory Browser** is perhaps the most used component of the XWF interface. It is where a listing of files and directories will be displayed as you select folders in the **directory tree**. Across the top of the **Directory Browser** are column headers that mirror the columns as configured in the **Directory Browser Options, Filters** dialog. As mentioned previously, while you can resize the visible columns using the mouse, you cannot reorder them by dragging and dropping the columns.

Column sorting

Clicking on a column will sort by that column. An arrow will indicate whether the column is sorted in ascending or descending order. XWF allows for sorting on up to three columns. For example, clicking the **Name** column will sort the **Name** column alphabetically. If you next click the **Ext.** column, the **Ext.** column will be sorted alphabetically, but for each unique extension, the files in the **Name** column will still be sorted alphabetically. The **Name** column will also have two *vertical* tick marks added to the right of the sort indicator, indicating that this column is the secondary sort column. Clicking a third column will result in yet another level of grouping and sorting and will place the corresponding number of vertical tick marks on the previous two columns. You can reset any secondary and tertiary sorting by holding the **SHIFT** key when clicking a column header.

Column filtering

In many of the column headers, you will see a filter icon just as we saw in the **Directory Browser Options, Filters** dialog. If a filter is inactive, the icon will be gray. If active, it will be blue. Recall that any time one or more filters are active the **caption line** of the **Directory Browser** will contain a blue filter icon to the left of the path.

When one or more filters are active, the right side of the **caption line** of the **Directory Browser** will change to reflect the number of files that are visible as a result of the filter as well as the number of files that have been filtered from view. You can click the blue filter icon to the right of this summary to deactivate all active filters.

To see the options available for a given column's filter, click the filter icon and a dialog will be displayed. If you wish to activate a filter without being shown the dialog for that filter, hold the **SHIFT** key while clicking the filter icon. To deactivate the filter, repeat the process.

Most of the filter options are self-explanatory, but a few have some additional options that are discussed below.

The **Name** filter allows for the use of wildcards (up to two if they appear at the beginning or end of the filter) or substring searches (no wildcards needed). Regular expressions are supported when substring searches are selected. Filters should be added one per line.

If you wish to negate an entry, prepend it with a colon. For example, entering *:apple** on one line and **oranges** on another will display all files that do not start with *apple* and have the word *oranges* somewhere in the file name. Negation does *not* work for substring matches. This filter dialog is also shared with the **Parent name** and **Child objects** columns. As such, only one of these three columns can be filtered at any given time.

The **Type** filter allows for either groups of files by type or individual extensions to be selected. Rather than browsing the list manually to look for a particular extension, use the **Expand all** button to expand all groups and then simply start typing the extension that you are interested in. You do not need to type the dot as the groups consist of extensions only.

The **Type Status** column's font color will reflect the results of the file type verification as follows: verified = black, mismatched = blue, and everything else = gray.

The **Category** filter serves two purposes. Selecting a category filters the files listed in the **Directory Browser** to list only those that match the selected category. You can also simply click the **Category** filter to get an overview of the number of files that are listed in the **Directory Browser** by category without activating the filter. The configuration file that sets forth categories can be edited as needed and this will be covered in Chapter 7.

The **Path** filter works on substring matches, so wildcards are not needed when entering items.

The **Created**, **Modified**, **Accessed**, **Record update**, **Deletion**, and **Int. creation** filters are date based and can be used to filter any of these columns to list files before, after, or between dates and times. You can also adjust the time zone as needed. These columns also share a single filter and as such, only one of these columns can be filtered at a time. In cases where different time zones are being used in different evidence objects, sorting is done based on the UTC date and time and not the converted date and time value.

The **Attr.** filter can be used to filter on a wide variety of object attributes. Filtering on this column is very powerful. The values of each of the abbreviations can be seen on the **Legend** tab that will be covered below when discussing the **Mode** buttons and **Details** pane. When sorting by the **Attr.** column, more important attributes will be listed first as opposed to attributes being sorted alphabetically.

The **Owner** filter can be used to display only files owned by a certain user, hide files owned by the operating system, etc. Clicking the **SIDs** button displays a list of SIDs and their associated usernames. The rightmost numerical value in the SID can be used in either of the **User ID** options in the **Owner** filter.

The **Int. ID** filter is very useful in that it can filter out any files NOT found as a result of the RVS process. By default, the **Int. ID** filter will display the number of files that have been recovered as part of the last RVS process which makes it easy to look at only the newly found files as opposed to having to look at newly found files mixed in with previously existing ones.

XWF TIPS AND TRICKS
Internal ID Internals
If you hide files via the **Directory Browser** context menu and then use the **Directory Browser** option to **Totally remove hidden items**, XWF will rearrange the **Int. ID** of the remaining objects to eliminate any gaps created by the removal process. As such, you cannot rely on the **Int. ID** to reflect the order in which items were added to the volume snapshot.

The **Hash** filter has several options including allowing up to four hashes to be entered at a time. This is often a more efficient option than creating a hash database should you be looking for a small number of files by their hash values. If you need to filter by a single hash, right clicking on a hash value in the **Directory Browser** allows for quickly filtering by that hash value.

The **Report table** filter allows for selecting one or more report tables to be selected. Using this filter allows for quickly locating a particular group of files assigned to report tables by an examiner as well as certain files identified (and assigned to report tables) by XWF that may require manual review (animated GIFs, files that caused XWF to crash, etc.). You can also use this filter to list files which have *not* been assigned to a report table.

The **Comment** and **Metadata** filters are similar in that they can quickly find any files or directories with a comment or metadata. If you are looking for particular words in either column, up to two different criteria can be used.

When one or more filters are active, the right side of the **caption line** of the **Directory Browser** will display additional icons that allow you to save the active filters to a file for later use as seen in Figure 3.10. These saved filters can then be quickly applied to the **Directory Browser** as a unit by reloading them via the folder icon.

FIGURE 3.10

Save active filters icon.

Directory Browser context menu

When one or more files and/or directories are selected in the **Directory Browser**, right clicking will display a context menu with options that allow further action to be taken against the selected objects. An example of this context menu is shown in Figure 3.11.

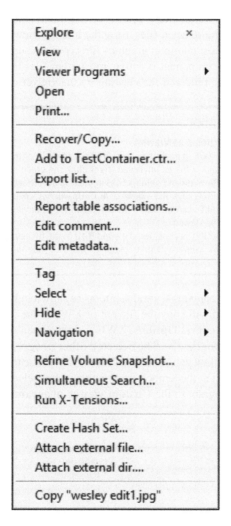

FIGURE 3.11

Directory Browser context menu.

The context menu will operate on the objects *selected* in the **Directory Browser** and not on objects merely *tagged* in the **Directory Browser**.

The contents of the context menu will change depending on what files and/or directories were selected before right clicking. For example, if you do not have an XWF container file or skeleton image (SI) open, you won't see the **Add to** option to add the selected objects to the container or SI. Similarly, if an object doesn't have metadata, the **Edit metadata** option will not appear.

Explore will "drill down" into an object to allow you to see any child objects that are contained in the file. For example, exploring an archive file would let you view the files and directories contained in the archive. If a jpg image contained a thumbnail, exploring the jpg would allow you to see the thumbnail.

View will display the selected files using the internal viewers inside XWF. Only registry files and the most common graphics file types are supported by the internal viewers. If the viewer component is active, most other files that XWF doesn't have internal viewers for are rendered for viewing by the viewer component.

XWF TIPS AND TRICKS
Shortcuts for Marking Items as Viewed
When a file is viewed in XWF, a green box is added to the far left of the entry in the **Directory Browser**. To manually mark a file as unviewed, right click the green square.

You can also manually mark and unmark files in the **Directory Browser** by using the **ALT** key in conjunction with the arrow keys. **ALT+Down** or **ALT+Up** will mark each item as viewed as the selected line advances. **ALT+Left** will mark the selected files as unviewed and **ALT+Right** will mark the selected files as viewed.

As a side note, a directory is considered viewed if all of the files and subdirectories that it contains are marked as viewed. Unlike tagging, there is no half-viewed indicator for directories.

Viewer Programs contains several subitems as shown in Figure 3.12. The **Associated program** option will copy the file out of XWF to the temporary directory as defined in **Options | General Options**. XWF will then open the file using the Windows default program for the file. The **Selected other program** option will bring up a dialog box that will allow you to choose the program to use to open the selected file once XWF copies it out to the temporary directory. After selecting a program to use, XWF will add this program to the **Custom viewer programs** section of **Options |**

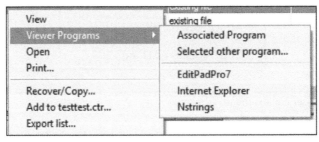

FIGURE 3.12

Viewer Programs submenu.

Viewer Programs menu and to the bottom of the **Viewer Programs** menu. Below **Selected other program**, all programs listed in **Options | Viewer Programs** will be displayed, including the program entered (if any) in the **Text editor** option.

Open will display the contents in hex of a file or a directory in a new tab in the **tab control**. Opening a file will *not* cause it to be marked as viewed.

Print will bring up a dialog, allowing you to customize what information is printed about the selected file along with other information specific to the file being printed. For example, an image file will include the image itself, an archive file will include the contents of the archive, and so on.

Recover/Copy allows for copying of the selected objects from your case to a directory of your choosing. When this option is invoked, a dialog will be displayed with several options as shown in Figure 3.13.

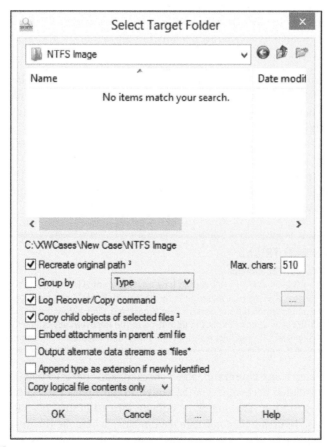

FIGURE 3.13

Recover/Copy dialog.

By default, XWF will save recovered files to a subdirectory of the case directory that corresponds with the name of the evidence object where the files reside (C:\XWCases\New Case\OCZ-AGILITY3, P2, for example).

Recreate original path has three options:

Fully checked: The full path for each selected object will be recreated inside the destination directory.

Half-checked: Any directories that have been selected are preserved and copied, as are any files that have been selected into the destination directory. The immediate path of the chosen file is copied, as opposed to the path from the root.

Unchecked: All selected files are copied to the destination directory (directories are not created at all). When copying objects from the **Case Root** (when viewing in recursive mode), an additional top-level directory will be created to reflect the name of the evidence object that the objects originated from. If files and/or directories are selected with the same name, XWF will make the names unique by appending a number to the end of the file so nothing is overwritten.

When **Recreate original path** is fully or half-checked, a button is available between the **Cancel** and **Help** buttons that contain settings related to the creation of artificial directories when objects being exported have one or more child objects.

While XWF supports paths up to a maximum of 510 characters long, Windows Explorer will not be able to view paths longer than 260 characters, so use the **Max chars.** option carefully.

The **Group by** option, when checked, creates subdirectories in output directories for such things as file extension, hash set, and so on. This serves as a timesaver when you have to categorize the recovered files for some reason.

XWF TIPS AND TRICKS

Embedded Object Timestamps

When exporting files in XWF, if a file doesn't have any timestamps (alternate data streams, for example) of its own, XWF will use a date and time of January 1, 1601 as a means to inform you the file that was recovered did not have its own timestamp. This behavior can be avoided by holding the **SHIFT** key while clicking the **OK** button in the **Recover/Copy** dialog. This may be necessary if any external programs refuse to open files that have such timestamps.

Log Recover/Copy command, when checked, adds the information as selected in the options dialog accessible via the button to the right of the command to the **Recover/Copy** log file. This log is, by default, located in the *_log* subdirectory of the active case. To create the log file in the directory where the file(s) are recovered to, click the button and uncheck **In case log subdir**. Unchecking this option is useful if you want to create a record of every **Recover/Copy** command in the directory where files were recovered to (as opposed to having *all* **Recover/Copy** commands ending up in one file when the option is checked).

Copy child objects of selected files has three options:

Fully checked: All files and/or directories below the selected objects will be recovered and copied to the selected destination directory.
Half-checked: Only child objects that are e-mail attachments will be copied.
Unchecked: No child objects of files will be recovered.

If **Embed attachments in parent .eml file** is checked, XWF will export the original e-mail message with the attachment still inside. When unchecked, XWF will export the e-mail message as well as the attachment that was found in the e-mail message during the RVS process.

By default, XWF will copy only the logical part of the file. You can adjust this by using the dropdown at the bottom of the dialog as needed.

Finally, any objects recovered will have their original dates and times reapplied after they are copied from the target location. Any files that could not be recovered will be added to a report table to allow for you to review the files that were not copied.

XWF TIPS AND TRICKS

Recover/Copy by Any Other Name Copies Just the Same

In other forensic tools, the option to copy files and directories from an image file is usually called something like *Export*, but in XWF, export means something very different as we will see later.

Add to (Container) allows for copying the selected objects to the currently open container file. In Figure 3.11, a container named *TestContainer.ctr* has been opened, so the menu indicates **Add to TestContainer.ctr**...

After choosing to add objects to a container, a dialog box is presented that has several options as shown in Figure 3.14.

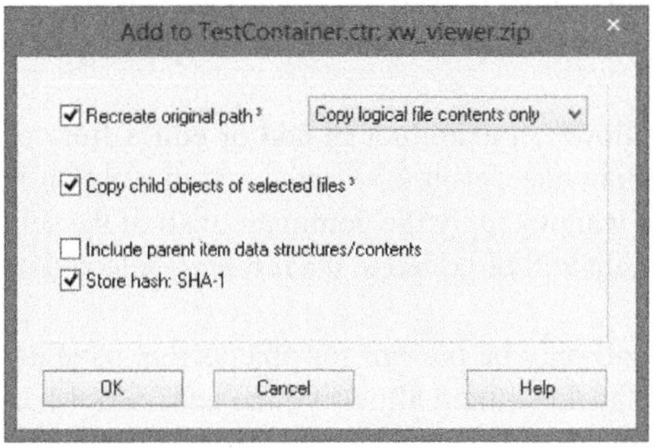

FIGURE 3.14

Add to container dialog options.

The **Recreate original path** and **Copy child objects of selected files** options work in the same manner as the **Recover/Copy** options discussed earlier. Similar to the **Recover/Copy** option, when adding objects to a container from the **Case Root** (when viewing in recursive mode), an additional top-level directory will be created to reflect the name of the evidence object where the objects originated.

When a SI is open, the **Add to** option will point to the SI. Selecting this option causes the sectors of the items selected in the **Directory Browser** to be read and therefore copied into the SI. When adding objects to the SI in this manner, it is helpful to change the state of the SI to *Idle*. When an object is then added to the SI via **Add to**, XWF will enable the SI for writing as the file is read and then set the state back to *Idle* again once the read operation is finished.

Note that you can have either a container or an SI open for writing at a given time.

Export list allows you to generate a report of selected objects and include the data in selected **Directory Browser** columns. A dialog box will be shown that allows you to select the columns to include as well as the format of the exported list. This is useful when a simple summary of objects is needed, as shown in Figure 3.15. Another example would be generating a file inventory for a trial that outlines every file of a relevant type, including dates, times, and paths.

Name	Size	Created	Modified
WinHex.exe	2,883,072	01/26/2013 18:47:17 -7	01/25/2013 16:08:02 -7
WinHex64.exe	4,737,536	01/26/2013 18:47:18 -7	01/25/2013 16:08:00 -7
xwforensics.exe	2,880,512	01/26/2013 18:47:17 -7	01/25/2013 16:08:02 -7
xwforensics64.exe	4,734,976	01/26/2013 18:47:18 -7	01/25/2013 16:08:00 -7

FIGURE 3.15

Export list example with four fields selected in HTML format.

Report table associations is used to assign objects to one or more report tables. An in-depth discussion will be deferred for now as reporting will be covered in detail in Chapter 8.

Edit comment allows an examiner to add or edit a free-form comment for an object. When more than one object is selected and this option is chosen, XWF will ask you whether you want to apply the comment to all of the selected objects. If you choose no, the comment will be added to the *top-most* selected item in the **Directory Browser**.

Edit metadata will only be present for objects that have data in their metadata field. Editing the metadata column allows you to add, remove, or update sections of the metadata field (to avoid excessive irrelevant information in the case report and focus on the main metadata fields, for example).

Tag will mark the selected objects in the **Directory Browser** with a blue square or checkbox in the leftmost column (the tag area) of the **Directory Browser**. **Untag** reverses the process. Tagging can be used to select a set of objects on which to selectively run an RVS operation. *Middle clicking* a directory in the **directory tree** will recursively tag and untag all objects under the selected directory. *Right clicking* the tag area will mark the selected object as viewed.

Select contains several subitems as shown in Figure 3.16. The options act as shortcuts for quickly selecting various categories of objects in the **Directory Browser**. In order for the **Listed hidden items** to work, make sure the **List hidden items** option is checked in **Directory Browser Options, Filters**.

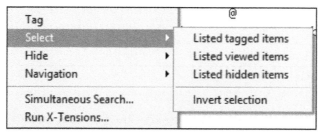

FIGURE 3.16

Select menu.

Hide contains several subitems as shown in Figure 3.17. The options act as short-cuts for quickly hiding various objects in the **Directory Browser**. The **Duplicates in dir. Browser based on hash** option will hide any duplicates of the selected files that *are visible in the* **Directory Browser**. To hide all such duplicates, recursively explore an object before choosing this option, if applicable. When deciding which files to hide, XWF will favor keeping existing files visible and hide any duplicate or previously existing files.

FIGURE 3.17

Hide menu.

XWF will offer to apply special rules when dealing with e-mail attachments. If you choose to use these rules, XWF will mark identical attachments as duplicates, but will not initially hide these duplicates, as their parent e-mail messages may be different. If a file doesn't have a hash value in the **Directory Browser**, this option has no effect.

Navigation contains several subitems as shown in Figure 3.18. The options act as shortcuts for quickly moving to various places in relation to the selected file. Depending on the kind of item selected in the **Directory Browser**, certain menu options may not be shown.

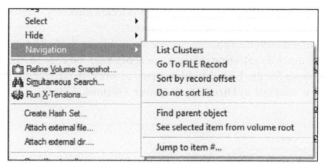

FIGURE 3.18

Navigation menu.

List Clusters will display a list of every cluster the selected file occupies. By default, the list will show every cluster number, but to shorten the list, XWF can omit contiguous cluster numbers. Right click on the list and select **Shorten contiguous cluster list,** then close and reopen the list to see the shortened version. You can also export a list of the clusters to a file by right clicking the list and choosing the appropriate option.

Go To FILE Record will, on NTFS file systems, display the FILE record of the selected object in the Master File Table (MFT). By default, XWF will color code various sections in the FILE record as well as display tool tips for the various attributes in the FILE record. You can disable or change the color-coding in the **Options | General Options | Auto coloring for FILE records** option. On Ext* file systems, the menu becomes **Go To Inode** and functions in the same way, but without color coding.

Sort by record offset causes XWF to sort the **Directory Browser** by the offset of the record that defines the selected file in the file system (if any such record is available). On NTFS, the FILE record is used; on FAT, the directory entry is used; and on Ext*, the Inode is used.

Do not sort list removes any active sorting from the **Directory Browser** columns.

Find parent object causes the **Directory Browser** to move up a level (unless in the root directory already) and select the parent file or directory of the object upon which the command was initially initiated. Repeating this command multiple times will continue in the same way until the **Directory Browser** is displaying the root directory (the left-side **caption line** of the **Directory Browser** will display a backslash when in the root directory). This command is useful when exploring recursively to quickly jump to the location where a file or a directory of interest is located. You may need to clear any filters to view the parent object.

Find related file causes the **Directory Browser** to jump to any files that XWF has determined are related to the selected file. Examples where you will see this option are when looking at files with hard links or for files found in VSCs. In the case of a file found inside a VSC, using this option causes the VSC host file to be selected (i.e., where the new file was found).

When not exploring recursively in the **Directory Browser**, **See selected item from volume root** selects an object after automatically switching the **Directory Browser** to explore the volume recursively. If exploring a volume recursively, the option becomes **See selected item in its directory** that will reverse the process in that the **Directory Browser** will display the selected file in its parent directory.

Jump to item # causes the currently selected line in the **Directory Browser** to move to the item # as entered in the dialog. For example, if 10 files are listed in the **Directory Browser**, entering 5 in the **Jump to item #** dialog will cause the fifth file in the list to be selected (highlighted in blue).

RVS allows you to perform an RVS operation on only the selected files. This is quicker than tagging a few files and then performing an RVS on tagged files.

Simultaneous search allows you to search the contents of the selected objects. Since searching will be covered in detail in Chapter 6, it will not be covered here.

Run X-Tensions allows you to run one or more programs that use the X-Tensions API on the selected objects. Since X-Tensions will be covered in Chapter 7, it will not be covered here.

Create Hash Set allows you to create a new hash set based on the selected objects in the **Directory Browser**. Once the hash set is created, the **Tools | Hash Database | Manage** dialog will be displayed that allows for merging with other hash sets, etc. The new hash set can then be used as a part of the RVS process. Chapter 4 will cover this in much more detail.

Attach external file and **Attach external dir** allow for attaching files and/or directories to an object in the **Directory Browser**. The attached files or directories become *virtual files* in the **Directory Browser**. A virtual file is one that doesn't exist in a forensic image, but rather is added to the volume snapshot and attached to a file or a directory that exists in a forensic image. Once added to XWF, virtual files can be the target of a RVS, added to reports, assigned comments, etc. This is an extremely powerful and flexible concept that sets XWF apart from other tools.

For example, consider the case where a Windows artifact is found and is relevant to your case. You know there is a specialized parser for the artifact and you wish to run the parser against the evidence in your case. After using the **Recover/Copy** feature to export the artifact, running the parser, and saving the results, you can then attach those results to the original artifact in XWF. Alternatively, you can attach the parsed file to your case as an external file and add comments if you wish. It may be helpful to attach such files or supplementary reports to the root directory, so they will be kept together in one location.

When attaching an external file, XWF will, by default, make the attached file a child object of the selected file. If you hold the **SHIFT** key after selecting a file (but before clicking OK), XWF will suggest a name for the virtual file and then create the virtual file as a sibling of the selected file (i.e., in the same directory as the selected file).

Any files or directories attached to objects will have an attribute of (**virtual attached**) in the **Attr.** column. By filtering **Attr.** on this value, all virtual files in a case can quickly be found.

XWF TIPS AND TRICKS

XWF's Virtual Object Capabilities Set It Apart
As mentioned above, virtual files are extremely powerful and useful for a wide variety of reasons. Because XWF has the concept of a virtual file, it is not necessary to "mount" compound files to view their contents. In other forensic suites, memory is used for each compound file that is mounted which can quickly exhaust memory.

The RVS process in XWF creates new objects for files initially found in the volume snapshot. Once this happens, a recursive file listing will show a listing of EVERY file and directory found in evidence objects regardless of whether they are found in archive files, Word documents, and so on.

Virtual objects are an elegant and clever solution that provides a significant improvement in the traditional methods of dealing with compound files as well as objects that are not part of, but are relevant to, your case.

If the context menu is invoked while in the **Hash** column, a **Filter by (hash value)** menu will be displayed as shown in Figure 3.19. This serves as a shortcut to quickly filter the **Directory Browser** by the selected hash. If this option is selected a second time, the first hash is replaced in the filter with the second selected hash. If you have more than one hash you want to filter on, right click and select the **Copy (hash value)** option on the first file and the **Filter by (hash value)** option on the second. After the **Directory Browser** is filtered, you can click the blue funnel and paste the first hash into the list of hashes.

Finally, **Copy** is a dynamic menu that will change depending on which column the mouse is in when right clicking the **Directory Browser**. For example, if right clicking in the **Name** column, the **Copy** command will contain the file name. If right clicking in the **Created** column, the **Copy** command will contain the date and time the file was created. This is handy for copying data to be used in a filter or to add to an external report or program.

FIGURE 3.19

Filter by hash example.

MODE BUTTONS AND DETAILS PANE

Below the **Directory Browser**, several **Mode** buttons are visible as shown in Figure 3.20. These **Mode** buttons control what information is displayed about the selected object in the **Directory Browser**.

FIGURE 3.20

Mode buttons.

Legend mode

Before discussing the **Mode** buttons from left to right, click on the **Legend** button. As you interacted with files and directories in the **Directory Browser** in the **Directory Browser** section, you no doubt noticed that files and directories had different icons as well as attributes. After clicking the **Legend** button, XWF will display a list of all these icons as well as an explanation of what some of the **Mode** buttons do. The **Legend** is shown in Figure 3.21.

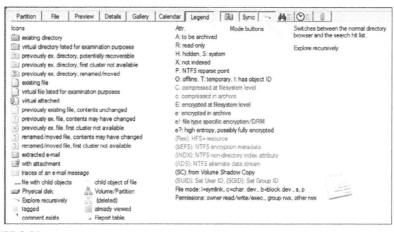

FIGURE 3.21

XWF icon **Legend**.

Use the **Legend** often as you are learning XWF as it serves as a quick reference for what each icon and attribute abbreviation means.

Volume/Partition mode

Jumping back to the leftmost **Mode** button, we will start our discussion with **Volume/Partition** mode. If you add an image of a partition to a case, XWF will use the term **Volume** in the button. If you add an image of an entire hard drive, XWF will use the term **Partition**.

When in **Volume/Partition** mode, the contents of the object selected in the **Directory Browser** will be shown in hexadecimal.

The leftmost side of the window contains the offset of the selected file from the beginning of the partition. Clicking the numbers in the **Offset** column toggles between the offsets being displayed in hexadecimal and decimal notation.

Scrolling up or down allows you to see the currently selected object in the context of the entire partition. As you click different areas of the file, notice that the **information pane** on the right side is updated to reflect the current cluster number, physical and logical sector numbers, etc. Clicking the info pane causes it to scroll in order to be able to view all the details contained in the info pane. Right clicking the info pane allows for copying of certain pieces of information to the clipboard.

Right clicking while in **Volume/Partition** mode will display a context menu. The options in this context menu will be discussed in Chapter 7.

Disk mode

When an evidence object that represents a disk is selected, **Disk** mode will be active. This mode works essentially the same as **Volume/Partition** mode does, but the items contained in the **Directory Browser** are partitions, unpartitionable space, etc.

File mode

The next mode is **File** mode. File mode works exactly like **Volume/Partition** mode with the exception that the hex viewer will only display the contents of a single file. Slack space is displayed in green unless **Specialist | Highlight slack space** is unchecked or **Directory Browser Options, Filters | Open and search files incl. slack** is unchecked. Additionally, areas at the end of a file that are declared as uninitialized by an NTFS or exFAT file system are displayed in red.

File mode will take any file system-level compression into account when displaying the file. The file will also be displayed contiguously regardless of whether the file is fragmented.

Preview mode

In **Preview** mode, if XWF has a built-in viewer for the selected file, that viewer will be used to display a preview of the file. For example, selecting a jpg image will result in the internal XWF viewer displaying the image unless **Options | Viewer Programs | For pictures, too** is checked.

If XWF does not have a built-in viewer for a particular file type, **Preview** mode behaves differently depending on whether the viewer component is active. If the viewer component is active, it will provide a preview of the selected file if the viewer component knows how to decode that file.

XWF TIPS AND TRICKS

To View or not to View

The quickest way to know if you are using an internal viewer vs. the viewer component is to right click the **Preview** mode pane. If you get a context menu, the viewer component is providing the preview. If no context menu is available, an XWF internal viewer is being used.

Using the viewer component's context menu allows you to print, copy the selected text to the clipboard, etc.

If the viewer component doesn't understand how to decode a file or if the viewer component is not being used at all, **Preview** mode will show a partial preview of the file by displaying the ASCII characters of a portion of the file.

Preview mode is also used to see the internal structures of such things as Windows shortcut (.lnk) files in an easy to read format.

When in **Preview** mode, an extra button will be displayed that, when clicked, allows for a noninterpreted view of the file to be seen. Clicking on the **Raw** button toggles between the interpreted and noninterpreted view of the selected file. For example, this is useful if you want to view HTML code as opposed to a rendered Web page.

Details mode

Details mode displays the information contained in all of the **Directory Browser** columns regardless of whether they are hidden. Other information, such as a summary of the object's permissions and an object's internal metadata, is also displayed (regardless of whether it was extracted as part of the RVS process).

Details mode works in conjunction with the viewer component. If the viewer component isn't active, **Details** mode will display raw HTML.

Gallery mode

Gallery mode will display any files in the **Directory Browser** that have been determined to be image files of a supported type as thumbnails. For nonimage files, a summary is displayed that includes the file name and file size. **Gallery** mode uses XWF internal viewers to display images. To view an image in a separate window, double click the thumbnail. Click anywhere in the window to close it.

When the mouse cursor is over the **Gallery** window, the mouse wheel will scroll the gallery up or down one page at a time. A page is determined by how many thumbnails are visible in the gallery at once.

In the upper left of each thumbnail is a tag area that can be used to tag files of interest from the gallery. Right clicking a thumbnail in gallery mode will display the same context menu as if the file was right clicked in the **Directory Browser**.

It is recommended to filter on the **Type** column before using gallery view as it will hide nonpicture files from the **Directory Browser** which makes reviewing many images easier.

Calendar mode

Calendar mode allows for a form of timeline analysis and will be discussed in Chapter 7.

Directory Browser mode

When active, the **Directory Browser** window will be displayed. When inactive, the **Directory Browser** window will be hidden.

Sync mode

When **Sync** mode is active, the **directory tree** is kept synchronized with the parent directory of the object that is selected in the **Directory Browser**. When in **Volume/Partition** mode, **Sync** mode can also be used to select a file or a directory in the **Directory Browser** based on where in the partition the cursor is. If the **Sync** mode is active, deactivate it by clicking it, then reactivate it in order for the **Directory Browser** to be updated.

Explore recursively mode

Clicking this button toggles whether the **Directory Browser** recursively displays all objects or not.

Search hit list mode

Search hit list mode will be explained in detail in Chapter 6.

Events mode

Events mode allows for another form of timeline analysis and will be discussed in Chapter 7.

Position manager mode

Position manager mode will be explained in Chapter 6.

XWF can take advantage of multiple monitors by detaching the **Mode** buttons and viewer pane from the main interface. Clicking the three dots to the far left of the **Mode** buttons will display the **Details** pane in its own window that can be moved to a separate monitor. These three dots are shown in Figure 3.22. Click the three dots again to reattach the **Details** pane to the main XWF window.

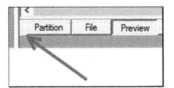

FIGURE 3.22

Three dots location.

STATUS BAR

Across the bottom of the XWF interface is a **Status bar** that will change depending on which mode is selected. Figure 3.23 shows the **Status bar** in **Volume/Partition** mode.

| Sector 119076 of 530082 | Offset: | 3A24800 | = 73 | Block: | n/a | Size: | n/a |

FIGURE 3.23

Status bar in **Volume/Partition** mode.

When in **Volume/Partition** mode, the **status bar** will display several additional fields:

Sector: The logical sector number where the cursor is and the total number of sectors in the volume or partition.
Offset: The offset from the beginning of the volume or partition in either hex or decimal notation depending on how the offset column is displayed.
Selected value: The decimal representation of the selected byte.
Block: The beginning and ending positions of any highlighted data.
Size: The number of bytes selected in hex or decimal notation.

When in **File** mode, the **status bar** is exactly the same as when in **Volume/Partition** mode with one exception:

Page: Displays the current and total number of pages of data the file contains as opposed to sectors.

When in **Preview**, **Details**, or **Gallery** mode, the path to the selected file is displayed in the **status bar**.

Right clicking the status bar

Right clicking on any of the sections of the **status bar** displays a context menu that allows you to copy information related to the viewer pane to the clipboard.

When right clicking the **Offset** section, an additional menu, **Relative record offsets,** is available which is shown in Figure 3.24.

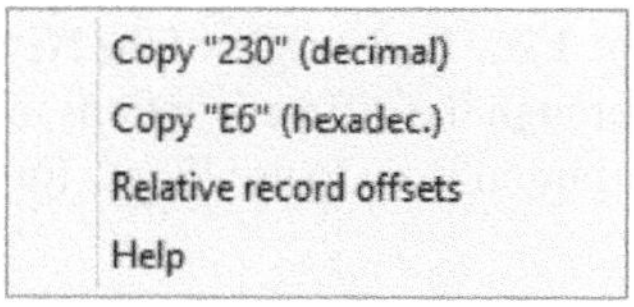

| Copy "230" (decimal) |
| Copy "E6" (hexadec.) |
| Relative record offsets |
| Help |

FIGURE 3.24

Offset context menu.

Clicking **Relative record offsets** brings up the **Record Presentation** dialog box that is shown in Figure 3.25.

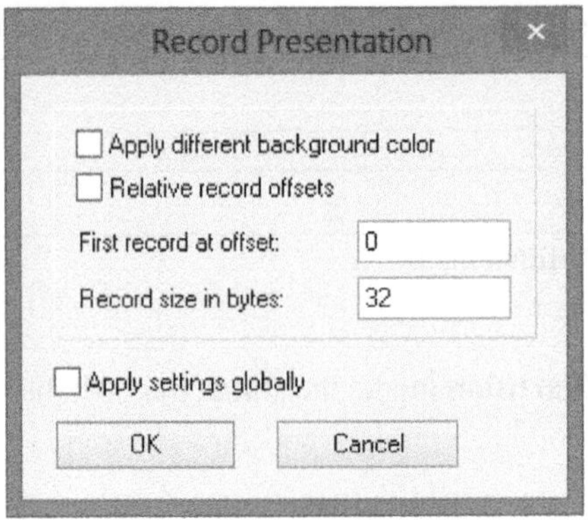

FIGURE 3.25

Record Presentation dialog.

If you are working with a file that uses a fixed length for a data record (for example, the MFT, where each record is 1024 bytes in length), this dialog allows you to set parameters such as the size of a data record so that XWF can display every other record in a different color, etc.

If **Apply different background color** is checked, XWF will display every other row in a different color so as to easily visualize each record. The color can be configured by selecting a color for **Record background color** in **Options | General Options**.

If **Relative record offsets** is checked, XWF will show the offset as it exists from the beginning of the record where the cursor is vs. from the beginning of the file itself. The **status bar** will also reflect the fact that this option is enabled.

Record Presentation only affects the display pane when in **Volume/Partition** mode.

Left clicking the status bar

Left clicking on any of the sections of the **status bar** will bring up context menus with options related to the section that was clicked. Most of the dialogs are self-explanatory.

When left clicking the *Offset* section of the **status bar**, the **Go To Offset** dialog is displayed as shown in Figure 3.26. To the right of the **New position** value is a button that, when clicked, cycles through the different options to use when moving to a new position. In Figure 3.26, the button is set to use *Words* for the value of **New position**.

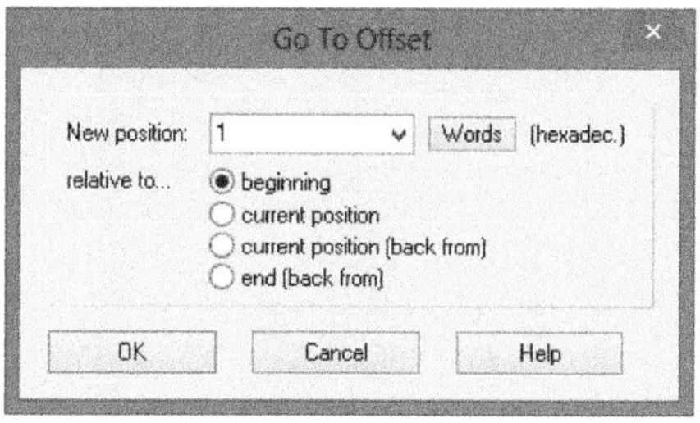

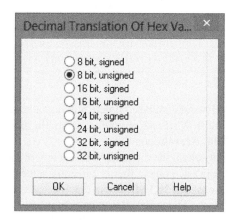

FIGURE 3.26

Go To Offset dialog.

If using the **Record Presentation** option, a **Records** option will be available when clicking this button.

When left clicking the *Selected value* section of the **status bar**, a dialog appears that lets you choose how the hexadecimal value will be interpreted. This dialog is shown in Figure 3.27.

FIGURE 3.27

Selected value dialog.

Left clicking either *Block* or *Size* results in the same dialog being shown that lets you enter the beginning and ending of a block of data.

Data Interpreter

The **Data Interpreter**, shown in Figure 3.28, will convert the appropriate number of bytes from the position of the cursor into a wide variety of values. The **Data Interpreter** will be covered in detail in Chapter 7.

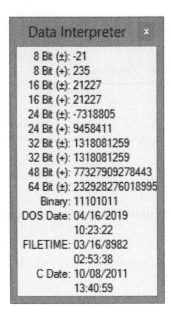

FIGURE 3.28

Data Interpreter.

MAIN MENU

A discussion of the XWF would not be complete without at least a brief discussion of the main menu. Like most Windows programs, the main menu contains common menus such as **File**, **Edit**, **Search**, etc.

The key thing to know about the main menu is that any of the options in the main menu affect the entire evidence object that is currently selected in the **tab control**. Using main menu options has NO effect on the files selected in the **Directory Browser** as that is what the **Directory Browser** context menu does.

Many of the options in the main menu have been discussed in this chapter, and others will be covered in chapters to come.

Before we conclude this chapter, let's revisit the remaining options we haven't covered in detail.

GENERAL OPTIONS CONTINUED

Recall from Chapter 1 the **General Options** dialog, shown again in Figure 3.29, that can be accessed via **Options | General Options**.

In Chapter 1, we covered some of these options. Some of the options are self-explanatory and need no elaboration. Note that the description of an option may change as you apply various checkmark states.

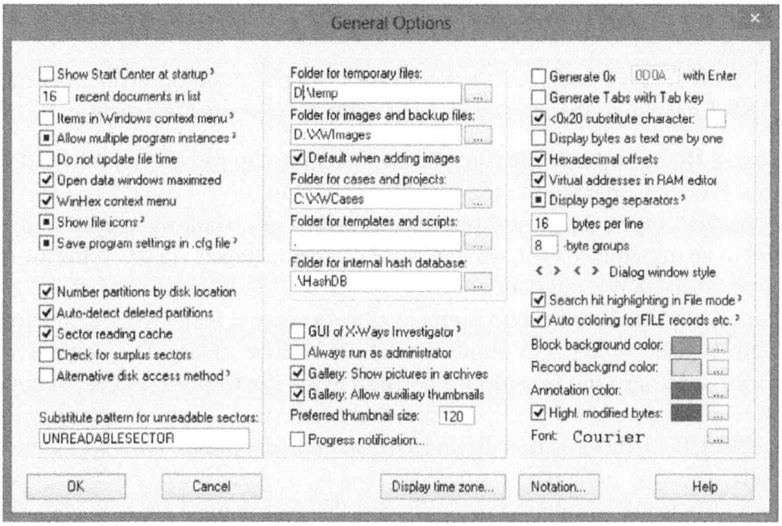

FIGURE 3.29

General Options dialog.

Show Start Center at start-up has three options:

Fully checked: The **Start Center** window will be displayed when XWF opens
and allows you to open a file, disk, ram, etc. The **Start Center** also maintains a
list of recently opened objects and cases that allows for quickly opening a
particular item.
Half-checked: XWF will remember the positions of its windows and restore them
the next time XWF is started. This includes restoring the search hit list
or event list mode and as well as selecting the last active search hit or event.
Unchecked: The **Start Center** will not be shown, nor will XWF restore the
previous locations of its windows.

Items in Windows Context menu has three options:

Fully checked: XWF will add an option to Windows Explorer context menus when
right clicking a file or a directory that allows that item to be opened in XWF.
Half-checked: Same as when fully checked (in WinHex, when this option is half-
checked, only directories will have the extra context menu items, not files).
Unchecked: XWF will not add any menu items to Windows Explorer context
menus when right clicking a file or a directory.

Allow multiple program instances has three options:

Fully checked: A new XWF session will be created without prompting the user to
confirm the operation.

Half-checked: XWF will ask the user to confirm whether to open a new XWF session.

Unchecked: XWF becomes a single-instance application. Subsequent execution of XWF results in the already running copy of XWF gaining focus.

If checked, **Do not update file time** the original timestamps will be preserved when saving a file after opening via the **File | Open** menu.

If checked, **Open data windows maximized** forces windows opened in the **tab control** to be maximized. The window state can be managed via the **Window** menu at the top of the XWF interface.

If checked, **WinHex context menu** displays a context menu when right clicking the **Details** pane when in **Volume/Partition** or **File** mode. The context menu allows for defining a block, adding a position to the **Position Manager**, or copying the selected values. If unchecked, right clicking results in a block being selected from offset 0 to the position of the cursor. These options will be covered in Chapter 7.

Show file icons is not used in XWF. See the user manual for how it is used in WinHex.

Save program settings in .cfg file has three options:

Fully checked: XWF saves all program options any time a dialog box is dismissed via the **OK** button.
Half-checked: XWF saves all program options when XWF exits cleanly.
Unchecked: XWF will never save program options unless holding **SHIFT** when exiting.

Alternate disk access method has three options. It is recommended to leave this option unchecked as this is the most efficient access method. When fully or half-checked, XWF allows for entering a "timeout" value that is used when reading data. See the XWF manual for a full description of these options and when you may need to use them.

GUI of X-Ways Investigator has three options:

Fully checked: XWF uses a simplified user interface that allows for opening of case files.
Half-checked: XWF uses a simplified user interface and is only capable of opening XWF container files, not regular images or actual disks.
Unchecked: The full XWF interface will be used.

If checked, **Gallery: Allow auxiliary thumbnails** forces any embedded thumbnail images inside larger images to be used when in **Gallery** mode. This can speed up the gallery when viewing high-resolution images. If stills are extracted from video files, one of the still frames will be used as a thumbnail for the video.

Checking **Progress notification** brings up a dialog that allows for the configuration for various types of notification events such as a text file log and an e-mail message. This is useful for time sensitive but long-running operations in that you can be notified of progress at the interval specified.

The **Generate Tabs with Tab key** is used with WinHex more than with XWF. If unchecked, pressing TAB moves the focus between the hexadecimal display and the text display of a file. In XWF, the TAB key changes focus between the **directory tree**, **Directory Browser**, and **Details** pane. When checked, WinHex will insert a tab character when the TAB key is pressed. In XWF, nothing happens when the TAB key is pressed.

Display page separators has three options:

Fully checked: XWF will show separators between pages in a file (when a file opened and has a tab in the **tab control**) and between sectors when in **Volume/ Partition** or **File** mode.
Half-checked: XWF will only show separators between sectors.
Unchecked: No separators will be shown.

The arrows to the left of **Dialog window style** allow for changing of the visual style XWF uses when drawing certain components of the user interface.

Search hit highlighting in File mode has three options:

Fully checked: XWF will highlight search hits whether or not the search hit list is visible when in **File** mode.
Half-checked: XWF will only highlight the search hit when the search hit list is visible.
Unchecked: XWF will not highlight search hits at all.

Auto coloring for FILE records etc. has three options:

Fully checked: XWF will, for certain files such as NTFS FILE records, timestamps in registry hives, and shortcut files, color-code different pieces of data regardless of the file system where such files are found.
Half-checked: FILE record highlighting is not attempted on partitionable disks or non-NTFS volumes, but only on NTFS volumes/partitions.
Unchecked: No color highlighting will be performed.

Clicking the **Notation** button allows for setting things such as the format to use when displaying dates and times, time zone bias, etc.

Checking the **Seconds**: **digits after decimal** option will show fractions of a second (when timestamps have a high level of resolution). We recommend enabling both the **Seconds** and **Display time zone bias** options.

Display file sizes always in bytes has three options:

Fully checked: File sizes will always be displayed in bytes and not rounded at all.
Half-checked: Only items listed inside partitions will have their file sizes listed in bytes, but items outside partitions including individual partitions, start sectors, unpartitionable space, etc. will use the common notation suffixes such as KB, MB, and GB.
Unchecked: XWF will always display file sizes using suffixes of KB, MB, GB, etc.

If you wish to revert *all* settings to their default values, not just those in the **General Options**, use the **Help | Setup | Initialize** menu item.

VOLUME SNAPSHOT OPTIONS

These options will be discussed in detail in Chapter 4.

VIEWER PROGRAMS OPTIONS CONTINUED

We also saw most of the **Viewer Programs** options when we initially configured XWF in Chapter 1. The remaining options that were not discussed are explained below.

View multiple pictures simultaneously, when checked, allows for viewing more than one graphics file in its own window at a time. If unchecked, only one file will be viewable at a time.

Alternative preview of .eml has three options:

Fully checked: The e-mail headers are displayed in a table for easier viewing.
Half-checked: The e-mail headers (subject, date, sender, etc.) of e-mail files are excluded in **Preview** mode (but you can always see the headers in **Raw** mode). You can see subject, sender, recipient, and dates already in the **Directory Browser**, and attachments are listed when exploring the parent .eml file.
Unchecked: The e-mail headers are displayed as they exist in the .eml file without formatting.

Crash safe text decoding has three options:

Fully checked: Additional background processes will be used when decoding files via the viewer component. This protects the main XWF process from crashing should the viewer component encounter a file that causes it to crash.
Half-checked: Same as when fully checked with the exception that e-mail (.eml) files will not use an additional background process when being decoded.
Unchecked: No background processes will be used when rendering text and as such, should a file be unable to be decoded, XWF itself may crash.

If **Buffer decoded text for context preview** is checked, XWF will remember text extracted from files as a result of certain operations, so searching and indexing will be more efficient. The extracted text is stored in the volume snapshot.

SECURITY OPTIONS

The last set of XWF options to discuss is **Security Options** that can be viewed via **Options | Security Options**. The **Security Options** dialog is shown in Figure 3.30.

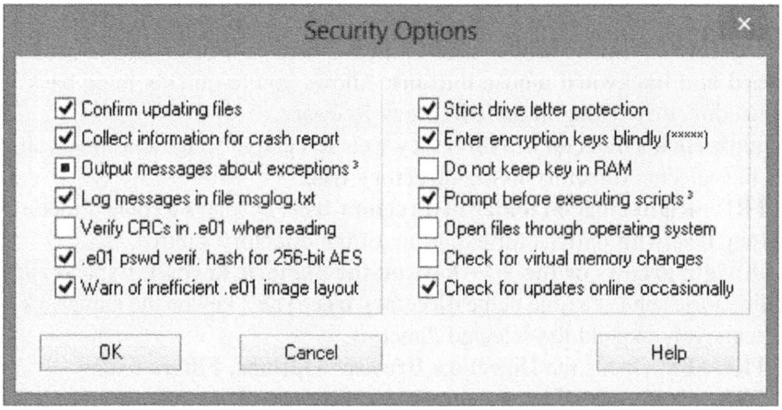

FIGURE 3.30

Security Options.

Output messages about exceptions has three options that control how much detail is output in the messages window:

Fully checked: All messages will be displayed including those that have no impact on XWF's stability.
Half-checked: This option strikes a balance between full verbosity and only reporting significant errors.
Unchecked: Only errors that can significantly affect the stability of XWF will be displayed.

Regardless of which option is selected, all exceptions will be logged to a file named *error.log* in the main XWF directory.

If **Verify CRCs in .e01 when reading** is checked, XWF will calculate and compare each internal CRC value in the e01 file as the image is read.

XWF will, by default, add entries to the messages window when inefficient compression is detected as it processes image files. If you do not wish to see these messages, uncheck the **Warn of inefficient .e01 image layout** option. If you do run into an image that uses inefficient compression, you can use XWF to create a new image and, of course, XWF will use much more intelligent options when creating the new image.

Finally, the **Strict drive letter protection** option, when checked, limits XWF in **Recover/Copying** files out of XWF. As outlined in the XWF manual and Help file, when enabled, XWF will limit files being copied to the following locations:

- The drive letter that hosts the active case if one is active
- The drive letter with the directory for temporary files
- The drive letter from which XWF was run
- The drive letter that contains the directory for image files.

Disabling **Strict drive letter protection** removes any such restrictions on where files are recovered.

SHORTCUTS

Forward and backward mouse buttons: Allows you to quickly jump back to the previous directory listing in the **Directory Browser**.

Middle click a directory in directory tree: Recursively tags and untags all items under the selected directory in the **directory tree**.

CTRL+Right click on folder in directory tree: Displays a context menu in the **directory tree** with options for exporting of the directory subtree, etc.

Left/right arrows or the +/− keys on the numeric keypad: Expand and contract directories one at a time in the **directory tree**. The * key on the numeric keypad will recursively expand the selected directory.

CTRL+F5: Opens the **Directory Browser Options, Filters** dialog.

CTRL+Q: Closes all open items in the **tab control**.

CTRL+W: Closes the active item in the **tab control**.

SHIFT+tag file: Reverses the behavior of the **Tag and hide recursively** option when tagging files.

SHIFT+click on column name: Removes any secondary and tertiary sorting on columns in the **Directory Browser**.

SHIFT+click on column filter icon: Activates or deactivates the column filter without displaying the column filter dialog.

ALT+Left arrow: Marks items as unviewed in the **Directory Browser**.

ALT+Right arrow: Marks items as viewed in the **Directory Browser**.

ALT+Up/Down arrow: Marks item as viewed in the **Directory Browser** and moves to the next item.

SUMMARY

This chapter has thoroughly discussed almost every aspect of the XWF user interface.

We started with how to interact with the **directory tree** after adding one or more evidence objects to a case. We saw how to set properties of evidence objects, efficiently expand and contract the **directory tree**, export a listing of directories, and view directories recursively.

Next, we covered one of the most used component of XWF, the **Directory Browser**, in conjunction with the **tab control** and **caption line** of the **Directory Browser**. We discussed every available option in **Directory Browser options** including how to add or remove columns from the **Directory Browser**. We saw how to sort the **Directory Browser**, filter on certain columns, and interact with objects displayed in the **Directory Browser**.

We then looked at the various modes that XWF can display files and directories. These modes included limiting the display to a single file or directory, previewing a file with and without the viewer component, and displaying a gallery of files that allows for quickly reviewing many graphics files.

Once we selected a file, we saw how to interact with that file by using the **status bar** and its various options when right or left clicking the mouse.

Finally, we discussed the remaining options that were not covered in a previous chapter, including the remaining **General Options**, **Viewer Options**, and **Security Options**.

Now that you have a thorough understanding of every aspect of the XWF user interface, we can move on to discuss some of the features that really set XWF apart from any other forensic program.

Acknowledgments

Eric Zimmerman and Jimmy Weg are two forensic examiners that are true X-Ways Forensics practitioners. I am humbled to have their efforts attributed to this book, as both Eric and Jimmy are two of the most competent forensic examiners around. After Eric agreed to coauthor the Practitioner's Guide to X-Ways, I knew this would be the go-to guide for all current and new users of X-Ways Forensics. To have Jimmy Weg as the Tech Editor only solidified this book's credibility. Eric and Jimmy, thank you for your support in this endeavor.

Stefan Fleischmann of X-Ways Software Technology has been a constant support of my personal use of X-Ways Forensics since the forensic version was first released. Little did I know that by asking Stefan in 2004 to teach an X-Ways Forensics class in Seattle (the first class in the USA) that I would be introduced to the best forensic utility available, with amazing support, both personal and professional, from Stefan. Additionally, Stefan's support of this book has been a tremendous help in ensuring the information is up to date and accurate.

I also thank Craig Ball for his kind words for the foreword of this book. I first met Craig Ball in the first X-Ways class and, since then, have followed his witty and intelligent writings on forensics and electronic discovery. Craig has an amazing command presence and superb knowledge of the law surrounding electronic discovery and forensics (he is an attorney...), but he is also an advocate and longtime user of X-Ways Forensics.

As for my number one supporter, I thank my wife Chikae, as she not only listened to my endless jabbering of all things digital forensics at home but has also supported me in this second book even before I finished writing my first book. When looking at the success of our children, or even my personal success, I look no further than to my wife and I know how it is all possible.

Brett Shavers

I would like to start by saying thank you to all of the dedicated men and women in both law enforcement and private industry that go to work every day and tirelessly pursue the truth in the realm of digital forensics. While we may at times have different missions, the goal is the same: to tell the story of what happened as it relates to a computer. It is my belief that X-Ways Forensics can help you tell that story in an efficient and succinct manner.

I want to extend a special thanks to Brett and Jimmy, my coauthor and tech editor. I am grateful for being given the opportunity to write this book and work closely with you over the past few months. Your passion for X-Ways Forensics comes through in every chapter.

I too want to thank Stefan Fleishmann and all the X-Ways employees for putting together such a fantastic and capable tool. Your dedication to making the best software available has made more impact in the world than you know.

Finally, I would like to thank my wife Michele for supporting me when it came time to add writing a book to my already crazy schedule. Thank you for being a constant source of encouragement. You are a fantastic wife and mother. Wesley and I are blessed to have you.

Eric Zimmerman

Refine Volume Snapshot

INTRODUCTION

The Refine Volume Snapshot (RVS) is perhaps the most important and powerful feature of X-Ways Forensics (XWF), yet it is also one of the simplest to configure and use. The value of the RVS cannot be overstated.

Back in Chapter 2, the concept of a volume snapshot (VS) was introduced. A VS is a database created by XWF that is used to store all of the information related to items in an evidence object. Each evidence object gets its own VS. As you navigate the XWF GUI, the VS is queried and the results are displayed in the **directory tree**, **Directory Browser**, etc. As XWF interacts with files or other objects in a case for certain functions, the results are stored in the VS. This includes such things as marking files as viewed, tagged files, hidden files, etc.

XWF TIPS AND TRICKS
The Rest of the Story
For more detail on the types of information stored in a VS, refer to the *Case Data Storage* section of http://www.x-ways.net/winhex/setup.html.

The VS serves as the starting point for the RVS process. Essentially, the VS contains everything XWF "knows" about evidence objects (as it pertains to files and directories) in a case. By using RVS, XWF can add even more data to a VS by performing certain actions against evidence objects. This includes such things as finding embedded thumbnails, exploring archive contents, extracting file metadata, displaying the contents of database tables, extracting e-mail, etc.

This chapter gives a brief overview of each option of an RVS so as not to duplicate the official XWF manual. The intention of this chapter is to get you quickly up to speed with the knowledge to properly choose RVS options to maximize your efficiency in working a case. Although the number of options may seem overwhelming, the default selections work well for the vast majority of examinations.

Figure 4.1 is an overview by Ted Smith (http://xwaysclips.blogspot.com) that visually depicts both the initial VS and the RVS processes. The individual phases of creating and adding to the database of files from an evidence object can be seen as you move down each tier. As you can see, the result of an RVS is the sum of all files and directories, including items found inside other files, such as PDFs and zip archives. Because of this, it is possible to exceed the physical size of a volume as reflected in other tools.

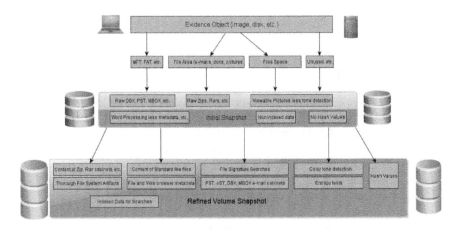

FIGURE 4.1

Graphic courtesy of Ted Smith, http://xwaysclips.blogspot.com.

Several other core XWF functions rely upon the data contained in the VS. Logical searches, indexing, and actions taken in the **Directory Browser** reference the contents of the VS, so it is essential to employ an RVS to find additional data.

VOLUME SNAPSHOT OPTIONS

There are two concepts: *taking* a VS and *refining* a VS. VS options are chosen via the **Options | Volume Snapshot** menu. Figure 4.2 shows the default selections, most of which take effect when taking a new snapshot. As with most features in XWF, the default settings are usually the best choices. Unless you have a valid reason to change these options, we recommend leaving the defaults intact.

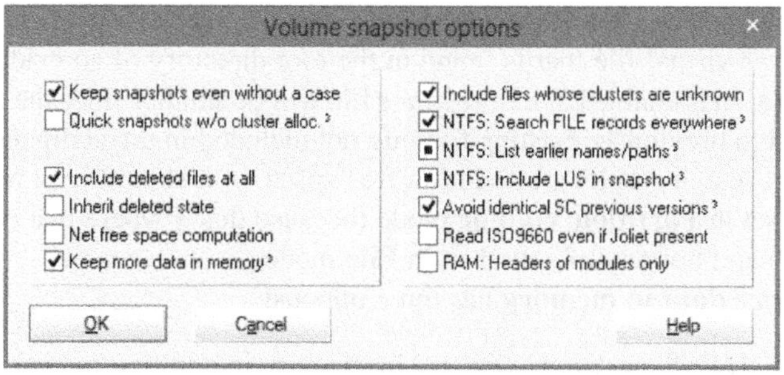

FIGURE 4.2

Volume snapshot options.

The **Keep snapshots even without a case** option allows all information gathered to be saved in temporary files even after closing XWF. These temporary files, including VSs, can be used in later sessions. When reusing an existing VS, XWF will tell you how old the VS is in case you want to update the VS.

Keep snapshots even without a case does not affect VSs or files collected when an evidence object has been added to a case as snapshots of evidence objects are always kept in subdirectories of the main case directory. The directory where the temporary files are created is controlled via **Tools | General Options | Folder for temporary files**.

Quick snapshots w/o cluster alloc has three options:

Fully checked: Quick allocation is used for all file systems
Half-checked: Quick allocation is used for Ext* and ReiserFS file systems
Unchecked: Quick allocation is disabled

Enabling this option causes XWF to lose the ability to determine the file allocation for a cluster. Disabling this option and taking a new RVS will update the VS to contain cluster allocation information.

XWF TIPS AND TRICKS

Defaults Are Defaults for a Reason

Don't forget! XWF has been tweaked over many years of user input and advanced development for ease of use and efficiency of operations. Every option that is checked, unchecked, or half-checked by default is probably the best selection needed in most cases unless your needs call for tweaking the preferences for certain examinations. When in doubt, use the defaults.

Inherit deleted state prevents deleted partitions to pass their deleted state to all items contained in their partition. Enabling this option prevents XWF from being able to differentiate between existing and deleted files. This also prevents deleted e-mail archive files to pass on their deleted state to all e-mails and attachments that they contain.

Net free space computation determines what free space XWF will gather into the *Free space* virtual file that is found in the root directory of an evidence object. When this option is enabled, the *Free space* file will be smaller since the clusters that are allocated to previously existing files are not included in the computation of free space. When search results are found in free space, you should only reference the physical offset in **Partition/Volume** mode (because that's where that data actually live on disk) and not any offset when in **File** mode.

Keep more data in memory has three options:

Fully checked: Timestamps are kept in memory in addition to everything kept in memory when half-checked
Half-checked: Additional VS data (start sector number, hard link count, skin color percentage, etc.) are kept in memory
Unchecked: No additional data are kept in memory

NTFS: Search FILE records everywhere has three options:

Fully checked: Searches in all sectors of the partition
Half-checked: Searches in only volume shadow copy (SC) host files
Unchecked: Disable searching for FILE records

NTFS: List earlier names/paths has three options:

Fully checked: Earlier instances of names/paths are added to the VS
Half-checked: Earlier instances of names/paths are annotated via comments, but the names and paths themselves are not added to the VS as additional files
Unchecked: Earlier names/paths are not reported at all

NTFS: Include LUS in snapshot has three options:

Fully checked: Include all logged utility streams (LUSs) in the VS
Half-checked: Include only non-$EFS (Encrypting File System) streams
Unchecked: Do not include any LUS information in the VS

A LUS is similar to a data stream but logged in the NTFS log file.

Avoid identical SC previous versions has three options:

Fully checked: Prevents exact duplicates of files from being added to the VS where duplicates are determined by the contents of files only, not by modification dates. Up to 128 MB of files are compared
Half-checked: The same as when fully checked with the exception that only 16 MB of data are compared
Unchecked: Duplicate files from volume SCs will be included in the VS

For read errors on a CD/DVD during a snapshot or during disc imaging, using the **Read ISO9660 even if Joliet present** option gives an additional chance to recover directories and files if the data structures are located in readable sectors in the ISO9660 area.

The **RAM: Headers of modules only** option enables allocation of memory pages in RAM mode to compute hashes for comparison against known hash sets.

STARTING RVS

Like many features in XWF, there is more than one way to accomplish a task and starting an RVS process is no exception. RVS can be started in one of four ways. Figure 4.3 shows three different ways to bring up the RVS dialog.

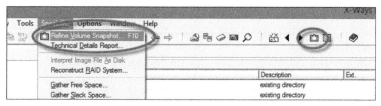

FIGURE 4.3

Three ways to open the RVS dialog (Menu, F10 shortcut, or the RVS icon).

The fourth way to initiate an RVS is to select files in the **Directory Browser** and choose the RVS option from the context menu. This last option allows for quickly focusing the RVS against the selected items.

The RVS dialog is shown in Figure 4.4. The RVS dialog is broken up into two primary sections: file recovery and file processing. The file recovery section (beginning with *Execute now*) contains options that apply to free space (including slack space), unpartitioned sections of disks, partition gaps, etc. The file processing section (starting with *Compute hash*) contains options which apply to files in a VS.

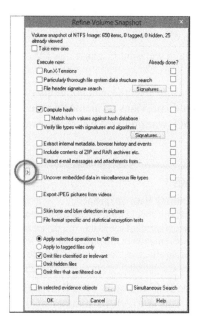

FIGURE 4.4

Refine Volume Snapshot dialog.

Before explaining the options in these two sections, a few other items merit discussion.

Take new one and default RVS options

The **Take new one** option is used to force the generation of a new VS. Checking the box brings up a warning message that asks you to confirm your decision. As shown in Figure 4.5, taking a new RVS will cause a loss of all previously gathered, refined data as well as any comments, report table associations, etc. In short, this option resets the VS to its original state.

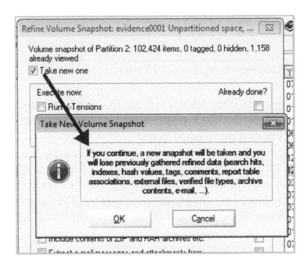

FIGURE 4.5

Before selecting OK, make sure you want to take a new RVS.

This one selection, if hastily selected, can potentially result in a significant loss of time as you will have to redo previous refinements unless you restore from backup. Therefore, as with any XWF warning, make sure you want XWF to do what you are telling it to do.

XWF TIPS AND TRICKS

Do You Really Want an Entirely New Snapshot?

If, after an RVS, you find that you should have selected additional options, you can easily run RVS again with only the new options that you need. You do not have to lose your previous RVS results because the snapshot remembers the processes that were completed (as well as the individual files those processes affected), so it does not have to process the same data again.

On the center left of the RVS dialog is a small arrow that is circled in Figure 4.4. When clicked, this small button toggles a number of options as a way to quickly select all options that relate to files in the VS. These selections may or may not fit your needs and it is best to understand each option before enabling every possible option.

Finally, down the right side of the dialog are checkboxes with a heading of *Already done?* These checkboxes are used to denote which options have already been applied to a given evidence object. As different RVS options are applied to evidence objects, these checkboxes will either be half-checked (indicating some, but not all, of the files in the VS were processed with that option) or fully checked (indicating all files have been processed with that option). It should be noted that certain options, like **File header signature search**, will only ever be half-checked as its possible to rerun this option with different selections.

Once certain options have taken place (computing hashes for instance), selecting the same option will present different options allowing you to either verify an option (in the case of hashing) or reapply a given RVS option. You can also uncheck the checkbox to clear the related data from all items in the VS when implementing an RVS. This is only supported for some RVS operations. For example, if you calculate hash values and then uncheck the box, XWF will ask you to confirm your choice. If you choose *Yes*, the hash values will be completely removed from the VS.

RVS OPTIONS

Selecting every option is not necessarily an incorrect method of refining a VS, but doing so will result in longer processing times as well as potentially more data created in the VS than you need. By knowing the effect of each option, the RVS can be configured to target the specific types of data needed rather than finding everything possible from an evidence object that you must then review.

The X-Ways manual explains the overall power and elegance of the RVS process as follows:

> *Imagine someone tries to conceal an incriminating JPEG picture by embedding it in a MS Word document, misnaming that .doc file to .dll, compressing that file in a Zip archive, misnaming the .zip file to .dll, compressing that .dll in another Zip archive, misnaming that .zip file again to .dll, and then sends this .dll file by e-mail as an attachment using MS Outlook. If all the respective options are selected, Refine Volume Snapshot does the following: It extracts the e-mail attachment from the PST e-mail archive. It detects that the .dll attachment is actually a Zip archive. Then it includes the contents of it in the volume snapshot, namely, a file with the .dll extension. That file is found to be actually another Zip archive. Consequently that archive will be explored, and the .dll file inside will be detected as a .doc file. Searching for embedded pictures, X-Ways Forensics finds the JPEG file in the .doc file and can immediately check it for skin colors if desired. All of this happens in a single step.*

> **(Fleischmann, 2012)**

File recovery options

The **Run X-Tensions** option allows for the execution of DLLs which adhere to the XWF API. X-Tensions are compiled code that has been programmed by anyone wishing to do so using a programming language of your choice. X-Tensions will be further explained in Chapter 7.

The **Particularly thorough file system data structure search** extends the initial VS process. Because this option can take a considerable amount of time depending on the amount of data in an evidence object, it is not used when generating the initial VS. However, this option is critical in gathering additional data found in evidence objects, so we recommend using it in most cases.

XWF locates different types of data depending on the file system being used. Table 4.1 summarizes the kinds of information XWF recovers for the specified file systems through a particularly thorough search.

Table 4.1 Results of Particularly Thorough File System Data Structure Search Based on Type of File System

File System	Recovered Data
FAT12/16/32	Orphaned subdirectories
NTFS	Traces of files in FILE records in sectors not belonging to the current MFT or to a volume shadow copy (VSC)
	Traces of files in INDX buffers and $LogFile, including earlier names and/or paths
	Files referenced by existing/previously existing VSC host files
	Traces of files in old versions of $LogFile found in existing/previously VSC host files
ReiserFS, Reiser4	Deleted files
UDF	Additional sessions of multisession UDF CDs/DVDs (in addition to the first and last session)
CDFS	All sessions on a multisession CD/DVD
RAM	Terminated processes and rootkits
Others	No difference

In many instances, files located in volume SCs are of particular interest. Any files XWF finds in volume SCs are marked with *SC* or *SC prev. version* in the Attributes (**Attr.**) column of the **Directory Browser**. This allows for quickly filtering for files that were found in SCs. Other benefits of the **Particularly thorough file system data structure search** are the recovery and reconstruction of deleted files as well as the ability to reveal previous names of files (including paths of renamed and moved files and directories).

The **File header signature search** is XWF's mechanism for file carving. Employing this option allows for finding files in free and/or used drive space based on their file header signature. Enabling this option and clicking OK in the RVS dialog will display the **File Header Search** dialog as shown in Figure 4.6.

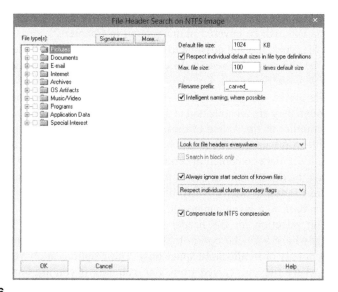

FIGURE 4.6

File Header Search options.

The tree on the left contains categories of file types. Checking the box next to the folder name will select all related file types. For example, checking *Pictures* will include all file types specified under the *Pictures* folder. Every file type can be selected without increasing processing time. However, doing so would be unnecessary unless the case objectives called for a file header search of every file type possible. Expanding a category allows for individually selecting one or more file types.

The two buttons above the tree open the files that define file types. Customizing these files will be covered in detail in Chapter 7.

XWF TIPS AND TRICKS

RVS Speed Tip!

If your objective is the recovery of user-created word processing files, only select those options for **File header signature search**es that benefit that objective. XWF will carve for the word processing files of your choosing, even specific to one file format if need be, and in doing so, XWF will recover only what you have decided is pertinent to your case and this results in less data you have to review.

The **Default file size** is used in cases where a particular file type has a well-defined header, but not a well-defined footer (or, if a footer is typically available, cannot be found). In these cases, XWF will use the exact value of **Default file size** when recovering files. **Max file size** is used in conjunction with **Default file size** and serves as the upper limit for a file. The values used here serve as a global default, and it is recommended to customize a given file's definition with a more accurate file size if it is known. This will be covered in more detail in Chapter 7.

For most file types, it is not possible to determine the filename of files recovered during a file header signature search. **Filename prefix** provides a means to name such files as they are recovered. Entering a value for this option gives carved files a common file prefix. This may make it easier to find such files in the **Directory Browser** (though they are all collected in a special virtual directory) as well as serve as a visual reminder of the source of these carved files. With **Intelligent naming, where possible**, XWF creates file names based on metadata in files it has recovered. For example, EXIF data contained in certain image files will be used when naming files to include the digital camera model that created the image and, in some cases, the internal time stamp of the recovered file. This is a powerful option that helps tie deleted photos back to a given camera or individual.

The default selection for file header search locations is **to look for the file headers everywhere** with the option to change this to either **searching headers in free clusters only** or **in allocated space only**. These options allow you to change the focus of where files are carved from. For example, if you are limited to only searching active files, change this to **in allocated space only. Search in block only** becomes available after selecting a block of data when in **Volume/Partition** or **File** mode. This serves as another way to limit the scope of a file header signature search. To prevent duplication of files, any files that are already part of the initial VS are not carved again.

Always ignore start sectors of known files is a means for XWF to prevent duplicates in that it will not bother to carve files when an existing or previously existing file already starts in a given sector.

Respect individual cluster boundary flags and the other options available in the dropdown determine how and where XWF searches for file headers. Changing this option to **Search at all sector boundaries** results in a more thorough search in that partitions with different cluster layouts can still be searched since the search will work on a per sector vs. per cluster basis. **Extensive byte-level search** is helpful to find artifacts that are not ordinary files, like memory artifacts or individual records within certain file formats. The options referencing *boundary flags* are controlled in the file type definition files that will be covered in Chapter 7.

Finally, **Compensate for NTFS compression** often allows the file header signature search to find NTFS-compressed files, mark them as compressed, and attempt to decompress them.

As with all RVS options, if XWF crashes during a file header search or if the search is intentionally canceled before completion, XWF can resume from the point where it was intentionally interrupted or last saved before a crash (e.g., because of the autosave interval in the case) as opposed to having to start the RVS process all over again.

File processing options

Before discussing the various file processing options, let's take a look at the different ways to limit the files that XWF processes in a given RVS operation. Several options are displayed at the bottom of the processing section as shown in Figure 4.7.

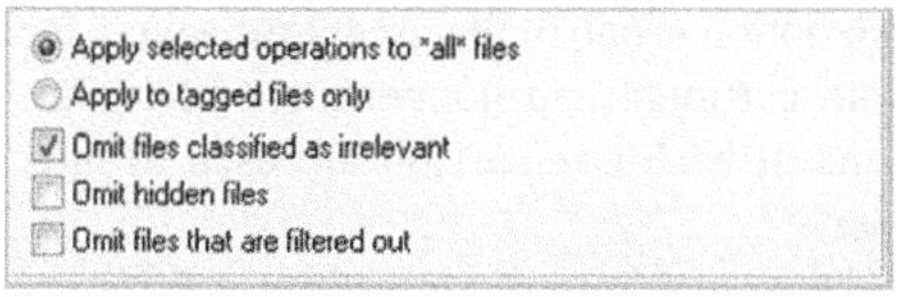

FIGURE 4.7

Choose the targeted files wisely for efficiency and accuracy.

Since efficiency is a key feature of XWF, it should come as no surprise that XWF allows you to focus an RVS operation on a subset of files vs. all files in the VS.

Whenever you start an RVS operation, the default is to **Apply** the **selected operations to *all* files** in the VS. If you tagged one or more files in the **Directory Browser** before invoking RVS, **Apply to tagged files only** will direct the RVS at the tagged files. This is useful if there are files located in different directories or in different evidence objects in that you can tag items in the **Directory Browser** and then perform an RVS operation against only those files.

The exception to this is when you invoke RVS through the context menu of the **Directory Browser**. In this case, the RVS will be limited to the files selected in the **Directory Browser**. This allows for very fine-grained control over the RVS process because you can specifically hone in on the exact data you wish to process.

Regardless of the method by which RVS is initiated, the bottom three options work the same. **Omit files classified as irrelevant**, when checked, tells XWF to ignore files that have been deemed nonpertinent as a result of a hash database match against an irrelevant or not-of-interest hash set. The last two options effect files that have either been hidden via the context menu of the **Directory Browser** or files that are not visible as a result of one or more filters being active in the **Directory Browser**. **Omit files that are filtered out** is also an efficient way to quickly target a set of files for an RVS operation.

Once you have selected which files to include in an RVS process, you can select the options you wish to perform against those files. Refer to Figure 4.8 as each option is discussed.

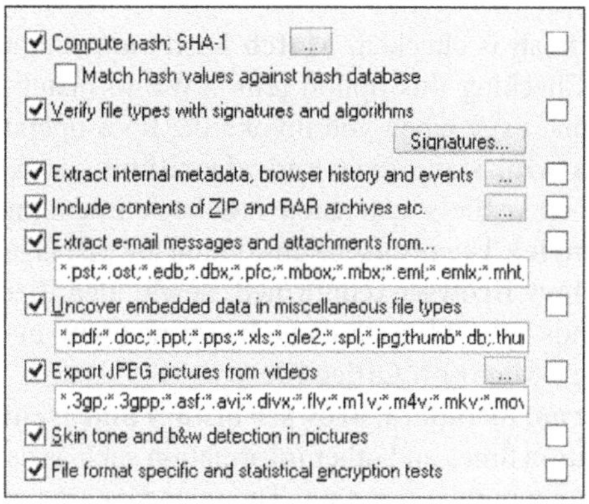

FIGURE 4.8

File processing options.

The **Compute hash** option is one of the great time savers for examiners because it can quickly locate both pertinent and nonpertinent files. Further time savings are gained when the results of hash comparison are used to hide duplicate files from the **Directory Browser**.

Figure 4.9 shows the available hash algorithms XWF can use to calculate hash values. Clicking the button next to the **Compute hash** option displays this list. When using hash databases (covered in detail in Chapter 5), select the hash algorithm that matches the hashes stored in the hash database. The reason for this should be obvious in that if your hash database contains SHA-1 hashes, choosing the MD5 hash is not effective as nothing will match.

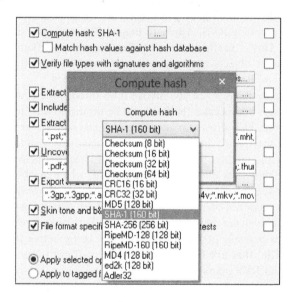

FIGURE 4.9

Option to create hash values of files.

When **Compute hash** is checked, **Match hash values against hash database** becomes available. Checking this option tells XWF to match hash values against any hash databases that exist when you invoke the RVS operation.

Verify file types with signatures and algorithms checks for file type mismatches such as when a file's extension has been intentionally changed (from JPG to TXT, for example). The results of this option are displayed in the **Type status** column in the **Directory Browser** (confirmed, newly identified, not verified, etc.). This function also finds hybrid files that can be opened with more than one application, such as a merged Microsoft Office file.

The **Extract internal metadata, browser history and events** option extracts the internally stored creation times and other information such as database tables, EXIF, etc., from files that contain this metadata. The metadata are extracted and stored in the **Metadata** column of the **Directory Browser**. Once populated, metadata can be edited, filtered, sorted, or output as part of the case report with their host files.

Figure 4.10 shows the suboptions available after clicking the button to the right of the option. Some of the options are self-explanatory and will not be covered.

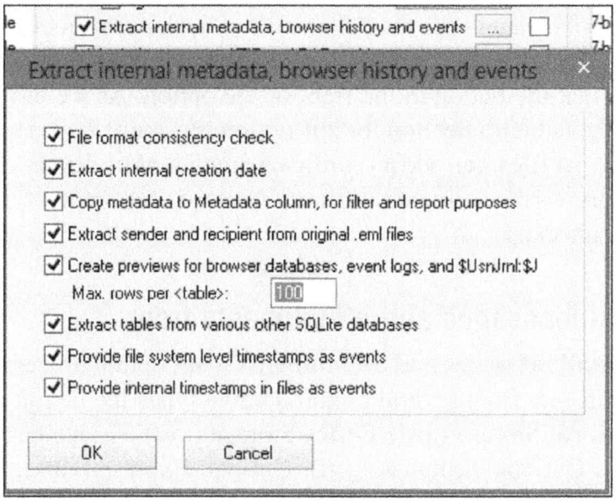

FIGURE 4.10

Extract internal metadata options.

File format consistency check can detect corruption in certain types of files. The results of this check are displayed in the **Type status** column of the **Directory Browser**.

Any extracted creation timestamps are shown in the **Int. Creation** column of the **Directory Browser**. Typically, the internal creation date is the earliest timestamp available and is the closest to the original creation date of the file. XWF contains custom algorithms not found elsewhere that can extract such timestamps with high reliability.

When processing e-mail messages, the sender and recipient fields are extracted and shown in the **Directory Browser** in columns of the same name. These columns are dynamically displayed in the **Directory Browser** if **Directory Browser Options, Filters | Dynamic e-mail columns** is checked.

Create previews for browser databases, event logs, and $UsnJrnl:$J unpacks such things as SQLite databases and other binary storage files into HTML files that can be included in reports. For a complete list of supported formats, see the XWF manual section entitled *Extract internal metadata*.

Finally, the last two options enable XWF to create *events* (which are the basis for timeline examinations) based on various timestamps, both at the file system and metadata levels. Events will be covered in Chapter 7.

Include contents of ZIP and RAR archives, etc. enables XWF to examine the contents of archived files, such as ZIP files, and create child objects for every item in the archive files. If an encrypted file is found, it is marked with an *e* in the **Directory Browser Attr.** column. There is no limit on the number of archived levels, such as a ZIP file compressed into another ZIP file, etc., but split/spanned/segmented archives are not supported. This option is affected by the selected case code pages in that the filenames inside archives will not be displayed properly if the code page used by the archive is not selected. In most cases, using UTF-8 and the default code page will suffice.

As many modern document files are usually zip archives (such as recent Microsoft Office documents), they are processed as archives by XWF. These can be excluded if you only want to see the documents as a whole without showing embedded data, such as pictures, separately. To select the types of archive files that this option affects, click the button to the right of the option. As we have seen in other areas of XWF, the default selection for this option is usually the best choice because archives, such as .jar files, can add a significant amount of irrelevant child files to the VS. Unless you have a need to examine the contents of such archives, we recommend leaving these unchecked.

Extract e-mail messages and attachments from...

The **Extract e-mail messages and attachments from** option processes e-mail messages and attachments from several e-mail archive types including:

Outlook Personal Storage (.pst), Office Storage (.ost), Exchange (.edb), Outlook Message (.msg), Outlook Template (.oft), Outlook Express (.dbx), Kerio Connect (store.fdb), AOL PFC files, Mozilla mailbox, generic mailbox (mbox, Unix mail format), and MHT Web Archive (.mht).

E-mail messages from these archives are extracted as .eml files. The creation date and time is taken from the timestamp in the *Date* line in the e-mail message's header. The last modification date and time is taken from the timestamp in the *Delivery-Date* line in the message header. The **Directory Browser** also will have two additional columns populated (**Sender** and **Recipient**) for each of the extracted e-mails and e-mail attachments.

Viewing the contents of an e-mail archive without refining the VS can still be done by selecting an e-mail archive. However, XWF will suggest you perform an RVS as shown in Figure 4.11.

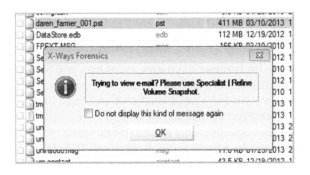

FIGURE 4.11

XWF gives a suggestion to create an RVS when trying to view e-mail.

Closing this dialog box without taking an RVS will allow viewing the e-mails in the e-mail store, such as the .pst file seen in Figure 4.12. Changing to **Preview** mode renders a view of the e-mail store that contains information about the messages. At this point, if an RVS was not taken, the e-mails will not have been extracted as .eml files. For this reason, it is not the most effective means of reviewing e-mail. We recommend always performing an RVS when your case involves e-mail as it makes reviewing e-mail messages much easier.

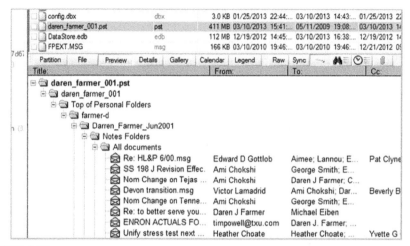

FIGURE 4.12

XWF allows for viewing of e-mail without an RVS, but not as .eml files.

XWF also attempts to find traces of e-mail messages in unallocated (double-deleted e-mail) space within the PST files in addition to providing data from Calendar/Contact/Notes/Tasks/Journal entries. It also supports non-English Unicode characters, overlong paths, and processes password-protected PST archives without needing the password.

The **Uncover embedded data in miscellaneous file types** option extracts files that are embedded in files of other types through a byte-level file header signature search. These files are then added as child objects of the files in which they were found. An example would be the extraction of .emf files embedded in multipage printouts (.spl spooler files). See the XWF manual for complete details on the types of embedded data this option uncovers.

The **Export JPEG pictures from videos** is a time-saving feature for those examinations involving digital video files. If the video player application of either MPlayer (http://www.mplayerhq.hu) or Forensic Framer (http://www.kuiper.de/index.php/en/) is configured as a viewer in XWF, JPEG pictures are exported from the following types of media formats (in addition to any other formats that MPlayer or Forensic Framer support):

.3gp;.3gpp;*.asf;*.avi;*.divx;*.flv;*.m1v;*.m4v;*.mkv;*.mov;*.mp4;
.mpeg;.mpg;*.nsv;*.nut;*.nuv;*.qt;*.rm;*.rmvb;*.vob;*.wmv

Clicking the button to the right of the option brings up a dialog that allows for adjusting how often frames are generated for each given video.

Depending upon the video's compression or encoding, selecting intervals smaller than the interval between completely stored new frames may not create additional pictures from the videos. In addition, videos protected with Digital Rights Management are unable to be processed by XWF and will be marked with an *e!* in the **Attr.** column of the **Directory Browser**.

This feature helps speed up the review of videos by allowing you to view thumbnails from a video without having to play each video to find relevant portions of the file. By being able to scroll through still images rather than having to watch every video, you can quickly identify "of interest" videos. This feature also allows you to "print" a movie in that you can include the still frames of a movie in a report table. Finally, still frames from movies can be further analyzed for skin tone which allows you to locate movies that contain a high percentage of skin tones (this is yet another example of the people behind XWF putting a great deal of thought into the order of operations).

The **Skin tone and b&w detection in pictures** option can be applied against the following file types: JPEG, PNG, GIF, TIFF, BMP, PSD, HDR, PSP, SGI, PCX, CUT, PNM/PBM/PGM/PPM, ICO. XWF computes the percentage of skin color pictures to allow sorting by percentage in the **Directory Browser**'s **SC%** column. In addition to skin tone, black & white detection helps when looking for documents that were scanned or faxed.

By calculating skin tone percentage, child pornography examinations can be made more efficient because you can sort by percentage of skin color in order to quickly find the most potentially relevant pictures. In some cases, there may be false positives because of colors in pictures that match skin tones.

In the majority of cases, the odds of having the most likely relevant pictures sorted at the top for quick identification are increased with skin color detection. Pictures unable to be scanned due to corruption or other issues are marked with a question mark instead of skin color percentage.

The **File format specific and statistical encryption tests** option checks files larger than 255 bytes for potential signs of encryption. Encrypted files found through this entropy test are flagged with *e?* in the attribute column. Table 4.2 shows the file types that XWF can check for encryption. Compressed files are not checked, as the contents are compressed internally and cannot be distinguished from random or encrypted data.

Table 4.2 Types of Files Checked for Encryption

File Type	Checked for Encryption?
Encrypted container files	**Yes**: TrueCrypt, PGP Desktop, BestCrypt, DriveCrypt (as drive letters)
Documents	**Yes**: .doc; .xls; .ppt; .pps; .mpp; .pst; .xlsx; .pptx; .ppsx; .odt; .ods; .pdf
Digital rights protected	**Yes**: Microsoft Office Documents
eCryptfs-encrypted files	**Yes**: Linux Enterprise Cryptographic File System (*flagged with "E" in attributes column*)
Compressed files	**No**: .zip, .rar, .tar, .gz, .7z, .arj, .cab, .jpg, .png, .gif, .tif, .mpg, and .swf (*archives are detected as encrypted already when/if included in the volume snapshot*)

While this option can be used to determine whether files are encrypted, if you are looking for encrypted containers such as those created by TrueCrypt, it is often much more efficient and effective to recursively list all files in a case, sorting the **Directory Browser** by the **Size** column, and then looking for the largest files.

In selected evidence objects allows for choosing the evidence objects to include in the RVS process. Clicking the button to the right of the option results in the dialog as shown in Figure 4.13 that allows for selecting one or more evidence objects for the RVS process.

FIGURE 4.13

Option to select one, multiple, or all evidence objects.

RESULTS OF AN RVS

XWF TIPS AND TRICKS

Do You Really Need to Select Everything?

Although XWF is very efficient and quick, understand that selecting unneeded options will add to processing time and increase the number of items in the VS. Do you really need skin tone and black & white detection if your case has nothing to do with images? Try to choose only what you need to minimize processing time. If need be, you can always go back to select additional RVS options later.

After the RVS is completed, you will, in most cases, notice a remarkable difference in the number of files that have been added to your case. As an example of the number of files added as a result of a single RVS, Figure 4.14 shows the total number of files before the RVS process and Figure 4.15 shows the total number of files after the RVS process.

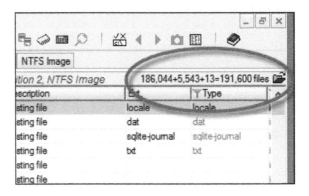

FIGURE 4.14

Object counts prior to an RVS.

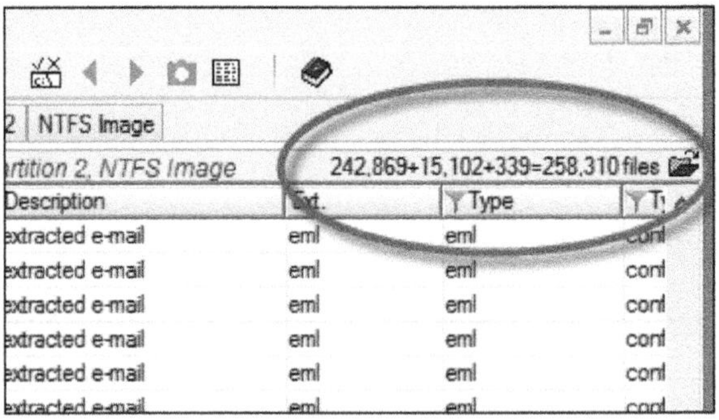

FIGURE 4.15

Object counts after an RVS.

In this example, there were 191,600 objects in the initial VS. The RVS process added an additional 66,710 objects to the snapshot. Recall from Chapter 3 that the breakdown of the numbers in the circled area equate to:

$$\text{Existing} + \text{previously existing} + \text{virtual} = \text{total objects}$$

If no virtual files are listed, then no number for virtual files will be shown. If no previously existing files are listed, then a number for previously existing files will not be shown either.

The **Simultaneous Search** option seen in the RVS dialog box invokes the **Simultaneous Search (SS)** dialog seen in Figure 4.16 and its use is detailed in Chapter 6.

FIGURE 4.16

Simultaneous Search dialog box.

SHORTCUTS

F10: Opens RVS dialog
CTRL+DEL: Resets selected files in the **Directory Browser** to the *still to be processed* state

SUMMARY

The RVS is one of the most significant features of XWF and provides capabilities that distinguish it from other forensic tools. Although the default settings are generally more than sufficient for most examinations, having an understanding of the inner workings of XWF as it pertains to the VS is important. Rather than pressing a button that simply finds evidence in a manner that cannot be controlled, curtailed, explained, or exploited, the RVS puts that control in the hands of the examiner.

By having control in refining a VS, the time needed for processing can be minimized, the amount of data recovered can be targeted, and an analysis can be more efficiently conducted. XWF gives us the option to work with defaults or run the tool like a finely tuned machine.

Reference

Fleischmann, S., 2012. X-Ways Forensics/WinHex Manual. Retrieved January 21, 2013, from X-Ways Forensics Computer Forensics Integrated Software. http://www.x-ways.net/winhex/manual.pdf.

About the Authors

Brett Shavers is a former law enforcement officer of a municipal police department and has been an investigator assigned to state and federal task forces. Besides working many specialty positions, Brett was the first digital forensics examiner at his police department, attended over 1000 hours of digital forensic training courses across the country, collected more than a few certifications along the way, and set up his department's first digital forensics lab in a small, cluttered storage closet.

Brett has been an adjunct instructor at the University of Washington's Digital Forensics Program, an expert witness and digital forensics consultant, a prolific speaker at conferences, and a blogger on digital forensics and is an honorary member of the Computer Technology Investigators Network. Brett has worked cases ranging from child pornography investigations as a law enforcement investigator to a wide range of civil litigation cases as a digital forensics expert consultant. This is Brett's second book, with *Placing the Suspect Behind the Keyboard*, being his first.

Brett is also a Former Corporal of Marines.

Eric Zimmerman has been involved with computers in some form or fashion since the days of the Commodore 64. Initially pursuing a mathematics degree at Youngstown State University, Eric moved to Chicago for work in 1997. For the next 9 years, Eric worked at a third-party logistics company where he was a lead systems administrator. His duties included programming and systems integration work.

While living in Chicago, Eric received his Bachelor of Science in Computer Science. In 2007, Eric joined the FBI as a Special Agent and is currently assigned to the Salt Lake City field office.

X-Ways Forensics and Electronic Discovery

INFORMATION IN THIS CHAPTER

- Introduction
- Review of relevant data with X-Ways Investigator
- Summary

INTRODUCTION

The case studies chapters put to use the information in this book in a practical way. As every analysis is different, and every analyst conducts examinations differently, the suggestions in this chapter are only ideas of a workflow process using XWF.

CIVIL LITIGATION

The range of civil cases varies just as much as criminal investigations, and although some rules may be different, there are still rules to follow. At times, a case may be litigated concurrently in civil and criminal courts, or one case may follow the other. Although the electronic data involved in both cases may come from the same source, the processes involved have differences. It is not the intention of this chapter to describe legal differences, but rather to focus on the practical application of XWF in these cases.

CASE STUDY

Scenario: *civil litigation*
Plaintiff and Defendant are involved in civil litigation involving one employee's workstation. Electronic data are to be collected from the workstation for analysis and review.

This is a broad example of civil litigation and can apply to nearly every case. As every case is different, particularly in civil cases where additional restrictions affect the methods and processes involved, this section gives recommendations on handling varying types of these constraints using XWF.

Figure 9.1 shows the model used for processing an electronic discovery case using XWF. This graphic is the Electronic Discovery Reference Model (EDRM), which shows each stage of the electronic evidence process from identification through production. XWF is capable of fulfilling the phases of *Identification* through *Production*, in both logical and physical acquisitions of data collection.

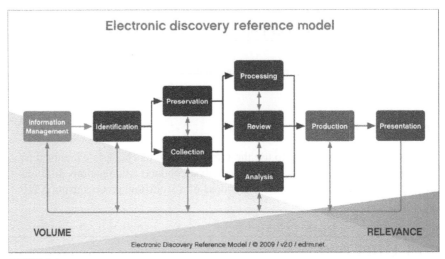

FIGURE 9.1

The EDRM visual graphic of the electronic discovery process (http://www.edrm.net/resources/edrm-stages-explained).

A common issue in civil litigation is whether the parties failed to preserve information pursuant to a "litigation hold." At times, litigants are accused of destroying information, contrary to document retention policies and litigation holds. One such case was *Liebert Corp. v. Mazur* (Liebert Corp. v. Mazur et al., 2005), where thousands of electronic files were deleted after a party was served with an injunction motion.

Preparing XWF

Preparing XWF for an eDiscovery collection effort will help organize data collection to minimize the time needed to be onsite. Using an external USB hard drive, copy the XWF program files and create a case on the hard drive (refer to Chapter 1 for details on creating a case with XWF). The result is a portable storage device that contains all files needed to execute XWF as well as a destination for collected data. We recommend using relative paths any time you have XWF on removable media as you will not know the drive letter of your external device in most cases. Figure 9.2 shows the folders created in this example.

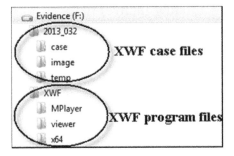

FIGURE 9.2

External USB drive containing the XWF program files and case folders for data collection.

Accessing the data

In the most basic case, simple file copying may suffice in an electronic document collection. However, this is neither the best method nor the most efficient approach. On the other end of the spectrum, creating a forensic image of an entire storage device is the most complete method, but may be overkill when only a small percentage of data may be required. Some cases may specifically prohibit forensic imaging (refer to Chapter 2 for imaging methods using XWF).

Your choices for data access can include forensic imaging, live collection on a running computer, or booting the computer to a forensic boot media such as the Windows Forensic Environment (http://winfe.wordpress.com). The most efficient method is booting to the Windows Forensic Environment, where the custodian media is write protected. XWF then has access to the physical hard drive without risk of altering any data during the collection. This also lessens the risk of the custodian machine crashing due to unknown operating system problems if the collection is conducted on a live machine.

XWF TIPS AND TRICKS

Running XWF on a non-Windows custodian machine

As XWF is a Windows-based tool, if the custodian computer is running an operating system other than Windows, you can still use XWF to collect the data. The hard drive can be removed and placed behind a write-blocking device, or, when the drive cannot be removed, just boot the custodian machine to Windows FE (http://winfe.wordpress.com) and execute XWF.

Whichever method is chosen to access the custodian data, the processes involved to collect responsive data with XWF are similar. From this point, no matter which method of accessing the data is chosen, XWF will see the data in the same way. This includes a forensic image as well as data collected from a live (running) machine.

User created files—Existing (active) files

The most common eDiscovery collection method is collecting only user-created files, such as word processing documents, spreadsheets, email, and other files typically created and maintained by a computer user. Previously existing files are not always a factor for collection in eDiscovery cases. Since only existing files are typically collected in eDiscovery cases, this may sound like a situation where copying files to an external hard drive will suffice; however, that would not be efficient, practical, or as thorough compared to using XWF.

The key feature in XWF that supports this task of collecting electronic data is through filtering. If you recall from Chapter 3, the **Directory Browser Options, Filters** (the shortcut is CTRL+F5) gives several dozen options for filtering data. In Figure 9.3, The **Directory Browser Options, Filters** shows a way to implement a **Type** filter. XWF lists a multitude of predefined and categorized file types. If the collection goal is the capture of all word processing file types, then every file type listed can be selected. Conversio, if the data collection requires specific word processing file types, then only those types can be selected. Depending on the file types required, you can select additional categories, such as spreadsheets, presentations, etc.

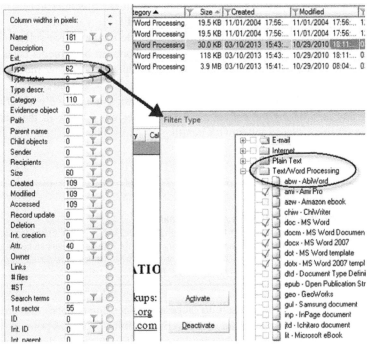

FIGURE 9.3

Filtering by file type using the Directory Browser Options.

Once the **Directory Browser, Filter** has been activated, only those files meeting the selected file type criteria will be shown in XWF.

You can also apply the **Type** filter directly from the **Directory Browser** as well (assuming the **Type** column is visible)

If the collection project has additional criteria or limits, you can apply additional options. One common example is that of file date/time stamps criteria. Figure 9.4 shows the popup dialog to filter by dates of creation, modification, access, record update, deletion, and initial creation, through which there can be one or multiple selections.

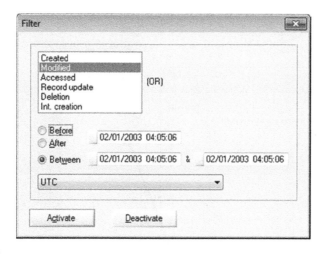

FIGURE 9.4

Filtering files by date/time.

As our first filter restricted all files to specific file types, this filter applies an additional restriction. More filters can be applied against the subject medium as needed. Search terms can be applied at this point if necessary to restrict relevant data (refer to Chapter 6 on the XWF search capabilities). Now that you have filtered the data to be collected, there are a few more steps you can take to create the best data collection.

As you recall from Chapter 4, the Refine Volume Snapshot (RVS) adds more information about files to the volume snapshot, such as file metadata. In the case of eDiscovery file collections, metadata may be quite important, so use the RVS against the remaining filtered files. Refer to Chapter 4 on configuring the RVS as you only want to apply the RVS to the filtered files and not to the entire system. This can include extracting metadata, computing the hash of each file, and eliminating irrelevant files (refer to Chapter 5 for details on "de-NISTing"), and other functions, such as email processing if e-mail is part of your collection.

The RVS will complete quickly on your filtered file dataset. Thereafter, you will have the metadata extracted, a hash value for every file, and you will be able to hide irrelevant files if you choose to compare against a hash set.

Copying the filtered files

At this point, select all the filtered files in the **Directory Browser** (shortcut is CTRL + A) and right-click to bring up the **Recovery/Copy** context menu option. Choose the options needed for your specific situation as seen in Figure 9.5. XWF can create a log (*copylog* file) of the copied files in either a .tsv or .html file with user-selected fields. The *copylog* file is customizable as the default format or can be input into a spreadsheet. The *copylog* is a critical component of file management and allows cross-referencing between the *copylog* file and copied files.

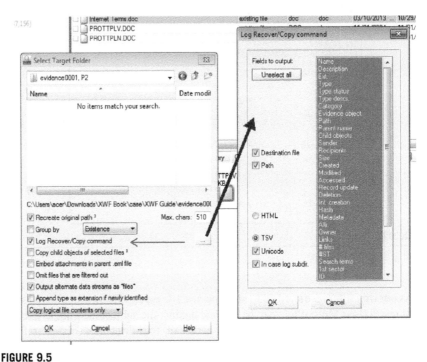

FIGURE 9.5

File listing selection fields.

Optional method of creating a file list

If files are not copied and only a file listing is desired, XWF can create a list of files similar to the list in the XWF *copylog*. Select the files of interest and right click to open the context menu. Select **Export list** and, in the popup menu, choose the desired fields for the files that you highlighted, the output file type, and the destination for your file list. Figure 9.6 shows an exported file list as a spreadsheet. With the exported list, you have a complete listing of the exported files and information from the fields selected from Figure 9.5, such as hash values, metadata, and timestamp data. As a spreadsheet, the data are sortable, searchable, and customizable to your preferences.

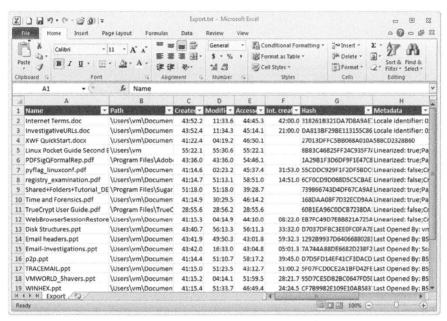

FIGURE 9.6

Exported file listing viewed as a spreadsheet.

Keep in mind that with recovered/copied files, a *copylog* can be generated with your preferences without having to export a separate file listing.

Printing the relevant files

Depending upon needs and requests, one or more files can be printed directly from within XWF for manual review. Obviously, printing a large number of files to a physical printer will probably require more paper and time than creating one or more PDF files.

Again, with all relevant files selected (just as you did when copying the files and exporting the file list), right-click and bring up the popup dialog. Choose the **Print** command. To create PDF files, you will need a PDF printer. One popular application that can print to PDF is PDFCreator (free from http://www.pdfforge.org/pdfcreator). As you can see in Figure 9.7, there are options to consider before printing. If you have several thousand pages of printable material, it may not be the best choice to print every page. Reductions in the number of pages can be made by not printing a cover page or by printing only the first page of each file. Other options include printing each document as individual PDF files, or printing all documents as a single PDF file. It is important to be aware that printing even a small selection of documents can result in thousands of pages. Printing is best done after reviewing the files for relevance.

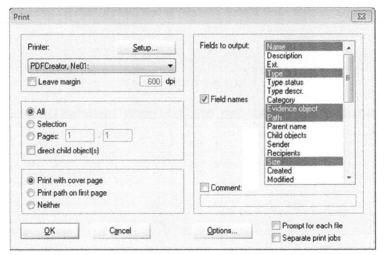

FIGURE 9.7

Printing files within XWF with PDFCreator.

XWF container

Container files (refer back to Chapter 2 for details on creating containers) are an excellent method of collecting data in eDiscovery cases. After filtering, refining a volume snapshot, searching for keywords, and determining the files to be collected, the XWF container will preserve all captured files in an encapsulated file format, protecting each file from modification.

The container file is also useful as a backup to the native (original) files that were copied. As the metadata and content of native files are fragile, inadvertent changes can occur. Having a container file creates a safety layer of data protection should native files lose original data.

More importantly, container files can be imported back into XWF as evidence items if needed. As an example, given a large collection of custodian files that were exported natively, a review and analysis can be conducted on the container of those native files rather than analyzing the native files and potentially modifying data.

XWF TIPS AND TRICKS

Want more than just file copying in an eDiscovery case? Don't forget about the skeleton disk image!

Recall from Chapter 2, that XWF can create "Skeleton Disk Images" that contain sectors specific to the data that you need to copy for eDiscovery. These sectors can be from partition tables, file system data structures, and even registry hives. The Skeleton Image also makes it easy to compare the data with the original disk as the original offsets and distances between various data and metadata are preserved.

Redacting files within an image

In almost every eDiscovery case, there are files protected by privilege or privacy on electronic storage media such as hard drives. Traditionally, these files are manually removed from an image through an arduous process of hex editing the image file with WinHex or similar tools. Alternatively, rather than a manual editing of an image, nonprivileged files are copied out of an image for production, which is still a labor-intensive process with risk of inadvertently altering file metadata.

In order to address these issues, XWF has the ability to create a **Cleansed Image**. A **Cleansed Image** allows the forensic acquisition of storage media with the ability to exclude data that needs to be redacted. The imaging process is identical as described in Chapter 2, but before acquiring an image, hide the files to be excluded from imaging (refer to Chapter 3 on hiding files). You may use one or more **Directory Browser** filters to display the files you do *not* want to include (use the negation options for various filters to achieve this) or you may target individual files as needed without filters. Once the filters are in place, explore recursively, select all items and hide them via the **Directory Browser**'s context menu. Once the files are hidden, create the image as outlined in Chapter 2; however, in the image creation dialog, select **Omit hidden files** from the **Scope: sectors** option. If you choose to use a watermark, it will be written to all affected sectors. XWF will prompt to make sure you want to **omit hidden files** because this will not capture any of the hidden data from the evidence drive (Figure 9.8).

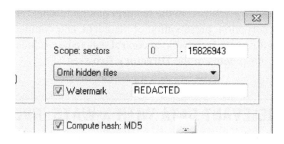

FIGURE 9.8

Creating a "Cleansed Image" with "REDACTED" watermark.

The results of a cleansed file using the watermark "REDACTED" is shown in Figure 9.9 (**volume** view) and Figure 9.10 (**Preview**).

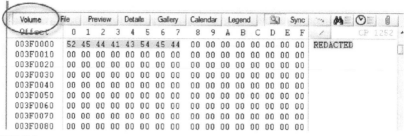

FIGURE 9.9

Volume view of a watermarked ("REDACTED") file.

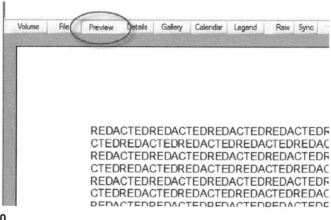

FIGURE 9.10

Preview of a watermarked ("REDACTED") file.

A **Cleansed Image** gives you all the features of a traditional forensic image such as compression, encryption, preservation of metadata, and compatibility with other forensic tools in addition to being able to control data to be excluded from the image by simply hiding those items in the **Directory Browser**.

REVIEW OF RELEVANT DATA WITH X-WAYS INVESTIGATOR

X-Ways Investigator, based on XWF, is a scaled-down version of XWF designed to assist in the review of electronic evidence by those specialized in areas of the investigation other than digital forensics. In eDiscovery, reviewers of the results of an analysis are typically paralegals and attorneys (this is also true in criminal cases). X-Ways Investigator is a solution to consider as a review platform as it continues the functionality of XWF from collection of electronic data through review and finally to production.

X-Ways Investigator offers a review platform that has less functionality than XWF in that it restricts features that nonexaminers may find confusing. However, many important and useful features remain to streamline the review process. Some of these features include logging and case management, reporting, keyword searching, tagging relevant files, filtering, and hash comparisons.

A further reduced version of XWF, X-Ways Investigator *CTR*, allows opening only evidence file containers created by XWF and X-Ways Investigator. A few other restrictions, such as hash computation, are also removed to further reduce complexity and increase the number of potential reviewers able to use X-Ways Investigator *CTR* as a review platform without needing expertise in digital forensics. Each reduced version of X-Ways Forensics (Investigator and *CTR*) also comes at a reduced price of the full version.

Refer to Chapter 8 for methods of tagging files, inserting comments, and adding files to report table associations. X-Ways Investigator gives the reviewer these powerful review and tagging capabilities combined with reporting features, just as in XWF. Although other commercial review platforms exist, there are few, if any, that can compete with the price and functionality of X-Ways Forensics, Investigator, and Investigator *CTR*.

Bates numbering

Through the menu command **Specialist | Bates Number Files**, XWF can add a user-defined, unique number (*Bates number*) between the filename and extension. The renaming applies to all files of a folder and those files in sub-folders. Figures 9.11 and 9.12 show the popup dialogs for numbering choices. As an example, the file **evidence.doc** could appear as **evidence."prefix_1".doc** using the XWF Bates-numbering feature.

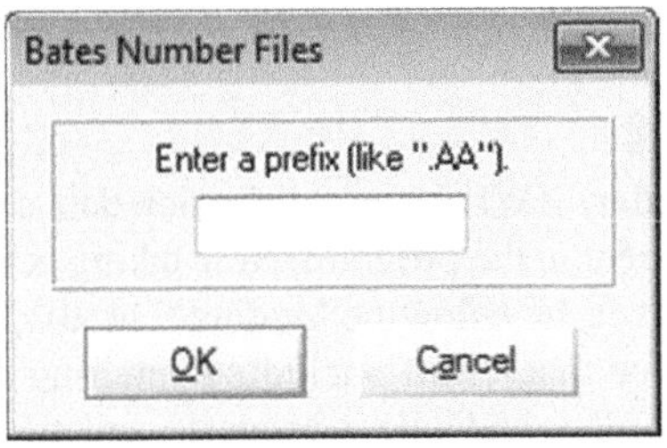

FIGURE 9.11

User-created prefix to be inserted between the filename and serial number.

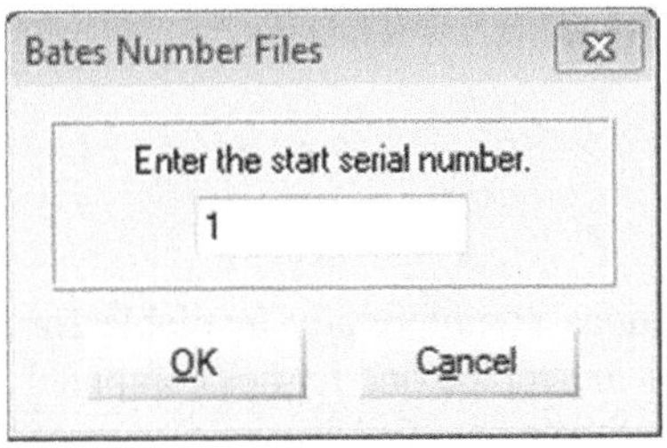

FIGURE 9.12

User-created serial number inserted between the user-created prefix and the file extension.

Attorney review of data

When X-Ways Investigator and X-Ways Investigator *CTR* are not an option as a review platform for attorneys, the copied files along with the *copylog* may be sufficient. Either the active (native) files can be reviewed using the applications that created them, such as a word processing application, or the data can be imported into a law firm's choice of eDiscovery tools.

A benefit of using either X-Ways Investigator or X-Ways Investigator *CTR* is that the reviewers are prevented from making inadvertent changes of file metadata because they will be accessing the files from an XWF container.

XWF does not produce load files needed to import data into eDiscovery review platforms. It is possible to manually create load files using the export features of XWF; however, load file creation is beyond the scope of this guide.

Forensic analysis and electronic discovery

This example showed a basic method of collecting targeted, existing files (user created files). We did not discuss methods that are more analytical or forensic in nature, such as data carving and registry analysis. Since most collections simply involve user created files and not conducting an analysis on the operating system, we limited our discussion to the basics.

This is not to say that eDiscovery cases do not ever employ a forensic analysis. In those events where a forensic analysis is warranted, we can employ the methods described in this book in an eDiscovery case as well.

Log file and reporting

Another safeguard offered by XWF for civil litigation data collection is the reporting and logging features inherent in the program. Note taking is time intensive and prone to error or neglect. However, by using the logging function, all actions taken during the collection can be added to a report, including detailing the steps taken to verify compliance with court orders and client requests and to document the chain of custody.

As part of your eDiscovery data collection and reporting, the responsive files can be added to the XWF case through the **Report table associations** (refer to Chapter 8 for more details on **Report table associations**).

SUMMARY

There are many applications commercially available for document collection in eDiscovery, wherein files are copied and hashes computed. When used in eDiscovery, XWF gives you the power of a full forensic suite of tools that not only does everything an eDiscovery collection requires but also gives you the complete functionality of a forensic tool. From identification to production, XWF delivers more than just file copying in civil litigation.

Reference

Liebert Corp. v. Mazur, 357 Ill. App. 3d 265, 283 827 N.E.2d 909, 929 (Ill. App. Ct. 2005). (Appellate Court of Illinois, First District, Second Division. 2005). Retrieved April 22, 2013, from http://scholar.google.com/scholar_case?case=16708488608786485277& q=Liebert+Corp.+v.+Mazur,+827+N.E.2d+909&hl=en&as_sdt=2,48&as_vis=1.

Foreword

I've been waiting for this book for nearly a decade.

As a devoted user of X-Ways Forensics since its introduction, I turn to X-Ways Forensics more than any other tool in my lab. I've watched X-Ways Forensics mature from a brilliant hex editor to a digital forensics tool of incomparable depth, power, and flexibility. Yet, after years of daily use, X-Ways Forensics still manages to amaze and daunt me with its wealth of features and options.

I'm an old-school forensic examiner. I honed my skills in DOS using a hex editor, so I feel a deep kinship with X-Ways Forensics' old-school emphasis on the data notwithstanding its being one of the most advanced digital forensic analysis platforms on the market. Though it greatly simplifies the forensics workflow, it best serves those who understand the evidence. X-Ways Forensics is built atop WinHex, surely the finest hex editor ever written. It's the tool of choice for the digital forensic examiner who wants to be close to the evidence and truly, deeply understand how data live.

The X-Ways Forensics product manual is an invaluable resource, but what's been missing is a guide to X-Ways Forensics written from the user's perspective; ideally, a volume looking at the many capabilities of the tool through the eyes of experienced examiners and aiding both novice and veteran users in understanding how to configure the tool and choose wisely among its many options. X-Ways Forensics can do virtually anything, and its name reflects that tasks need not be accomplished in just one way, but can often be approached in a multitude of ways, i.e., in "X" ways. Sometimes, the challenge of having "X" ways to accomplish a task is deciding which to choose.

This book does a splendid job helping users understand the program's many options and make wise choices. Because it's the work of experienced computer forensic examiners, it focuses on the basic tasks examiners must accomplish and the features of greatest practical value. This book introduced me to features of X-Ways Forensics I'd not noticed before or had forgotten. Far from being a recasting of the program's help files, every chapter of this volume contains golden nuggets, many in the form of tips and tricks to aid your exploration of X-Ways Forensics.

X-Ways Forensics manifests the vision and extraordinary programming acumen of Stefan Fleischmann, who has nudged, nurtured, and supported the product from its inception. One marvels at the speed with which Stefan investigates any bug report and the swiftness with which fixes are instituted and wished-for features appear in new releases. Where so much software product support today is scripted and impersonal, Stefan's support is deeply personal. When a new release exhibits an infrequent glitch—as any complex software will do—that glitch is quickly acknowledged and corrected. But when the product is unfairly criticized, it is vigorously defended. It is a tool so deep and rich that many support requests seek features already in the product or complain that the program can't do something it's been able to do for years! When that happens, Stefan suffers no fools gladly.

Still, an application needs more than just a gifted developer to endure and grow; it needs a passionate community of experienced and devoted users. This book reflects the work of some of the strongest contributors to the X-Ways Forensics community. Brett Shavers brings boundless experience in computer forensics gained as a law enforcement officer and private practitioner. Brett's longtime use of X-Ways Forensics coupled with his experience defending its results in and out of court makes him an ideal guide to the power and intricacies of the tool. Eric Zimmerman is both a computer scientist and an FBI Special Agent. Eric has written numerous free tools to aid the digital forensics community. Together, Brett and Eric bring a first-rate mix of practical, technical, and investigative skill and experience to their X-Ways Forensics Practitioner's Guide.

I recommend you read this book with your copy of X-Ways Forensics running and data loaded. Try out each of the features described and keep the many shortcuts shared at the ready. Whether you are exploring X-Ways Forensics for the first time or you're an old hand with the program, you will benefit from letting this fine book be your guide.

Craig Ball
Attorney and Forensic Technologist
Certified Computer Forensic Examiner

Installation and Configuration of X-Ways Forensics

INTRODUCTION

Before you get started with XWF, there are a few basics to understand about the installation, user interface, and basic configuration of XWF. We are not fans of using the term "basic" because, for many of us, we sometimes want to skip the "basics" and go right into "advanced" work, even when we may not be ready. Nevertheless, there are a few basic pieces of information that will be helpful to know before you begin using XWF.

SYSTEM REQUIREMENTS

This chapter begins with one of the most incredible aspects of XWF: its system requirements. When running on average 64-bit hardware with multiple processors and 4 GB of RAM, XWF can handle extreme numbers of files and does so in a *very* efficient and fast manner. However, XWF will also run on older computers such as a 32-bit machine running Windows XP with just 256 MB of RAM! XWF is not resource hungry and will use only the resources necessary to get the job done. This means your workstation remains usable while XWF is working. Contrast this to other forensic tools that consume all resources on a computer, effectively rendering it unusable for anything else.

So there you have it. XWF is a full-featured forensic software utility that can run on just about anything. This is an impressive ability and comes into play in situations where live machines with minimal resources might be the target of an analysis or where an older forensic workstation can be kept in service instead of being discarded. Plus, XWF can run on a running target machine, either to preview the machine or to fully analyze it, all while using as little as 100 MB of RAM. Of course, the examiner must understand that running any program on a live evidence machine must be based on the circumstances at the time, such as when the machine cannot be turned off. Finally, XWF's ability to run from a directory vs. being installed on a computer means that you have full-blown forensics capabilities with nothing more than a thumb drive and your XWF dongle!

Throughout this book, there will be tips and guidance to help you squeeze out every bit of XWF's power in terms of both speed and processing. Even though the processing speed is already quick, there are options and techniques to help it run even faster. Bear in mind that just because XWF runs on older machines, its forensic capabilities aren't diminished nor is it less powerful than any other forensic application. In our experience, the opposite is true.

INSTALLING XWF

There are several ways to install XWF. The first method we will cover is the traditional setup.exe method. The following steps outline installing XWF in this manner:

1. Download the XWF compressed program file.

    Licensed users can download XWF from http://www.x-ways.net. The download is in the form of a compressed file, generally named xw_ *forensics.zip.*
2. Extract the compressed file and then execute the setup file.

    Extract xw_forensics.zip and run the setup.exe file to start the installation process just like any other software application as seen in Figure 1.1.
3. Add supplement (add-on) programs and the viewer component.

    MPlayer (an optional video player/framer), WinHex, and the X-Ways Viewer component are simply extracted to the XWF program folder after downloading them. Links for these programs are available after checking your license status on the X-Ways Web site.

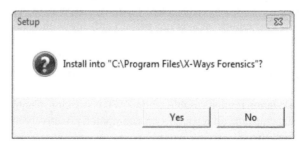

FIGURE 1.1

Installing XWF via setup.exe.

Alternative install methods

The second method for installing XWF is simply to extract each of the zip files to a directory and have that directory serve as the installation directory. We recommend using c:\xwf when installing via this method. By having XWF at the root of your C:\ drive, maintaining, upgrading, and accessing XWF is faster and simpler. In the context of this book, we refer to c:\xwf as the path for XWF. Once xw_forensics.zip is unzipped, you can run the *xwforensics.exe* executable without having to do anything else. Of course, you should also download and unzip the viewer component, MPlayer, and any add-ons. Installing via this method does not generate any shortcuts to the XWF executables, so this will have to be done manually.

Because XWF does not require a traditional installation via setup.exe, you can unzip *xw_forensics.zip* to almost any media, such as a USB device, and it will operate from that media. Similarly, XWF requires no uninstaller to remove it from your system; just delete the directory where it resides. This will come in handy later when used as portable forensic application. In addition, XWF can run from a compact disc or a flash drive.

After unzipping XWF, the next step is adding the viewer component add-on. Adding the viewer component entails unzipping the *xw_viewer.zip* file to the XWF folder. XWF expects the viewer files to be in the subdirectory of the program folder at c:\xwf\viewer (32 bit) or c:\xwf\x64\viewer (64 bit). The viewer component add-on allows viewing and printing of more than 270 different types of files directly within XWF. *xw_viewer.zip* already contains these expected directories, so simply extracting the contents of *xw_viewer.zip* to c:\xwf will put things where XWF expects them to be.

MPlayer (http://www.mplayerhq.hu/) is an optional, but recommended, add-on for XWF. MPlayer is a free and open source media player and supports a wide range of media formats. Similar to the viewer component, MPlayer must be extracted to a folder under c:\xwf. As we saw with the viewer component, the Mplayer archive has the necessary folders inside it to properly organize things, so extracting the contents of *MPlayer.zip* to c:\xwf is all that is required. After extracting MPlayer to c:\xwf, XWF is also able to extract JPEG pictures from videos files in addition to being able to play a wide variety of video formats. An alternative to MPlayer is the commercial product Forensic Framer (http://www.kuiper.de/) from Kuiper Forensics that is free to law enforcement.

Another available add-on is WinHex. Both XWF and WinHex share the same base code, and licensed XWF users can use WinHex with the same license. In recent versions of XWF, the WinHex add-on is included in the XWF zip file and does not need to be added or installed separately. To start WinHex, run the *winhex.exe* executable file in the program folder. The primary difference between XWF and WinHex is that WinHex allows you to alter data, whereas XWF cannot alter any data. It should be noted that newer versions of XWF already contain WinHex in the XWF zip file and as such, no add-on file is available.

XWF TIPS AND TRICKS

Getting WinHex in XWF versions 17.1 and later

Staring with version 17.1 of XWF, Winhex.exe is no longer distributed as a separate file. The reason for this is that there is a significant overlap in the code base between XWF and WinHex.

You can, however, access WinHex's write capabilities by making a copy of the *xwforensics. exe* file and renaming it *WinHex.exe*. If you need a 64-bit version, rename *xwforensics64.exe* to *WinHex64.exe*.

The user interfaces seen in Figure 1.2 shows whether you are running XWF or WinHex. The programs appear identical to each other, but there are subtle, yet significant differences. Most importantly, XWF interprets image files, disks, and physical RAM in a **read-only** mode, whereas WinHex is read-write. Always check the program you are using before touching your evidence. Those who wish to do so can simply delete WinHex.exe to remove any chance of inadvertently starting the wrong program.

FIGURE 1.2

Identification of XWF and WinHex.

The last and, in our opinion, best way to install XWF is by using a program we have written for this book: XWFIM or XWF Installation Manager (created by Eric Zimmerman). You can download XWFIM from the X-Ways forums. The only requirement for using XWFIM is the Microsoft .NET 4.0 runtime that should be installed on almost every Windows machine by default. If you need to install .NET, it can be downloaded from Microsoft's Web site.

When XWFIM is first run, it will inform you that it needs the credentials to the X-Ways Web site in order to download version information. These credentials can be found by querying your license status at http://www.x-ways.net/winhex/license. html. After entering the credentials, XWFIM will download a list of available XWF and viewer component versions. By default, XWFIM will install the latest available version of both XWF (to include previews and beta releases) and the viewer component. The XWFIM interface is shown in Figure 1.3.

Each option in the program is documented via tooltips that are visible when hovering over a particular option. After adjusting the options to suit your needs, simply click the **Install** button and XWFIM will download and extract all the necessary components for you.

In addition to downloading and setting up your XWF directory, XWFIM will also generate a file containing the SHA1 hash of every file that was installed. These data can be used later to verify the integrity of your installation.

We recommend using XWFIM to manage your XWF installation as it not only combines the best of both previously discussed installation methods but also takes

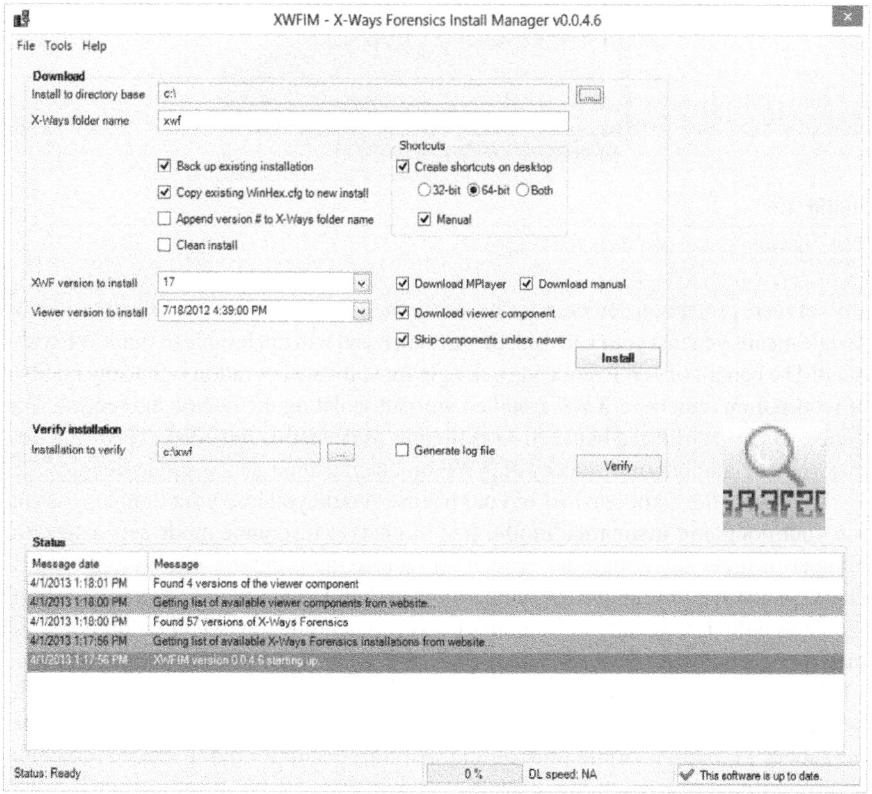

FIGURE 1.3

XWFIM dialog.

additional steps to ensure your XWF installations are properly backed up and upgraded as needed. With XWFIM, you can have a working installation of XWF in minutes!

THE XWF DONGLE

From version 13.2 onward, XWF uses a dongle as a software protection device. To start XWF, the dongle must be connected to the system as with any dongle-based software protection device. However, the XWF dongle is different when compared to the typical software protection device. The XWF dongle, seen in Figure 1.4, does not need any drivers installed, nor is a reboot necessary after attaching the dongle to your system. The XWF dongle acts like a human interface device (HID), similar to a mouse or a keyboard, and not as a storage device. This allows for use on machines that may have USB ports locked by system administrators.

More importantly, when XWF runs on a live evidence machine, there are only minimal changes to the evidence machine's registry as it relates to the dongle. As with

FIGURE 1.4

XWF software protection device (dongle).

any software protection device, your license to the software is the dongle, and losing the dongle means you lost your software license since you will not be able to run XWF without it. The benefit of XWF requiring a dongle for software operation is that any number of workstations can have XWF installed without violating the license agreement. The dongle can be transferred between workstations as needed to run XWF. However, you may run any number of instances of XWF on one machine with a single dongle.[1]

To prevent the complete loss of your license should you lose your dongle, you can run your dongle in **insurance mode**, free of charge. Insurance mode sets a specific number of times the dongle will run XWF before the program will no longer start. Once the number of remaining executions drops below 13, you can "top off" the dongle limit either manually or automatically (depending on whether or not your machine is connected to the Internet).

The worries of needing to purchase a new license to replace your lost dongle will be reduced because if an insured dongle is lost, X-Ways will replace it for a nominal fee (about $120.00 as of the time of this writing). Insurance mode can be turned on and off without restriction, but excessive conversions are not recommended. If you lose a dongle, report it to XWF, so the dongle ID can be recorded as lost. That way it will stop functioning once the number of executions reaches zero.

Insurance mode for dongles is managed through the X-Ways Web site or through the XWF program (**Help | Dongle**) if the workstation is connected to the Internet. Dongles that cannot be used in insurance mode are X-Ways Imager dongles and dongles programmed with an expiration date.

Insurance mode is designed for those who transport their dongles off-site. Others may not require that feature.

Starting with version 17, XWF supports using network based dongles. For details, see http://www.x-ways.net/forensics/dongle.html or contact X-Ways. Network dongles allow for a pool of XWF licenses to be made available to a network. As instances of XWF are started, the available license count is decremented. When XWF is shut down, the available license count is incremented. Such a setup removes the need for physical dongles being moved between machines in addition to providing centralized management of XWF licenses.

---

[1]Running XWF on a physical machine and a guest virtual machine *at the same time* requires two dongles.

Upgrading your dongle

XWF licenses are perpetual and do not expire. Rather, only the maintenance of a license expires. Therefore, a license that is not current still allows the operation of the software, but does not allow updating to newer versions after the expiration date. Since X-Ways constantly improves XWF, it makes sense to keep the license current via a maintenance subscription. After receiving an activation code for upgrading your dongle, you can run the latest version of XWF. You can update your dongle through the XWF menu option via **Help | Dongle** as seen in Figure 1.5. Entering the activation code will update the dongle with the new expiration date.

The dialog box for entering your activation code, shown in Figure 1.6, also contains a text box to store information in the dongle. This information can include ownership details or any other information that might be useful.

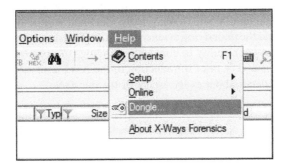

FIGURE 1.5

Menu option to upgrade the XWF dongle.

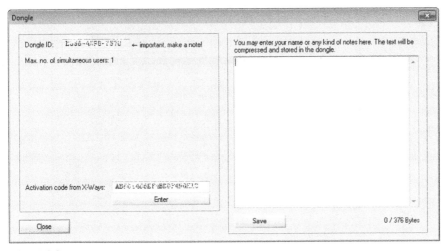

FIGURE 1.6

Dongle information dialog box.

THE XWF USER INTERFACE

Perhaps the first thing that makes potential users of XWF cringe is that XWF was born from a hex editor and therefore it must be difficult to use. This is far from the truth. In reality, it is quite the opposite of being difficult to use. To compare it to something you are already familiar with, XWF looks like an advanced version of Windows Explorer, but with more buttons and capabilities. As you can see in Figure 1.7, the user interface is not scary at all. A full size, color version of Figure 1.7 is available at http://www.x-ways.net/forensics/user_interface.jpg.

An unintended benefit to the use of XWF is that, as a user, you will be learning more about file systems, files, and forensic processes because of the ingenuity of design in the layout of the user interface. Using XWF to teach digital forensics in the classroom is also more effective since students are able to easily maneuver through data at any level of granularity required for the topic. The time spent analyzing electronic media with XWF greatly increases your understanding of the analysis process and the underlying science behind it. This directly affects the quality of your reports and your ability to convey the findings of your examinations.

What follows is a very brief introduction to the XWF user interface. Chapter 3 will go into great detail about every aspect of the interface.

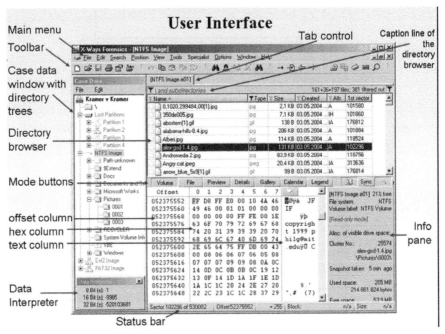

FIGURE 1.7

The XWF user interface.

The most commonly used areas of XWF are the **Directory Browser**, **Case Data** window (specifically, the **directory tree**), and offset/hex/text columns via the **Mode** buttons. These three panes of XWF function much like Windows Explorer, in that the offset/hex/text column pane (viewer) reflects the file selected in the **Directory Browser**, which reflects the contents of the selected folder from the **Case Data** window. In simple terms, choose a directory, highlight a file (or directory), and view the selected object as it sits on the volume or as it appears by itself.

Nearly all of the surrounding buttons, commands, and menus allow you to data carve, search, export, and analyze data. As one example, the **Mode** buttons change the current view of a file from the hex/text view as shown in Figure 1.7 to a preview of the file, a timeline calendar of files, or a gallery of images, based completely on the needs of the examiner. The functions and features will be detailed as we delve into future chapters.

So rather than detail every mode, feature, option, and function at this point, the most important sections of the interface are shown in Figure 1.7. Throughout this book, you will see how each function can be used for specific tasks. While we present several case studies at the end of the book, we do not explain how to do forensics but rather how XWF functionality can be brought to bear in those general kinds of cases.

Since any one piece of information in this book may not be of enough detail for your needs, you can obtain additional documentation of XWF from the software manual (Fleischmann, 2012) available freely from http://www.x-ways.net. While *The Practitioner's Guide to X-Ways Forensics* was developed to supplement the manual, there is a major difference in method of presentation. The official software manual details each feature with great granularity and leaves the user to decide how to process evidence. Our book gives suggested steps, recommended options, and proven workflow processes to get started immediately with a forensic analysis using XWF. The combination of the two will set you on the right track to using XWF to its fullest potential.

CONFIGURING XWF

One thing that will become apparent as you use XWF more and more is that the XWF team selected the default values through careful deliberation and user suggestions. While it is our aim to discuss every option in XWF in as much detail as possible, for most users, **simply keeping the default options will suffice in the vast majority of cases.**

With that said, there are a few options we recommend changing depending on certain circumstances or particular cases. We will point out these options as they are explained in each of the chapters. Until then, accept the defaults as we progress. The individual needs of a case and your personal preferences will ultimately determine the options needed.

At this point, your XWF program folder should look like Figure 1.8 if you chose the suggested add-ons and viewer component. Of course, you can name the program folder as you wish, but in this instance, we named it "xwf."

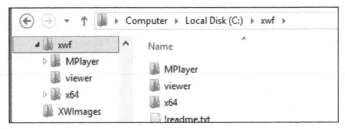

FIGURE 1.8

Completed program folder structure for XWF.

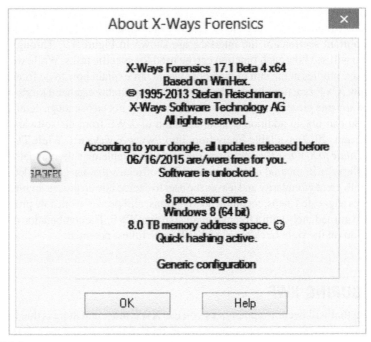

FIGURE 1.9

About screen.

Before wrapping up this chapter, there are a few more housekeeping steps that must be completed. We have already covered the basic XWF directory structure that we recommend above.

When XWF is first started, the About screen will be shown as seen in Figure 1.9.

After clicking OK, XWF will display the General Options window that allows you to change some basic settings. The General Options dialog can be displayed via the Options menu (**Options | General Options**) and is shown in Figure 1.10.

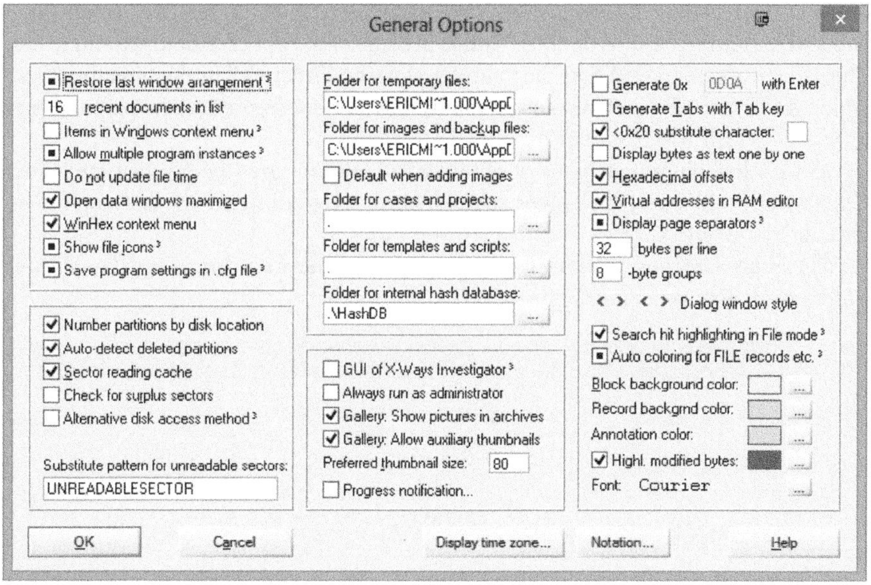

FIGURE 1.10

General Options dialog.

Notice some of the options have a superscript 3 after the description. This indicates that the option can be one of three values as opposed to the typical on or off usually associated with a check box. In most cases, when changing a tri-state option, the text description of the option will also change to indicate the new behavior. Most of these options will be further explained in Chapter 3.

While XWF will work as is, there are a few changes we recommend. In the middle column, there are options for directories for temporary files, images, and cases/projects.

In general, we recommend creating a directory on the fastest disk system you have for the **Folder for images and backup files** option. An SSD drive or fast RAID setup allows XWF to read forensic images as quickly as possible and therefore process information more quickly.[2] We recommend a directory named *XWImages* to keep things consistent. For similar reasons, the path for temporary files should be on a speedy disk as well. Again, for consistency, choose a directory name like *XWTemp*. Finally, we recommend creating a directory outside c:\xwf for storing cases and projects, such as *c:\XWCases*.

The last thing to change is the default time zone by clicking on the **Display time zone** button. Choose the desired zone and whether XWF should compensate for

---

[2]Remember that, with respect to RAID volumes, a trade-off exists with respect to speed and data safety. Consider your backup procedures and choose a setup that affords a good compromise. RAID is not a backup!

daylight savings time automatically. XWF can understand both relative and absolute paths when setting various options. Notice in some of the options there is a single dot. This is interpreted by XWF as the "current working directory" or the directory from which XWF started. XWF also understands that two dots represent the parent directory from which XWF started from.

As mentioned previously, most of the default options are fine for the time being. Clicking OK will save the changes and will allow us to configure the last step before we can start using XWF.

Click the **Options | Viewer programs** menu item to bring up the Viewer Programs dialog as seen in Figure 1.11.

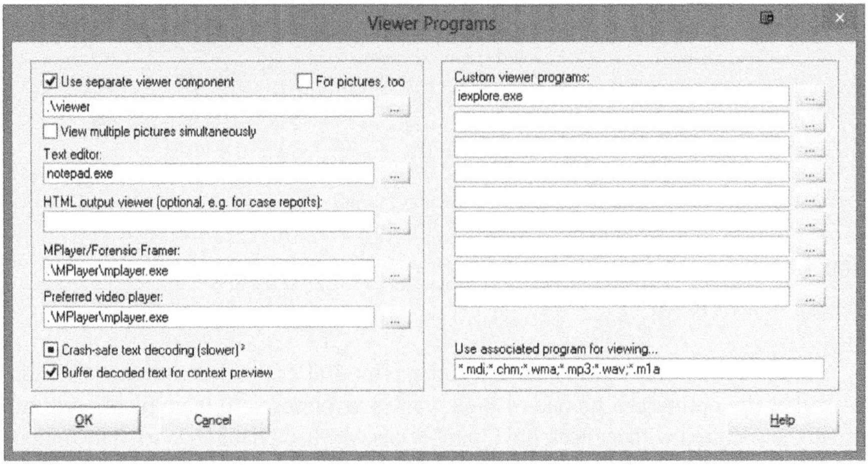

FIGURE 1.11

Viewer programs dialog.

Here, you can change such things as whether to use the viewer add-on, the default text editor, HTML viewer, etc. On the right side, you can set up various external viewer programs that can be invoked through a context menu in XWF.

XWF TIPS AND TRICKS

32 bit vs. 64 bit

If you are using the 32-bit version of XWF, the path in Figure 1.11 is correct. However, if you are using the 64-bit version, the path to the viewer component must be ".\x64\viewer" or XWF will be unable to load the viewer component. XWF should detect which edition of XWF is running and auto detects the correct path to the viewer component the first time XWF is started.

By default XWF will use MPlayer (if installed as recommended) for viewing videos. XWF will auto detect MPlayer if it is in a folder named *mplayer* in your XWF directory. In addition to MPlayer, we recommend using a media player like

VLC Media Player (http://www.videolan.org/vlc/index.html) for video playback as it supports a wide variety of video formats.

When you click OK, XWF is ready for use, but just to be safe, restart XWF to ensure the new settings take effect.

XWF TIPS AND TRICKS

Creating a portable installation

When creating a portable installation of XWF, you can use the "." and ".." options to configure XWF to work regardless of the drive letter assigned to the XWF medium. As an example, create the following folders on a thumb drive, as seen in Figure 1.12.

FIGURE 1.12

Folders for XWF files on a portable device.

You can copy your xwf folder from your c:\ drive to save time. After doing so, start XWF and open the General Options dialog as explained above. In the options for temp files, images, and cases, you can use paths as seen in Figure 1.13. This will allow XWF to find those folders regardless of whether your thumb drive is assigned drive F, G, R, etc.

You also will want to use similar options when setting up the Viewer programs on your portable installation, specifically for MPlayer (.\MPlayer\mplayer.exe for example). Notice that

Folder for temporary files:
.\XWtemp

Folder for images and backup files:
.\XWImages
✔ Default when adding images

Folder for cases and projects:
..\XWCases

Folder for templates and scripts:
.

Folder for internal hash database:
.\HashDB

FIGURE 1.13

Path entry in General Options dialog.

the viewer component uses the single dot notation by default. If you leave an absolute path anywhere, XWF will not be able to use the programs if the drive letter changes.

Finally, any external viewers can also be set up this way if they exist in folders on your thumb drive. Just use the correct invocation of ".." to allow XWF to find your external programs. For example, putting something like notepad on your thumb drive and setting the **Text Editor** option to this program can make your life a lot easier (if notepad.exe is in the root of the thumb drive, the **Text Editor** path would be *..\notepad.exe*).

Finally, when setting up a portable installation, be aware that using the viewer component creates files on the system being examined. This does not necessarily compromise a live examination, but you should look for and document these changes in your report. By default, XWF creates such files in the Windows profile of the currently logged on user.

SUMMARY

The installation and configuration of XWF are different from other forensic applications since it is a portable application that doesn't need an actual installation. The XWF dongle also has differences in that it does not require drivers and makes minimal changes to the system. These minor differences extend XWF into a more flexible and useful tool than you may have realized at first.

XWF is far more than a "forensically sound hex editor." XWF may be less of a push-button forensics application than other tools, but that doesn't mean XWF is harder to use. There are simply more functions and features available than some examiners may be accustomed to seeing together along with an amount of granularity for file analysis that is invoked by the XWF user as required. It is because XWF affords more control to an examiner that he or she can determine the best approach to an exam and save a great deal of time by making decisions instead of simply letting a tool decide everything.

Reference

Fleischmann, S., 2012. X-Ways Forensics/WinHex Manual. Retrieved January 21, 2013, from X-Ways Forensics Computer Forensics Integrated Software: http://www.x-ways.net/winhex/manual.pdf.

The XWF Internal Hash Database and the Registry Viewer

5

INFORMATION IN THIS CHAPTER

- Introduction
- XWF internal hash database and hash set
- The registry through X-Ways Forensics
- The XWF Registry Viewer
- The XWF Registry Report
- Shortcuts
- Summary

INTRODUCTION

Perhaps the quickest method to find files relevant to your case is through a hash comparison of files against one or more preconfigured hash sets. XWF makes it easy to import existing hash sets or create entirely new hash sets that you can use to conduct hash comparisons against files in your case. This process can significantly reduce the amount of data that you must review because you can eliminate irrelevant files through both filtering and hiding of duplicate files. This allows you to focus on the important data in a case.

A common use of a hash comparison involves importing a hash set consisting of known child pornography hash values to compare against hash values of files that exist in an image of a suspect's hard drive. Any hash values from the evidence image files that match any of the child pornography hash values are quickly located and documented. Another benefit when working with such a hash set is obviating the need to look at every image and video in a case. You can run similar hash comparisons with any set of known hash values run against evidence objects.

Another easy to use, yet comprehensive, tool is the XWF Registry Viewer. The Windows registry contains a treasure of forensically relevant information, yet it can be difficult to analyze because of the sheer volume of information present in registry hives. The XWF Registry Viewer gives you the ability to navigate and collect relevant information quickly and easily. The second part of this chapter focuses on efficiently using the XWF Registry Viewer and its ability to generate comprehensive reports of registry contents.

XWF INTERNAL HASH DATABASE AND HASH SETS

Before working with the internal hash database, you must select a location to store the hash database. The **General Options | Folder for internal hash database** property, shown in Figure 5.1, determines where XWF will create its hash database.

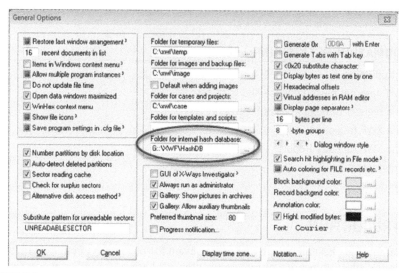

FIGURE 5.1

Choose a location for your XWF database in the General Options dialog.

XWF TIPS AND TRICKS

Speed tip!

To squeeze more speed out of XWF, store your internal hash database on a drive separate from the drive from which you execute XWF. This also makes it easier to manage your hash databases over time as you add hash sets and, depending on where you store them, share them with others in your office.

The XWF internal hash database consists of 257 binary files that XWF uses to store hash sets. XWF does not ship with any hash sets, and it is up to the user to import or create hash sets. A common misconception is that XWF maintains more than one hash database. Rather, the internal hash database contains multiple hash sets. Every hash set must consist of at least one hash value.

Hash categories

The XWF hash database consists of two categories of hash values: *notable* and *irrelevant*. Synonyms for *notable* hashes are known bad, malicious, and relevant. Synonyms for *irrelevant* hashes include known good, harmless, and ignorable.

Figure 5.2 is a visual representation of the XWF internal hash database as it relates to its hash sets and categories.

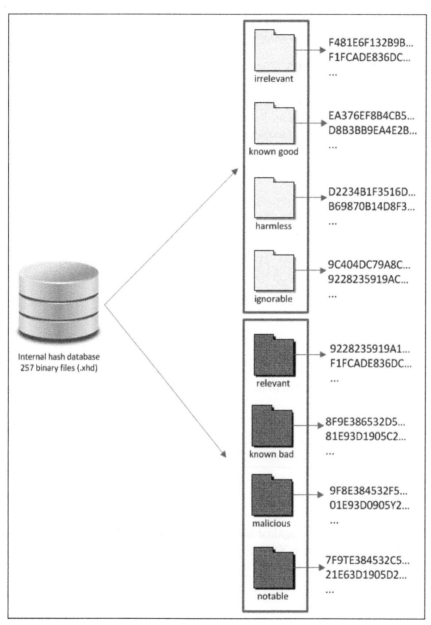

FIGURE 5.2

The XWF internal hash database contains two hash categories that contain individual hash sets.

Every hash set must be defined as one of these two categories in order for XWF to use it for hash comparisons. As mentioned above, every hash set must contain one or more hash values, but this does not mean that a hash is confined to only one hash set. Of course, you should not add the same hash to both a notable and irrelevant hash set if you plan to use them at the same time as doing so makes no sense (how can a file be notable *and* irrelevant at the same time?). Should this happen, XWF will detect it and inform you.

Computing hash values

Hash values are computed and optionally compared against hash sets by performing a **Refine Volume Snapshot** (RVS) operation. The **Compute hash option** does not require any preexisting hash sets, as this option does not control whether XWF compares a file's hash against a hash set.

XWF supports the following hash algorithms:

Checksum (8, 16, 32, or 64 bit)
CRC16 (16 bit)
CRC32 (32 bit)
MD5 (128 bit)
SHA-1 (160 bit)
SHA-256 (256 bit)
RipeMD-128 (128 bit)
RipeMD-160 (160 bit)
MD4 (128 bit)
Ed2k (128 bit)
Adler32

Which hash algorithm you use is determined both by the needs of your case and by the algorithm used to generate a list of hashes that can be imported into XWF. Figure 5.3 shows the two options related to hash calculation and hash comparison, respectively.

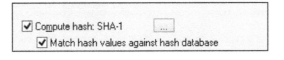

FIGURE 5.3

RVS compute hash options.

If **Match hash values against hash database** is checked, there must be at least one hash set against which XWF can compare hash values. If this is not the case, XWF will inform you of this via the error message as shown in Figure 5.4.

FIGURE 5.4

Without a hash database to compare, the RVS will not continue.

In many cases, using hash comparisons will save time by eliminating irrelevant files from view and finding relevant files through matching hash values, so we recommend spending the time to build up a robust collection of both notable and irrelevant hash sets.

Creating hash sets

In addition to importing hash sets from external sources, XWF allows for creating hash sets based on files selected in the **Directory Browser**. After using the filtering capabilities of the **Directory Browser** to locate the files you wish to include in a hash set, select the **Create Hash Set** option from the **Directory Browser**'s context menu as shown in Figure 5.5.

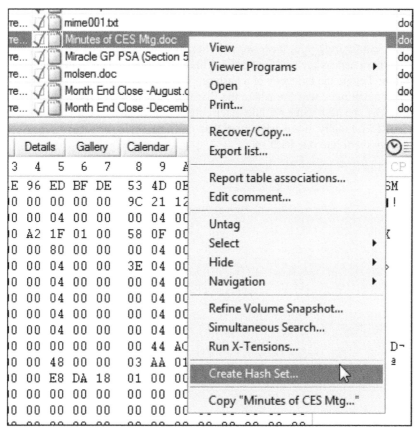

FIGURE 5.5

Creating a hash set by selecting files of interest and right-clicking to bring up the **Create Hash Set** option.

XWF prompts you for the hash algorithm to use and then generates the hashes for the selected files. After **Create Hash Set** is selected, the **Add Hash Set to Database** dialog, shown in Figure 5.6, is shown. The options in this dialog are self-explanatory. Note XWF's use of the primary hash category as well as the synonyms for that type in the dialog.

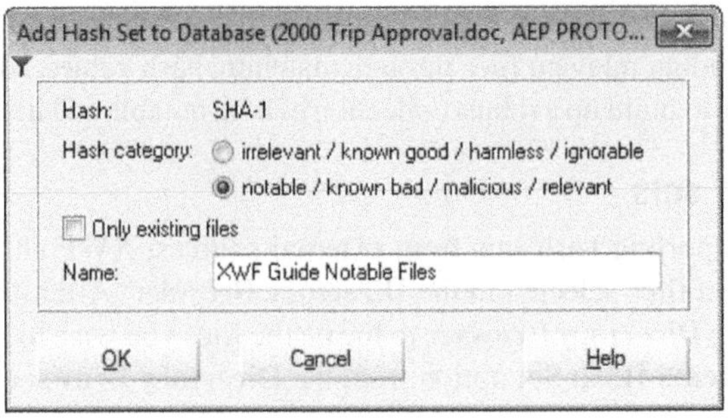

FIGURE 5.6

Categorizing and naming a new hash set.

After configuring your hash set and clicking **OK**, XWF shows a listing of all existing hash sets as seen in Figure 5.7. This dialog allows you to delete, rename, export, or **Toggle** the **category** of a hash set. When exporting a hash set, XWF will generate a delimited text file where the first line indicates the hash algorithm used followed by one hash value per line. Each entry is separated by a carriage return/line feed (CRLF). Finally, if you have more than one hash set of the same category, you can merge them into one hash set.

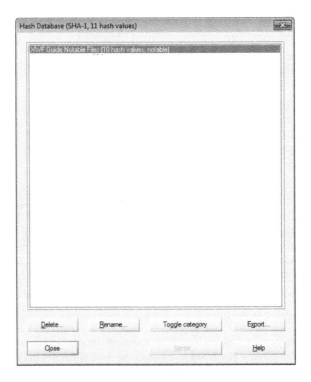

FIGURE 5.7

One user-created hash set in the internal hash database.

XWF TIPS AND TRICKS

How many hash sets did you say?
You do not have to worry about exceeding the number of hash sets that can be imported into XWF because the internal hash database can contain up to 65,535 hash sets.

Since we now have at least one hash set available, the **RVS** process can compare hashes against this new data set. Any files that are found to match the hash values are prominently displayed in XWF as seen in Figure 5.8. The **Hash set** column gives the name of the hash set name (in this example, *XWF Guide Notable Files*) and the **Hash category** column gives the category (in this example, *notable*).

Name ▲	Hash set	Hash category	Hash ▼
001.pst\farmer-d\Darre... ☐ ☐ Committee List 1108 .doc	XWF Guide Notable Files	notable	6A42A98B60136A165
001.pst\farmer-d\Darre... ☐ ☐ Compassion.doc			D7BB9DB138010D16
001.pst\farmer-d\Darre... ☐ ☐ Controls Review.doc	XWF Guide Notable Files	notable	05814D2D71AF661A!
001.pst\farmer-d\Darre... ☐ ☐ CoServ RFP Gas Supply eversio...			AB13B8C7A3DAB5A!
001.pst\farmer-d\Darre... ☐ ☐ Curtailment Memo.doc			CE8D625C578E1F18-
001.pst\farmer-d\Darre... ☐ ☐ Davis_Gloria_06142000_original...			C290C55A0000AEB6
001.pst\farmer-d\Darre... ☐ ☐ DEFS.pdf			8DDF3098A6D12C6B
001.pst\farmer-d\Darre... ☐ ☐ Different beliefs.doc			52CD402DC6E9921B
001.pst\farmer-d\Darre... ✓ ☐ Duke Resume.doc			3289B2FC3C0F7790A
001.pst\farmer-d\Darre... ✓ ☐ econnect.doc (6)			3C1A50D4909B03D8
001.pst\farmer-d\Darre... ✓ ☐ econnect.doc (6)			3C1A50D4909B03D8
001.pst\farmer-d\Darre... ✓ ☐ EEX Update (4.26.01).doc			F904A90583FDDAC6
001.pst\farmer-d\Darre... ✓ ☐ electricgasrfp6101.doc (2)			A5CEEAD9E2D67882
001.pst\farmer-d\Darre... ✓ ☐ Employee Referral Policy _ Form...	XWF Guide Notable Files	notable	F34682679FC9AC00F
001.pst\farmer-d\Darre... ✓ ☐ Employee Referral Policy _ Form...	XWF Guide Notable Files	notable	F34682679FC9AC00F
001.pst\farmer-d\Darre... ✓ ☐ enakerville.doc (1)			64A91C27CA9BD6B7

FIGURE 5.8

Results of a hash comparison.

In addition to creating hash sets from the **Directory Browser,** you can create hash sets outside of XWF and then import them into the hash database in various formats.

The simplest implementation of an external hash set is a plain text file where the first line in the file identifies the hash algorithm used (SHA-1 for example). Every subsequent line contains one hash value. Figure 5.9 shows an example of a hash set that was created using Notepad.

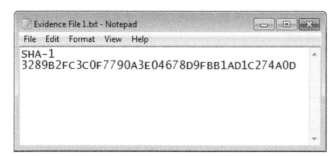

FIGURE 5.9

Example of a simple hash set with one hash value.

After creating and saving your hash set, select **Tools | Hash Database | Import Hash Set** as seen in Figure 5.10. After selecting the file containing your hashes, XWF will ask for the category. By default, XWF will name the new hash set after the file name (minus extension) from which it imported the hashes. You can always rename the hash set via **Tools | Hash Database | Manage** if need be. In addition to importing files one at a time, you can also choose import a folder (including sub-folders) containing multiple hash sets by using **Tools | Hash Database | Import Folder**. Once a folder is chosen, the hash sets can be imported as separate hash sets or as a single hash set. This is helpful if you have several hash sets that are of the same category as it saves time.

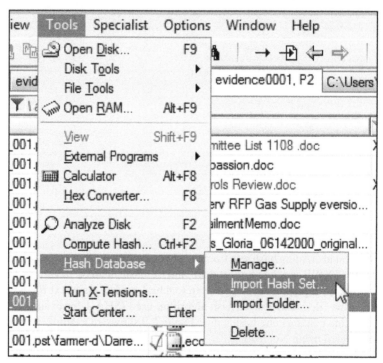

FIGURE 5.10

Importing a hash set.

Once imported, XWF will bring up the **Hash Database** dialog to show the newly imported hash set. Figure 5.11 shows a second hash set consisting of one hash, named *IP* and categorized as *notable*.

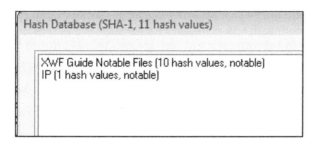

FIGURE 5.11

A second hash set created and imported into the XWF internal hash database.

The results of performing a new RVS operation using these two hash sets are shown in Figure 5.12. Since both hash sets are categorized as notable, the **Hash category** column is the same for *DukeResume.doc* and the duplicate files starting with *Employee Referral Policy*. However, the source of the hash sets is different (*IP* vs. *XWF Guide Notable Files*), giving a clear indication of the hash set that yielded the match.

Name ▲	Hash set	Hash category	Hash
CoastalAlbrecht.doc			FBA85EA8BF2
CoastalAlbrecht.doc			FBA85EA8BF2
DukeResume.doc	IP	notable	3289B2FC3C0
econnect.doc (5)			3C1A50D4909
econnect.doc (5)			3C1A50D4909
EEX Update (4.26.01).doc			F904A90583FI
electricgasrfp6101.doc (2)			A5CEEAD9E2I
Employee Referral Policy _ Form....	XWF Guide Notable Files	notable	F34682679FC5
Employee Referral Policy _ Form....	XWF Guide Notable Files	notable	F34682679FC5

FIGURE 5.12

Example using a comparison against two hash sets.

Finally, there are several sources of hash sets both freely and commercially available on the Internet. The National Software Reference Library (NSRL—http://www.nsrl.nist.gov/) is one source that provides downloads of hash sets containing millions of hashes computed from program installations and operating system files. Since the NSRL hash sets contain irrelevant hashes as well as relevant hashes, XWF checks the NSRL hash set for certain flags (*s* for special and *m* for malicious), so these hash sets are not wholly categorized as notable or irrelevant. Comparing known and irrelevant files to remove from unknown files is also known as "*de-NISTing.*"

Duplicate hash values

Since the same hash value can exist across multiple hash sets, XWF reports duplicates in a clear manner. If a file matches a hash value in multiple hash sets, XWF reports the name of each hash set that matched. Using the same example as above and adding a third hash set named *IPset2* containing the same hash value as hash set *IP*, XWF lists both hash sets as matches for the same file as seen in Figure 5.13.

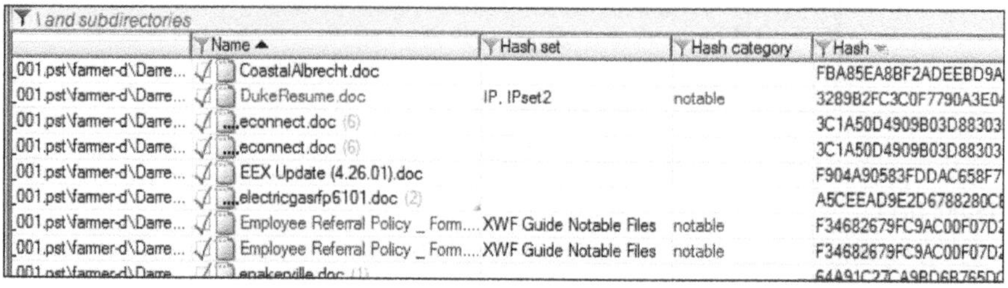

FIGURE 5.13

One file (DukeResume.doc) matching two different hash sets (IP and IPset2).

This should not be confused with duplicate hash values in a single hash set as that scenario is not possible because XWF checks hash sets for the existence of duplicate hash values before adding it. In other words, XWF deduplicates hashes as they are added to hash sets.

THE REGISTRY THROUGH X-WAYS FORENSICS

The following section details using XWF to examine the Windows registry. The registry is a hierarchical database that stores configuration settings and options for the Windows operating system in files called *hives*.

Entire books dedicated to the inner workings of the registry are available and such information will not be repeated here. As registry analysis as a whole requires more information than can be described in this chapter, we recommend examiners delve deeper into registry forensics through resources such as Harlan Carvey's *Windows Registry Forensics: Advanced Digital Forensic Analysis of the Windows Registry*. Resources such as this allow you to understand alternative methods of analysis of the registry as well as the scope of information stored in the registry.

In Chapter 3, we covered the **Directory Browser** and its columns including the ability to filter data contained in one or more columns. Before discussing how to use XWF to analyze registry hives, it would be helpful to hide everything from view that isn't a registry hive. Of course you always can navigate directly to where the hives are found on disk if you choose, but filtering allows for quickly seeing all available registry hives across entire evidence objects at the same time.

To begin registry analysis with XWF, click the filter icon for the **Type** column in the **Directory Browser**. Figure 5.14 shows the **Type** filter dialog that allows you to hide all files that are not of type *Windows Registry*. The quickest way to access this filter is via the funnel icon found in the **Type** column. Once the filter dialog is open, you can select one or more registry file types. If you want to find registry files of all types, filtering via the **Category** column is quicker than selecting all of the relevant file types in the **Type** filter dialog.

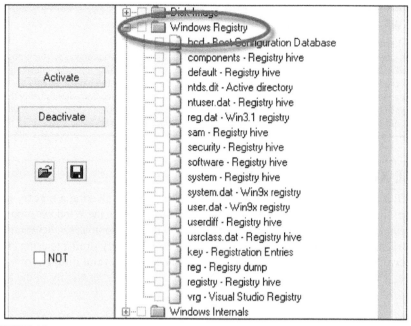

FIGURE 5.14

Filter by file type (registry).

Figure 5.15 shows several registry hives found in a forensic image after using the **Type** filter column as outlined above.

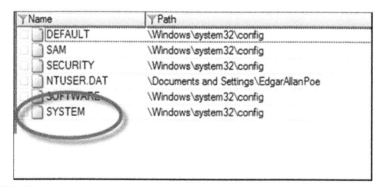

FIGURE 5.15

Filtered by registry file type.

XWF TIPS AND TRICKS

Filtering is your friend

By now, you have seen the usefulness of filtering data to expedite your analysis. The granularity of your filtering depends upon the type of case you are working and your knowledge of the files you need to analyze. As we have seen above, if you know the type of registry hives needed for specific information you can quickly eliminate all other files from view by using the **Type** column filter. If you were only interested in SYSTEM hives, you can then use the **Name** column filter to further refine the files shown in the **Directory Browser**.

THE XWF REGISTRY VIEWER

XWF includes a built-in viewer for registry hives. Double-clicking a registry hive opens that hive in the **Registry Viewer** (RV). If you have used the Windows program *regedit.exe*, the RV will look familiar. Figure 5.16 shows a comparison between RV and *regedit.exe*. Navigating a registry hive using the RV is very similar to using *regedit.exe*. Note, however, that while *regedit.exe* shows you several different hives at once, RV displays only the contents of hives that are opened explicitly in the RV.

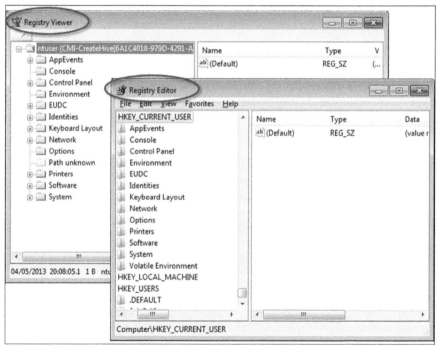

FIGURE 5.16

The XWF Registry Viewer shown behind the Windows Registry Editor.

Up to 64 different hives can be opened in the RV at the same time. Double-clicking another registry hive adds that hive to any currently open RV. In addition to browsing active records in hives, the RV also includes deleted keys in hives that contain unused space and lost keys/values in damaged/incomplete hives. Keys found under "Path unknown" are virtual keys where there is not a known, complete path for the keys.

A context menu is available in the RV that allows for finding text in different areas of the registry such as keys, value names, and data, as shown in Figure 5.17. After each search hit, the context menu provides a **Continue Search** option to move to the next instance of the text hit. A shortcut for **Continue Search** is SHIFT+F3.

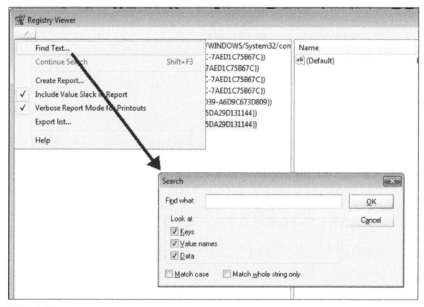

FIGURE 5.17

Searching the registry with the integrated viewer.

Viewing USB devices

For an example of using the XWF Registry Viewer, let's look at USB device connections that are contained in the SYSTEM hive. Figure 5.18 shows the items in the SYSTEM\ControlSet002\Enum\USBSTOR key that is used to store information about connected and previously connected USB devices. As keys are selected, the right side of the RV will display the contents of the key. A unique feature of the RV is its ability to decode certain values into easier to understand formats. As values are selected in the upper right side of the RV, any available decoded data in those values will be shown at the bottom of the RV. The value size and size of the slack can also be seen here. Refer to the XWF manual for a complete list of the types of data the RV can decode.

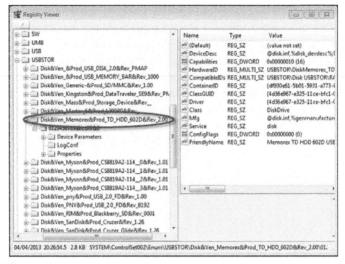

FIGURE 5.18

Device Class ID of a USB device viewed through the registry viewer.

The context menu also contains the command **Copy** when opened from the right-hand window after selecting the key to be copied. This command copies the selected element's value to the clipboard.

As you select values in the RV, XWF will highlight the corresponding block of data in the hive in the **File** mode window as shown in Figure 5.19. When you open a registry hive, XWF will switch to **File** mode if it is not already selected.

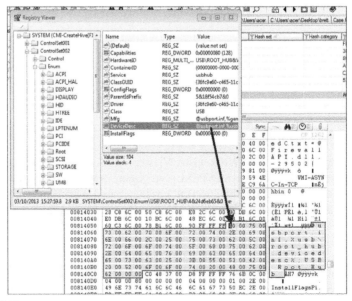

FIGURE 5.19

Double-clicking the value will cause the cursor to jump to the block, highlighting the value's contents.

This is a quick way to locate the selected value in the hive itself in cases where you need to include the raw contents of the hive. By using this technique, you can see the value in both hexadecimal and text. Right-clicking the block of data allows for such things as copying the block of data as binary, text, or Hex ASCII values. The options for working with blocks of data are covered in more detail in Chapter 7.

In many instances, it is important to know the last modified date of a registry key. To do this in the RV, select a key from the hive tree on the left and the last modified date will show at the bottom of the hive window. Selecting the name, type, or value in the right pane will show the last modification date plus more information about that key in the bottom right pane of the RV as shown in Figure 5.20.

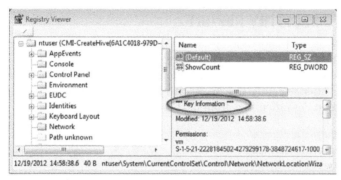

FIGURE 5.20

Key last modified example.

Exporting

In addition to interactively navigating registry hives, the RV allows for exporting the entire contents of the hive to a tab separated file. This can be done via the **Export list** option on the context menu. Once a hive is exported, it can be viewed in Excel or further processed by external analysis tools. Figure 5.21 shows an exported hive open in Microsoft Excel. Since the file is tab delimited, Excel displays the contents in an easy to read format.

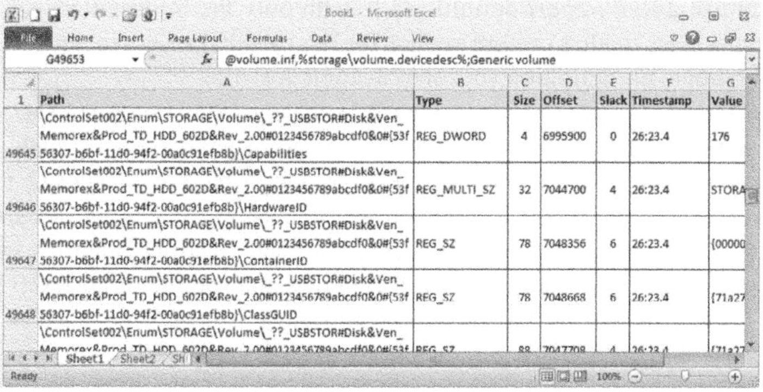

FIGURE 5.21

Exported list of a hive showing a selection of USB devices.

XWF TIPS AND TRICKS

Don't forget about the external analysis feature!

As discussed in Chapter 7, files in an evidence object can be copied outside the case and "handed off" to external programs (such as Excel). This technique can also be applied to registry hives, in that a program such as RegRipper (http://code.google.com/p/regripper/) can validate information obtained through XWF. In fact, the algorithm the XWF Registry Report uses in the table *Attached devices by serial number* is created according to the algorithm used in RegRipper. Thanks Harlan!

THE XWF REGISTRY REPORT

The XWF Registry Report is a HTML file listing of relevant registry keys and is created with the **Create Registry Report** context menu option. The data included in the report depend upon which report definition file or files are chosen when creating the report. After selecting **Create Registry Report**, XWF prompts to select one or more report definition files from the list below:

Reg Report Autorun.txt
Reg Report Devices.txt
Reg Report Free Space.txt
Reg Report Histories.txt
Reg Report Identity.txt
Reg Report Networks.txt
Reg Report Printer.txt
Reg Report Software.txt
Reg Report System.txt

Reg Report files are plain text files that contain information XWF uses to decode the data in hives into an easier to understand format. The registry keys in these text files can be modified to fit your needs through any text editor.

The XWF manual details the formatting rules for these files should you wish to customize the registry report definition files to fit your needs. As an example, you can customize a *Reg Report* definition file with only the information you wish to target from a hive, create a custom version for keys XWF does not include by default, or even combine all definition files into a single text file.

Once a report is created, it is viewable in any Web browser. The standard tables consist of four columns: description, extracted value, registry path, and last modification date. If more than one *Reg Report *.txt* file is chosen to create the registry report, the report lists hyperlinks to each registry report section in the beginning of the report (autorun, devices, free space, histories, identity, networks, printer, software, system, etc.). Figure 5.22 shows an example of an XWF Registry Report.

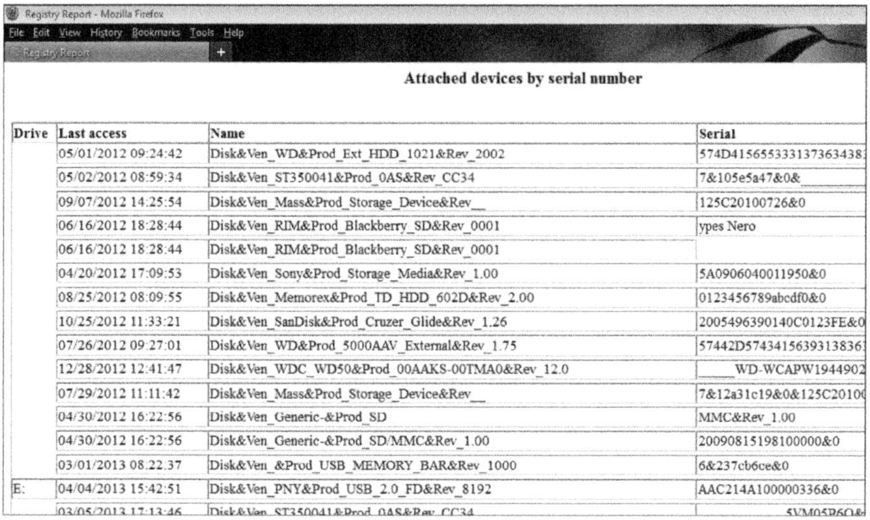

Attached devices by serial number

Drive	Last access	Name	Serial
	05/01/2012 09:24:42	Disk&Ven_WD&Prod_Ext_HDD_1021&Rev_2002	574D415655333137363438
	05/02/2012 08:59:34	Disk&Ven_ST350041&Prod_0AS&Rev_CC34	7&105e5a47&0&___
	09/07/2012 14:25:54	Disk&Ven_Mass&Prod_Storage_Device&Rev__	125C20100726&0
	06/16/2012 18:28:44	Disk&Ven_RIM&Prod_Blackberry_SD&Rev_0001	ypes Nero
	06/16/2012 18:28:44	Disk&Ven_RIM&Prod_Blackberry_SD&Rev_0001	
	04/20/2012 17:09:53	Disk&Ven_Sony&Prod_Storage_Media&Rev_1.00	5A0906040011950&0
	08/25/2012 08:09:55	Disk&Ven_Memorex&Prod_TD_HDD_602D&Rev_2.00	0123456789abcdf0&0
	10/25/2012 11:33:21	Disk&Ven_SanDisk&Prod_Cruzer_Glide&Rev_1.26	2005496390140C0123FE&0
	07/26/2012 09:27:01	Disk&Ven_WD&Prod_5000AAV_External&Rev_1.75	57442D5743415639313836
	12/28/2012 12:41:47	Disk&Ven_WDC_WD50&Prod_00AAKS-00TMA0&Rev_12.0	____WD-WCAPW1944902
	07/29/2012 11:11:42	Disk&Ven_Mass&Prod_Storage_Device&Rev__	7&12a31c19&0&125C20100
	04/30/2012 16:22:56	Disk&Ven_Generic-&Prod_SD	MMC&Rev_1.00
	04/30/2012 16:22:56	Disk&Ven_Generic-&Prod_SD/MMC&Rev_1.00	20090815198100000&0
	03/01/2013 08:22:37	Disk&Ven_&Prod_USB_MEMORY_BAR&Rev_1000	6&237cb6ce&0
E:	04/04/2013 15:42:51	Disk&Ven_PNY&Prod_USB_2.0_FD&Rev_8192	AAC214A100000336&0
	03/05/2013 17:13:46	Disk&Ven_ST350041&Prod_0AS&Rev_CC34	5VM05P6Q&

FIGURE 5.22

HTML output of the Registry Report.

As you navigate the report, you will notice certain data is color coded. Dates that are **gray** indicate the dates the *key* was modified, not the modification date of the value itself. Registry values in **red** text indicate that the registry values are deleted and are output with the *Reg Report Free Space.txt* definition file. If registry value slack contains text strings, the output will be **green**.

Once you generate one or more registry reports, they can be included easily in your final report using several techniques. Chapter 8 covers reporting in XWF in detail.

SHORTCUTS

SHIFT+F3: Continues a search in the XWF Registry Viewer.

SUMMARY

The XWF internal hash database is a powerful yet extremely easy-to-use feature. While XWF has only *one* hash database, the database can contain up to 65,535 separate hash sets. There are many sources of hash sets available online, both commercial and free, as well as hash sets forensic examiners create and share with each other.

The XWF **Registry Viewer** and **Registry Report** are two important features of XWF used for registry analysis. The searching, copying, and reporting functions allow finding and displaying relevant information in the XWF case report from registry hives.

Searching in X-Ways Forensics

INFORMATION IN THIS CHAPTER

- Introduction
- Simultaneous search
- Regular expressions
- GREP and regular expressions in XWF
- Indexed search
- Reviewing search hits
- Text search
- Hexadecimal search
- Shortcuts
- Summary

INTRODUCTION

Now that you have seen the power and capabilities of the **Refine Volume Snapshot** process, it is time to start drilling down into data beyond using **Directory Browser** filters.

XWF contains several very flexible and capable search features that, when used individually or in combination with each other, let you quickly and easily find the information you are looking for. XWF fully supports searching for simple strings, regular expressions, or any combination of the two, all at the same time.

Searching in XWF goes beyond simple linear physical searches in that it provides many options not found anywhere else, such as searching not only slack space, but in free space immediately following file slack. In addition, XWF can decode complex files to search their contents as opposed to simply searching the contents of files as they are stored on disk.

Once XWF locates the terms you have searched for, it allows you to review many different combinations of search hits to separate the relevant search hits from the irrelevant ones.

SIMULTANEOUS SEARCH

The most commonly used search feature in XWF is **Simultaneous Search** (SS). SS can be performed on entire evidence objects, individual files, or anything in between. SS includes a wide range of options including traditional keyword searches,

GREP-based searches, the ability to only match whole words (with a user-defined definition of what characters define a word), and the ability to search for text in encoded file formats such as PDF files and Word documents.

XWF is unique in that it allows any user-specified subset of files to be searched as dictated by the requirements of a case. Contrast this to many other tools that have a more "all or none" type approach. For example, if you have a need to search in Word documents, use the **Type** column filter in the **Directory Browser** to only include Word documents and then perform the SS on that set of files.

To perform an SS, use the **Search | Simultaneous Search** option or use the shortcut **Alt+F10**. The SS dialog is shown in Figure 6.1. You can also perform an SS on selected files by selecting one or more files in the **Directory Browser** and choosing **Simultaneous Search** from the context menu.

FIGURE 6.1

Simultaneous Search dialog.

Before actually performing a SS, a review of the various options available in the SS dialog is in order.

Search terms and code pages

In the upper left is the search term text box where you can enter search terms or regular expressions. By default, simple strings are used, but SS understands regular expressions as well if the **GREP syntax** option is used. This section focuses on using simple strings only. **GREP syntax** will be covered in its own section.

Above the search term text box are two icons that let you save the terms entered in the search term text box or open a file containing search terms that will then populate the list. This makes it easy to have predefined search term lists for drug, child pornography, white collar, etc., type cases.

Below the search term, text boxes are checkboxes that allow for selecting up to six different code pages that will be used for the search. As with most settings in XWF, the default code pages work in the majority of cases.

The right side of the dialog contains three groups of options: how to search, where to search, and additional search options.

How to search options

If **Match case** is checked, XWF will perform case-sensitive searches. When this option is enabled, XWF will search on the exact case (upper and lower) of each search term as it appears in the list. In most cases, this option's impact on search speed will be negligible, but we recommend using it only when needed.

The **GREP syntax** option will be discussed in its own section below.

Whole words only has three options:

Fully checked: Only words meeting the criterion as outlined below, based on the characters that are included in the **Alphabet to define word boundaries** option, will be considered search hits.
Half-checked: Same as fully checked but only for search terms that are indented with a TAB character. Hence, you can apply the whole word option to some terms, and not to others.
Unchecked: Words containing any of the terms will be displayed including words where a search term is a substring of a search hit.

As an example, consider searching for the term *range*. If **Whole words only** is unchecked, XWF will consider the word *orange* to be a search hit as it contains the word *range*. If this option is checked, *orange* will not be considered a search hit.

We recommend half-checking this option as it allows more flexibility in that you can find both substring and whole word matches at the same time by indenting the search terms you wish to match as whole words.

A word boundary is a boundary between two consecutive characters where one of the characters is a word character (as defined in the **Alphabet to define word boundaries** option) and one character is not a word character. If both characters are word characters, there is no possibility the second of the two characters is the start of a new word, as there was no nonword character between the two (recall the two characters in question were consecutive).

Likewise, if both consecutive characters are nonword characters, the position between the two words cannot be the beginning or ending of a word (since they are, by definition, nonword characters).

For example, with **Whole words only** fully or half-checked (and if half-checked, indented with a TAB character), if you were searching for the word *flow* within the string *her flower*, XWF will initially locate the first four characters in the word *flower* and apply some tests to see whether it is a whole word or not as follows:

XWF checks the character to the left of *f*, which is a SPACE character. XWF determines that the SPACE character is not a word character. It next checks to see if *f* itself is a word character according to the values configured in the **Alphabet to define word boundaries** option. Since there is a nonword character to the left of the *f* and *f* itself is a word character, XWF now knows there is a word boundary to the left of *f*. Since XWF has already identified the word *flow* as a possible search hit, it does not need to check every character in the word and moves to the last character, *w*. Now that XWF is at the *w* in flow, it again looks to the left and determines whether there is a word character or not. It then looks to the right of *w* and again, XWF sees that *e* is a word character. Since *e* is in our **Alphabet to define word boundaries** list, XWF now knows that the instance of *flow* in *flower* is not a whole word. Therefore, *flower* will not constitute a hit.

The Condition offset modulo (**Cond: offset mod**) option allows for looking for a given string at a given offset. Condition offset modulo, while seemingly intimidating, significantly reduces the number of false positives in many cases for certain types of data.

There are two available offsets. The first box is **X**, and the second is **Y**. **X** is used to denote the offset from the beginning of a record, for example, a partition or file. Once XWF moves to the **X** offset of a given object, the search term will be looked for at offset **Y** relative to offset **X**. It is helpful to think of **X** as the starting point or anchor for a search and **Y** as how far away from the anchor to actually look for a given search term. When entering values for both **X** and **Y**, use decimal notation rather than hexadecimal notation.

For example, master file table (MFT) FILE records are typically 1024 bytes in length. With this option disabled, an SS will find the beginning of every record in the MFT. To find every *other* FILE record, enable this option and set $X = 2048$ and $Y = 0$.

Another example would be a search of the MFT for a common value, such as the number *8*. Searching for *8* without this option enabled will result in hundreds of thousands of hits on an average MFT file. However, if you are only interested in finding the instances of *8* that are 20 bytes from the beginning of an MFT record, enable this option and set $X = 1024$ and $Y = 20$. This tells XWF to divide the MFT into 1024-byte chunks and, for each chunk, look 20 bytes from the beginning of the record for a value of *8*. If found, XWF will mark that instance as a search hit.

Run X-Tensions allows for selecting one or more plugins that use the X-Tensions API to be used as a part of the SS. We will cover X-Tensions in Chapter 7.

Where to search options

The radio buttons in this section define the scope of the SS as it pertains to which objects will be included in the SS. Depending on how SS was invoked, either two or three radio buttons will be visible. If SS is invoked on one or more objects via the context menu in the **Directory Browser**, a third option, **Search all selected objects**, will be shown. If not, this option is hidden.

If **All objects in volume snapshot** or **Search all tagged objects** is selected, an additional option is shown, **In selected evidence objects**, that allows for selecting which evidence objects from the case to include in the search. Individual objects can be selected by clicking the button to the right of the option. To select more than one object, press CTRL while clicking an object.

If a single evidence object is selected, the total size of the data to be searched will be shown in parenthesis at the end of the **All objects in volume snapshot** option. Similarly, the aggregate size of any tagged items or selected items is reflected after the appropriate option.

Open and search files incl. slack functions the same way we saw in Chapter 3 when discussing the **Directory Browser** options. This option can be used in several ways depending on how you went about selecting files to search. For example, use the **Directory Browser** to filter on all *.doc* files, tag them, and elect to search only tagged items in the SS dialog. In this scenario, half-checked would be best because, although nothing is hidden, there may be irrelevant files in your list (unless you verified file types via **Refine Volume Snapshot** (RVS) and then filtered for relevant files only in the **Directory Browser**). On the other hand, if you *hide* files in the **Directory Browser**, fully checked is the best choice because the file slack of the hidden files will *always* be searched. Having "X" ways of doing things can be tricky sometimes, but as you find the technique that works best for you, you will know how to best utilize the features of XWF.

When **Open and search files incl. slack** is fully or half-checked, the **Cover file slack/free space transition** option is shown. If **Cover file slack/free space transition** is checked, XWF will search into adjacent free space when searching file slack.

For example, a file is created that takes up almost two adjacent clusters. The string that you are interested in is split across the boundary of these two clusters. If this file is now edited such that the new file no longer contains the string you are interested in and the file needs less than one cluster to save its contents, the remaining part of the first cluster becomes slack space and the entire second cluster is marked as free space. With this option enabled, XWF will find the match because it is not blindly stopping at the cluster boundary but rather looks into the adjacent free space to see if a search hit exists. This is a unique and powerful option that allows XWF to find things other tools cannot.

To put it another way, if a larger file is overwritten with a smaller file, data from the larger file may remain in the slack of the smaller file and spill over into directly following free space. If the slack space and the free space are only searched separately, as in many forensic tools, any word spanning the cluster boundary that delimits slack and free space cannot be found. XWF does not suffer from this limitation and, by using this option, such search terms are easily found.

If **Decode text in files** is checked, SS will use the viewer component to decode the contents of files whose extensions are listed. XWF will inform you if the viewer component is not active and give you the opportunity to enable it. This option can significantly expand the amount of data XWF can look at while performing the SS as it decodes the contents of the most popular document types.

XWF TIPS AND TRICKS
Viewing Decoded Text Hits in Their Native Format
To view the decoded text that was extracted from a file when using the **Decode text in files** option, select the file in the normal **Directory Browser** (as opposed to the **Search Hit List**) and switch to **Preview** mode. Clicking the **Raw** button while in **Preview** mode results in many "garbage" characters being displayed. However, holding the SHIFT key and clicking the **Raw** button will show the decoded text without the extra characters.

Additional search options

The options found here allow for further filtering which objects the SS targets. Several of the options are self-explanatory.

Omit files classified as irrelevant, when checked, tells XWF to ignore files that have been deemed nonpertinent as a result of a hash database match against an irrelevant or not-of-interest hash set. The **Open and search files incl. slack** option affects this option, as XWF can search the slack of files deemed irrelevant.

Omit hidden files, when checked, will exclude any files that have been hidden via the **Directory Browser** regardless of whether they are shown in the **Directory Browser**.

The **Omit directories** option determines if directory records are included in the search. To clarify, **Omit directories** option does *not* exclude files found in selected directories from being searched. Rather, it excludes the data structures of the file system that define the directory from being searched (for example, on NTFS file systems, INDX records).

The **Omit files that are filtered out** option is useful because it allows you to use column filters in the **Directory Browser** to select the files you are interested in searching. This significantly reduces search time as XWF does not have to search an entire evidence object.

The **Recommendable data reduction**, when checked, allows XWF to intelligently omit certain files from a search. This is another example where XWF goes beyond the norm in terms of efficiency. When this option is enabled, one of the advantages is that XWF will not duplicate its efforts by searching both a file as a whole and each child of that file. For example, consider the case where an MBOX mailbox file is processed by XWF as part of an RVS operation. The RVS operation will result in child e-mail objects being associated with the MBOX file. When an SS includes the MBOX and its children, XWF will skip the MBOX as the same information is already available in the child objects. Archive files such as ZIP and RAR files work in a similar way after they have been processed as a part of an RVS operation.

XWF TIPS AND TRICKS
Less Isn't Always More
Recommendable data reduction is just that, a recommendation. There are times when you may not want to search only child objects of a given file. For example, there may be cases where not all data is extracted as e-mail messages from an MBOX file. With this option checked, you would miss any matching search terms found inside the MBOX file that aren't part of an extracted e-mail. As stated in the XWF manual, the use of this option is a compromise of sorts.

If **1 hit per file needed only** (**faster**) is checked, XWF will stop searching a file when any search term is found in a file. It should be noted that the search term found and highlighted in the file may not be the most relevant or useful search hit. For example, if you search for *dog* and *cat*, XWF will not search a file further if it finds *cat* before it finds *dog* in the file. As indicated by this option's name, enabling this option results in faster searching but at the expense of not being able to logically combine search term hits, that is, show files with *searchterm1*, *searchterm2*, etc. in them.

Search methodologies

The last option to cover is the methodology XWF will use when performing the search as it pertains to how data are stored in a given evidence object. This option is found between the **Cancel** and **Help** button at the bottom of the dialog.

Logical (**file-wise**) is by far the most powerful methodology and is the default choice. **Logical** simply means that the search is conducted on the contents of files regardless of whether the files are fragmented. Additionally, a logical search can search through decoded text in many file types such as Word and PDF documents and archive files.

Physical (**sector-wise**) tells XWF to search on a sector-by-sector basis in Logical Block Addressing (LBA) order. While this has its uses in certain situations, it is prone to miss data in many cases. For example, if a file is fragmented and the search term you are interested in is split across a fragment, it will not be found. A logical search avoids this issue.

When **Physical** (**sector-wise**) is selected, the *Where to search options* and *Additional search options* will not be available. A new set of options is displayed in place of *Additional search options* that includes options for the direction of the search, whether to list search hits, etc.

Unless you have a specific reason for doing otherwise, we recommend always selecting **Logical** (**file-wise**).

After you enter one or more search terms and set the various options to your liking, click the **OK** button to start the search. To cancel a search, press the **ESC** key or click the X in the upper right corner of the search progress window.

REGULAR EXPRESSIONS

A regular expression is a specific pattern that provides concise and flexible means to match (specify and recognize) strings of text, such as particular characters, words, or patterns of characters.[1] It can also be used to search for hex strings that represent non-ASCII characters.

Regular expressions (regex) come in several flavors or engines. Because of this, certain rules must be followed in order for a given engine to process a regex pattern. XWF uses its own engine to parse regular expressions, so its interpretation of regex patterns is tightly integrated to its internal searching algorithms.

---

[1] http://en.wikipedia.org/wiki/Regular_expression.

Mastering regular expressions is a daunting task. Entire books have been written about them. Being proficient in regular expressions is definitely one way to enhance your "geek" credibility. We understand that examiners have enough on their plates already and cannot spend an inordinate amount of time mastering another technology. Because of this, we will not attempt to cover every conceivable option or possibility when using regex in XWF.

Regex allows for creating patterns to match complex string and hex patterns. The following table summarizes the rules that must be followed when creating regular expressions in XWF:

.	Matches any single character
#	Matches any single digit
[]	Used to define a set of values. [a-z0-9] matches a single character between *a* and *z* or between *0* and *9* (inclusive). [abc18] would match a single instance of either *a*, *b*, *c*, *1*, or *8*. You can also define sets using a combination of both notations: [abc-gyz12-59]. Within square brackets, the characters .*+?{}()| are interpreted literally and as such do not behave as special characters.
[^]	Used to exclude a set of values. [^a-m] matches a single character **not** between *a* and *m*.
()	Used to define a group for use with logical operators
|	Logical 'OR' operator. (ez|bs) would match either the string *ez* or *bs*.
*	Following a character or a set, matches the character or set zero or more times. devic[es]* would match *devic*, *device*, *devices*, *deviceeeeessss*, etc.
+	Following a character or a set, matches the character or set one or more times. devic[es]+ would match *device*, *devices*, *deviceeeeessss*, etc.
?	Following a character or a set, matches the character or set zero or one time. devic[es]? would match *devic*, *device*, *devics*, but **not** *devices* (as a whole word. It would match the first 6 characters in the word however).
\	Used to 'escape' characters that have special meaning in a regular expression. For example, to match a backslash character, it would have to be escaped with another backslash (\\).
\b	Beginning or end of word anchor
^	Start of a file
$	Logical or physical end of a file
\xNN or \NNN	Byte values (hex or decimal notation). Can be used between []. Not case sensitive.
{X,Y}	Following a character or a set, matches the character or set between X and Y times. (ab){2,4} would match *abab* or *ababab*, but not *ab* or *ab ab*.

If you are looking for more information on regex, an excellent resource for all things regular expressions can be found at http://www.regular-expressions.info/index.html.

A very good program to help you create and test various regex patterns is RegexBuddy, found at http://www.regexbuddy.com/. RegexBuddy allows you to test a regular expression against a set of data, so you can see, in real time, what your regex matches as you adjust your regex. This is invaluable when learning how to build both simple and complex regular expressions.

Regular expression examples

When creating regular expressions for use in XWF (or anywhere for that matter), break down the information you are trying to find into smaller chunks. This helps prevent errors when trying to create a complex regular expression. By composing regular expressions in this manner, you will also create smaller expressions that can serve as "ingredients" in future regex "recipes."

Over the next few paragraphs, we will present several examples of common regular expressions. First, we will look at the expression as a whole and then, in several of the examples, deconstruct it into its relevant pieces. This will make the regular expressions easier to understand and allow you to reuse the building blocks of more complex regular expressions.

```
[a-zA-Z0-9\-_\.]+@(gmail\.com|hotmail\.com|yahoo\.com)
```

Finds e-mail addresses hosted by gmail.com, hotmail.com, or yahoo.com. Because the set of characters is followed by the plus symbol, the e-mail address must contain at least one character to the left of @. The left side can contain any letters a-z (regardless of case), a dash, an underscore, or a dot. Without the dot, the regex would find foobar@gmail. com, but not foo.bar@gmail.com (it would however match on bar@gmail.com). This regex can be easily adjusted to find all e-mail addresses by using a pattern similar to what we see to the left of @ in place of the three domain names.

[a-zA-Z0-9\-_\]+: This part of the regex will match the username piece of the e-mail address (the information to the left of the @ sign). It will match any character between a and z (inclusive) regardless of case, the numbers 0-9, the dash, and the period character. By using a plus sign after the range of characters, we ensure the username is at least one character in length.

@(gmail\.com|hotmail\.com|yahoo\.com): This part of the regex will first match the @ sign followed by one of the values in parenthesis. Since the parenthesis defines a set of OR conditions, there are three possibilities to match against: gmail.com, hotmail.com, or yahoo.com (case insensitive). As an alternative, this part of the regex could be simplified to *@(gmail|hotmail|yahoo).com* since the .com is redundant in our initial example.

```
(vacation|holiday)\.jp(g|eg)
```

Finds files where the file name to the left of the dot is *vacation* or *holiday* and the file extension is either *jpg* or *jpeg*. Notice the dot is escaped, so the regex looks for a dot as opposed to matching any single character. Without the backslash, the regex would match (in addition to finding files with a dot since it would match any single character) things such as *vacationYjpg* or *holiday_jpeg*. While an SS will find file names (if file system data structures are searched), this regular expression would be more applicable to be used in the **Name** filter as it also supports regular expressions.

(vacation|holiday): Matches either *vacation* or *holiday*

\.: Normally a dot matches any single character, but since we escaped it with a backslash, this only matches a period.

jp(g|eg): Matches *jp* followed by either *g* or *eg*.

```
\#[a-f0-9]{6}
```

Matches six digit hexadecimal numbers. Such numbers are often found in HTML documents for color codes (e.g., *<body bgcolor="#FF9900"*). In the string above, this regex would match *#FF9900*. Without the leading escaped number sign, any numerical value of at least six numbers would have been matched.

\#: Since the # sign is escaped, this matches the literal character #.

[a-f0-9]: Matches a single character between a-f and 0-9 which are the only valid characters for hex notation.

{6}: Restricts matches to strings whose length is exactly six.

```
(http|https|ftp):\/\/[a-zA-Z0-9-./]{5,50}
```

Matches any URL strings that start with *http*, *https*, or *ftp*. The range thereafter allows for letters and numbers, a dash, a dot, and a forward slash. Since we did not include the question mark, this regex would match URLs up to the beginning of the query string. The URL must also be between 5 characters and 50 characters long.

```
\x68\x74\x74\x70\x3A\x2F\x2F
```

Matches the string *https://* but does so by looking at the hexadecimal values in a file vs. an ASCII string.

```
^X-Account-Key
```

Looks for the string *X-Account-Key* at the beginning of a file as opposed to anywhere in a given file.

```
\baccount2\b
```

Looks for the string *account2* as an individual word. Without the leading and trailing \b, *account2* could be a part of any string and it would be considered a hit. Valid word boundary characters can be configured in the SS dialog via the **Alphabet to define word boundaries** button.

The examples above demonstrate several patterns and building blocks that can be used to create powerful and flexible regex patterns. These patterns greatly enhance your ability to find specific and relevant hits when searching while eliminating false hits at the same time. Because you will have fewer search hits to review, you become more efficient.

GREP AND REGULAR EXPRESSIONS IN XWF

To use GREP expressions in XWF, you must enable the **GREP syntax** setting in the SS dialog. If you enter a search term in XWF without telling XWF to use GREP, XWF will look for exact string matches and your results will most likely not be what you expect. The **GREP syntax** option, when enabled, tells XWF to use regular expressions either exclusively or in addition to string searches.

GREP syntax has three options:

Fully checked: All search terms will be treated as regular expressions.
Half-checked: Only search terms prepended with *grep:* are treated as regular expressions. This is useful to use both standard and regex searches at the same time.
Unchecked: All search terms will be treated as simple strings and will be searched as entered.

If **GREP syntax** is either fully or half-checked, it replaces the **Whole words only** option. When fully or half-checked, additional options become available.

Search window determines how many contiguous bytes XWF will look at when trying to match a regular expression. The default window is 128 bytes. Depending on the regex pattern used, this would list search hits up to the length of **Search window** even if there were more data that the regex pattern considers a match. In other words, this prevents overbroad regular expressions from finding matching patterns that are potentially thousands of lines long.

The value of **Search window** is also used when using a regular expression to find two strings within a given distance of one another (a proximity search). Note that this is *not* the preferred way to locate two terms that are close to one another. Rather than adjusting the **Search window** for terms that are close to one another, the preferred method is to look for search terms individually and then use the **Near** function in the **Search Term List**. The **Search Term List** will be explained in its own section below.

As explained above, the value of **Search window** determines the range of contiguous bytes XWF will look at when looking for matches. When used in conjunction with a proximity search, the potential search hit must fall inside this window.

The regular expressions used for a proximity search are of the pattern:

```
keyword1.{mindistance,maxdistance}keyword2
```

```
keyword2.{mindistance,maxdistance}keyword1
```

Breaking the regular expression into pieces, we get the following:

keyword1: the first keyword to look for as an exact string match.

.{mindistance,maxdistance}: A period (that matches any character) repeated between **mindistance** and **maxdistance** times. This is the number of characters that can separate **keyword1** and **keyword2** and still be considered a search hit.

keyword2: the second keyword to look for as an exact string match.

For example, **foo.{4,8}bar** would find matches where the string *foo* is at least four characters away from, but no more than eight characters away from, the word *bar*.

The total length of the proximity search regular expressions must be less than or equal to the value of **Search window** (length of **keyword1** + **maxdistance** + length of **keyword2**).

The second regex works just like the first one did, except that **keyword1** and **keyword2** are in opposite positions.

If **Allow overlapping hits** is checked, XWF will look for search hits if a given search term is found inside another string that also contains a search term. For example, if searching for *test* against the string *test testate testy testest*, with this option unchecked, XWF will find four search hits: *test*, *test*age, *test*y, and *test*est. With this option checked, XWF will find five search hits, the four as outlined above and an additional one, tes*test*. We recommend leaving this option unchecked as it can produce many additional search hits in certain cases.

INDEXED SEARCH

In most cases, an SS will be sufficient when looking for search terms. As you have seen, SS provides a powerful and flexible way to locate search terms in an evidence object. There are times when indexing can save a considerable amount of time but it is not necessary, nor do we recommend, creating an index in every case. XWF is flexible in that it allows you, the user, to make the determination whether to index or not.

Indexed searching differs from an SS in that, before conducting an indexed search, XWF must locate and record every word composed of characters (as selected by the user) that are contained in an evidence object (or subset of an evidence object).

By creating an index of words, considerable time can be saved if you know you will have a large number of search terms but do not necessarily know every search term that you will need at the onset of a case. In situations where you have a predefined set of keywords for which to search when conducting a particular type of forensic review, it may be more beneficial to use an SS as opposed to an indexed search.

XWF supports creating indexes of characters from all languages whose characters are contained in the Unicode character set, including predefined alphabets for over 25 languages. It is possible to combine character sets from different languages if your evidence objects contain more than one language. You can also create different indexes for different languages (preferable if the languages are not compatible).

To create an index, use **Search | Indexing** or press **CTRL+ALT+I** to bring up the **Indexing** dialog as shown in Figure 6.2.

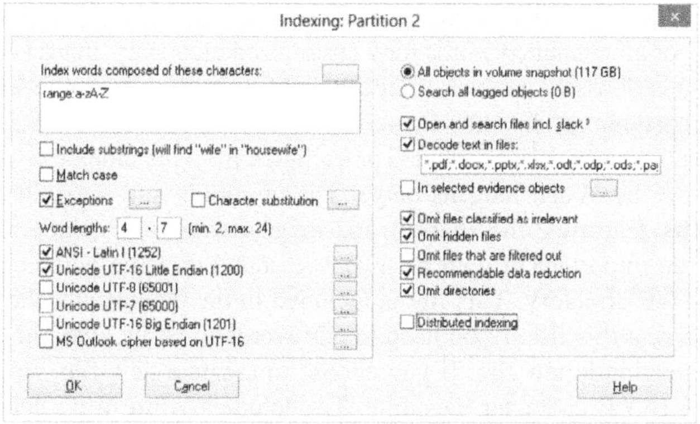

FIGURE 6.2

Indexing dialog.

Looking at Figure 6.2, we see a lot of familiar options from the SS dialog. There are also some new options that are explained below.

Index words composed of these characters defines the characters that are used when building an index. You can manually enter a value for this field or use the button above the right side of the textbox to select a character set for a particular language.

Include substrings, when checked, adds individual words found in compound words to the index. For example, with this option enabled, *time* would be found in the word *lifetime* and *ban* would be found in the word *abandon*. While it is possible to look for substrings when doing an **Indexed Search** without enabling this option, doing so can significantly slow down the speed at which the results of the search are found and the results will likely be incomplete. Therefore, enable this option if you are likely to require substring searches.

XWF TIPS AND TRICKS

You've Got to Keep 'em Separated

Recall from Chapter 1 the recommended layout of the directories that XWF uses when working with a case and evidence objects. Specifically, recall our recommendation to store your case files on a separate device from the evidence object images. Following this guideline will ensure index generation is as fast as possible as XWF will be able to read from one device (the source of the data) and write to another (the index files themselves).

The **Match case** option, when checked, results in the same words with different capitalization being stored as two different entries in an index. For example, consider a scenario where the words *superintendent* and *SUpErINtENDenT* are in a particular evidence object. With **Match case** checked, an entry for each version of the word would be added to the index. When unchecked, only one instance of the word would be saved. When searching the index with the **Match case** option enabled, only hits with the exact same capitalization will be displayed as search hits. Because of this, we recommend leaving this option off. This option is usually only needed if you create the index to produce a list of all contained words for a customized dictionary attacks on passwords where the assumption is the password may consist of a mix of lower and upper case letters.

The **Exceptions** option allows you to specifically include or exclude certain words that would normally be included or excluded from the index if a word's length falls outside of the **Word lengths** range. The minimum and maximum values for **Word lengths** determine the shortest and longest words to include in the index. Words that are important to your case can be added to a file named *indexwds.txt* in the root XWF directory. This file is included in the default installation, and we recommend using this file if you need to add words to be included in the index as opposed to creating a new file. If you choose to create a new file, be sure to save it using UTF-16 LE character encoding. To include a word in the index, prepend it with a plus sign. To exclude a word in the index, prepend it with a minus sign. Finally, if you enter words whose length is longer than the maximum length, those words will be truncated to a length equal to the maximum length.

Character substitutions allows for creating pairs of characters for use in an index. This is useful if you have characters with accents, umlauts, etc. By replacing such letters with one without the accent, searching becomes simpler in that you can use the standard ASCII character set when entering search terms as opposed to having to account for all possible spelling combinations. All character pairs must be entered in a file named *indexsub.txt*. This file is also included in a default installation of XWF. As in the case of the file used for **Exceptions**, we recommend using the existing file. If you choose to create a new one, the file must be saved using the UTF-16 LE character encoding.

You can open the corresponding files for **Exceptions** and **Character substitutions** by clicking the . . . button to the right of each option.

The **Code pages** checkboxes allow you to select up to six different index formats (one index per selected code page). For each code page selected, a directory is created in the metadata directory for a given evidence object. In Figure 6.3, the metadata directories are circled and are found in the *C:\XWCases\New Case* directory. Metadata directories are prefixed with an underscore. The directories without the underscores are the default paths used by XWF when using the **Recover/Copy** command.

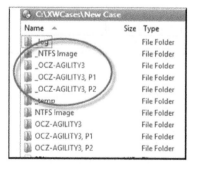

FIGURE 6.3

Metadata directories.

The directories containing the index are created as a subdirectory of the evidence object. Figure 6.4 shows the directories that were created as a result of the settings shown in Figure 6.2. Notice how the directories reflect the code page as seen in Figure 6.2.

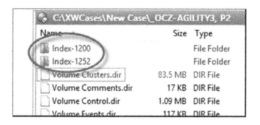

FIGURE 6.4

_OCZ-AGILITY3, P2 index directories.

To delete an index for an evidence object, simply delete the directories that correspond to the index you wish to delete.

Distributed Indexing allows for several copies of XWF to be used simultaneously to generate the index files.

XWF TIPS AND TRICKS

Two Instances of XWF Is Better Than One!

XWF has the ability to index a given set of data in a distributed fashion. In other words, you can tell XWF to distribute an indexing job across several instances of XWF by checking the **Distributed Indexing** option.

To use **Distributed Indexing**, store the case file and evidence objects on a shared drive, then start XWF on additional computers, and give each instance of XWF that will be processing the case a unique participant number. Because each instance of XWF is using the same case file, XWF knows to break up the indexing workload across each instance of XWF that is participating in the indexing process.

Using **Distributed Indexing** can significantly reduce the time required to create a complete index (assuming that your storage device is robust enough to handle the extra read operations required by the additional instances of XWF).

As with most things, it is best to know the limitations of your hardware before using **Distributed Indexing** in a live case. As such, we recommend spending some time experimenting with your hardware to determine the optimum settings before actually using **Distributed Indexing** on an actual case.

For complete details, see the XWF manual.

Once you have all the options configured, click the **OK** button to begin generating the indexes. Once the process starts, a progress dialog will be displayed as shown in Figure 6.5. You can adjust the memory used as well as the number of processes to match the capabilities of your hardware.

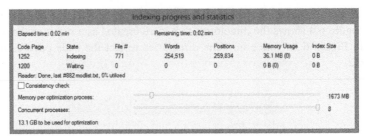

FIGURE 6.5

Indexing statistics.

Because each evidence object can have only one index per code page per evidence object, you may be asked by XWF if you want to overwrite an existing index if you indexed a subset of files in a particular evidence object. An example of this is shown in Figure 6.6.

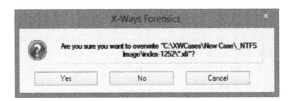

FIGURE 6.6

XWF asking to overwrite an index.

If you choose **Yes**, XWF will overwrite any existing index. If you choose **No**, XWF will generate new index files that can then be merged with the existing index file. As XWF builds the secondary indexes, additional index files will be created in the metadata folder as shown in Figure 6.7.

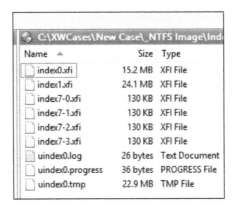

FIGURE 6.7

XWF creating additional index files.

If you choose **No,** an option to optimize the index will be displayed on the progress dialog. This option is circled in Figure 6.8. If this option is enabled, XWF will
combine all the index files into a single file (resulting in a more efficient index) at the
end of the indexing process. Compare this with Figure 6.5 which lacks the **Optimize
Index** option.

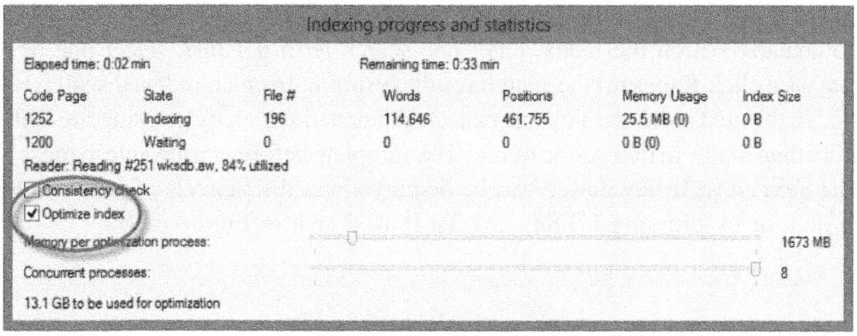

FIGURE 6.8

Enabling index optimization.

Once the index is created, the **Search in Index** dialog is displayed as shown in
Figure 6.9.

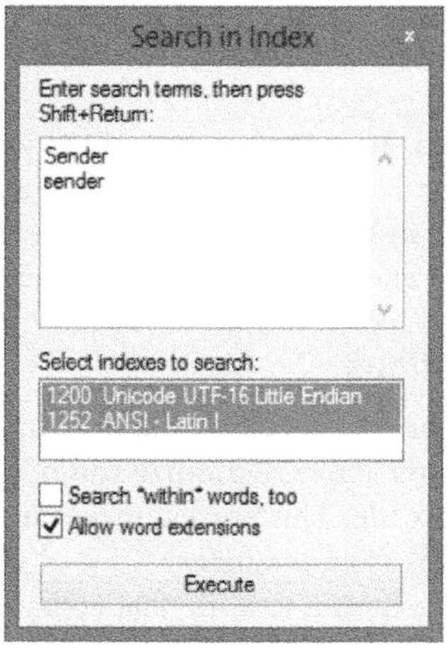

FIGURE 6.9

Search in Index dialog.

The **Search "within" words too** option allows for substring matches for search
terms. If you did not enable the **Include substrings** option when creating the index,
enabling **Search "within" words too** will incur a speed penalty when searching the
index as the substring searches must be generated on the fly. If you need to do

substring searches, we recommend enabling the **Include substrings** option when creating the initial index.

The **Allow word extensions** option enables XWF to treat words found in the index as the "base" of words when searching. For example, if the word *torrent* was in your index, with this option enabled, *torrents* is considered a search hit even though it is not an exact match. To put it another way, any word that starts with a word in the index will be shown in the **Search Hit List**.

To actually search the index, enter one search term per line, select one or more indexes, and click **Execute** (the search results resulting from an indexed search will be covered in the next section). You can cancel an indexed search by pressing the **ESC** key but more than likely an indexed search will be complete before you are able to press **ESC**.

The **Search in Index** dialog can be displayed via the **Search | Search in Index** menu item or by pressing **CTRL+ALT+F** as shown in Figure 6.10.

FIGURE 6.10

Additional index-related options.

As previously mentioned, an index can be created for each evidence object. As such, individual indexes can be searched by selecting a given evidence object and then bringing up the **Search in Index** dialog. To search all available index in a case, select the **Case Root** folder and then invoke the **Search in Index** dialog.

Other index-related options

In Figure 6.10, two additional index-related options can be seen.

As explained in the section above, **Optimize Index** will combine any individual index files into a single index file. This process makes index searches more efficient and removes duplicate words from the index.

Export Word List will export a text file that contains each unique word found in the index.

XWF TIPS AND TRICKS

Export Subtleties

As mentioned in the XWF manual, **Match case** can be used to generate a list of words that are case sensitive. In some cases, you may wish to generate a list of every word found on a computer for use in a dictionary attack against a password. Since any decent encryption program will use passphrases that are case sensitive, enabling the **Match case** option will ensure each unique instance of a given word is stored in the index, complete with specific capitalization, and, therefore, each of those words will be included when the words are exported.

REVIEWING SEARCH HITS

Now that we have covered the two primary search mechanisms in XWF, it is time to review the search hits. To toggle between the **Directory Browser** and the **Search Hit List**, click the binoculars icon on the mode bar as shown in Figure 6.11.

FIGURE 6.11

Binoculars button.

After an SS or Indexed Search is complete, the **Search Hit List** will be displayed automatically as shown in Figure 6.12.

Offset	Rel. ofs.	Descr.	Search hits ▲	Name	Typ	Size	#ST	Search terms
6D00040	49040	UTF-16	Umschlagabsenderadresse " 黳	Manual.doc	doc	429,056	1	Sender
6DE6284	46284	UTF-16	Umschlagabsenderadresse # 黳	Manuel WinHex.doc	doc	448,512	1	Sender
	42836	UTF-16	Umschlagabsenderadresse " 黳	Spanish Manual.doc	doc	402,944	1	Sender
74B249A	2BC9A	CP 1252	ng&index=4&sender=3&tag=sa8k	index.dat		1,949,696	1	Sender
767413A	13A	CP 1252	as permitted sender) client-ip=211	Trash		2,214	1	Sender
767439D	39D	CP 1252	message to sender: Message-Id	Trash		2,214	1	Sender
76AA8CA	CA	CP 1252	subject)(82 sender) (83 mess	Trash.msf	msf	2,191	1	Sender
76AAD95	595	CP 1252	message to sender) (8C=0MK	Trash.msf	msf	2,191	1	Sender
662CB25	325	CP 1252	ENT="umfassender interaktiver F	sendung[2].html	html	37,472	1	Sender
662CB89	389	CP 1252	ENT="umfassender interaktiver F	sendung[2].html	html	37,472	1	Sender
662D927	1127	CP 1252	ng&index=4&sender=3&tag=sa8k	sendung[2].html	html	37,472	1	Sender
6632211	5A11	CP 1252	1"> [Sender <a hr	sendung[2].html	html	37,472	1	Sender
6632277	5A77	CP 1252	%0&zeit <alle&sender=4" class="lr	sendung[2].html	html	37,472	1	Sender
6632CF2	64F2	CP 1252	m nach Sender oder Z	sendung[2].html	html	37,472	1	Sender
66348FF	80FF	CP 1252	gramm nach Sender</a> </	sendung[2].html	html	37,472	1	Sender
6B8580A	31580A	CP 1252	µý/à 2h 2! sender sendal	msgr2en.lex	lex	4,069,145	1	Sender
	(C05)	decoded	er und umfassender Rahmen für	gefstoffv_2005_flyer.pdf	pdf	71,936	1	Sender
	(107EA)	decoded	a message sender's data and r	rp99-020.pdf	pdf	186,027	1	Sender
	(1483D)	decoded	r instance, a sender of data canr	rp99-020.pdf	pdf	186,027	1	Sender
809AADD	62DD	CP 1252	en für die Absenderadresse. 1	mswkswp.hlp	hlp	56,826	1	Sender

FIGURE 6.12

Search Hit List.

XWF TIPS AND TRICKS

Location, Location, Location

The **Search Hit List** will only show search hits that are found in files contained in the currently selected directory (or directories if in recursive mode). To see all search hits, explore recursively at the topmost level of a particular evidence object or the **Case Root** folder.

Search Hit List columns

The **Search Hit List** adds several additional columns that do not exist in the main **Directory Browser** including the offset, the code page of the search hit, the location of the search hit, a contextual preview of the search hit, etc. A relative offset enclosed in parentheses indicates the search hit was found in the decoded text of a file. In addition, the offset displayed is relative to the beginning of the decoded text and not the beginning of the file in its encoded state. It should be noted that physical offsets are not available when viewing the results of an indexed search.

The **Search Terms** column can be displayed in both the **Directory Browser** and **Search Hit List**. As such, you can quickly see what search terms have been found in an object by displaying the **Search Terms** column in the **Directory Browser**. This can save time because you do not have to constantly toggle between these two modes to see which search terms have been found and where they exist in an object.

Interacting with the Search Hit List

To mark a search hit as **Notable**, right click on the search hit and select **Mark hit as notable** or simply press the **Space** bar. To remove a notable hit, select the search hit and press the **Space** bar again.

As we saw with the **Directory Browser**, several columns have filters that behave in much the same way as in **Directory Browser** mode. A unique column for the **Search Hit List** is the **Descr.** column. The filter for this column can be used to only show notable hits, user search hits, etc.

When in **Search Hit List** mode, the **Search Term List** will be displayed at the bottom-right of the **Case Data** window. An example of a **Search Term List** is shown in Figure 6.13.

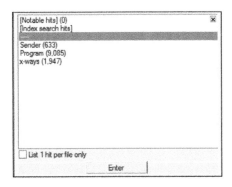

FIGURE 6.13

Search Term List.

After starting an SS or Index Search, search hits can be previewed before the search finishes by toggling **Search Hit List** mode. To refresh the list, click the **Enter** button at the bottom of the **Search Term List**.

Simultaneous search results vs. indexed search results

In Figure 6.13, the three terms below the hyphens are search term hits found as a result of an SS. To view the results of an index-based search, double-click **Index search hits** in the **Search Hit List** window.

The primary difference between these two kinds of searches is that the results of an indexed search are *not* recorded in the **Search Term List** unless a particular search hit is saved permanently. The reason for this is that it takes essentially no time to conduct an index-based search and saved search hits consume memory.

To save a *single* index search-based search hit permanently, select the search hit, right-click, and choose **Save hit permanently** from the context menu as shown in Figure 6.14.

FIGURE 6.14

Saving an index search hit permanently.

To save more than one indexed search hit, select all of the search hits you wish to permanently save before right-clicking. You can use **CTRL+A** to select all search hits at once if need be.

After saving an index-based search permanently, the search hit will be displayed like any other search term in the **Search Hit List**. Figure 6.15 shows the results of permanently saving two index search hits for the word *manual*.

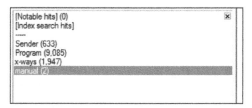

FIGURE 6.15

Permanent index search hits.

Search Hit List options

To permanently delete a search hit, select the search hit and press the **Delete** key. You can also right-click on a search hit and select **Delete** from the context menu. Deleting a search hit permanently removes it from your case.

To display all of the hits for a particular search term, **double click** the search term. To select more than one search term, hold the **SHIFT** or **CTRL** key while clicking search terms. **SHIFT** will select a range of terms while **CTRL** will select or deselect one at a time.

As you change directories in the **directory tree**, the number of search hits relative to the selected directory will be reflected in the **Search Hit List**.

The **Search Hit List** contains powerful options for combining search terms using Boolean operators (OR and AND). As usual, XWF has "X" ways to accomplish this task.

+ and − operators

In many cases, it is much more useful to find files where more than one search term has been located. This allows you to reduce a significant amount of false positives when reviewing search hits. In contrast, it is also useful to limit search results to certain files that contain one or more terms but do *not* have other search terms in them. The plus and minus operators allow you to create powerful filters based on search terms that make it much easier to find specific information very quickly.

By default, the **Search Term List** uses logical OR when more than one search term is selected. This simply means that a file can have *term1* or *term2* in it to be displayed in the **Search Hit List**.

The table below outlines the different combinations and how the **Search Hit List** changes depending on the options used. A plus sign means the search term should be included in files, and the minus sign means the search term should not be included. For the purposes of the chart, assume *x-ways* was found 1947 times and *manual* was found 9 times.

x-ways manual	Logical OR. Include files containing either search term. **Total search hits: 1956**
+x-ways manual	Let Group1 be the set of files where *x-ways* was found. Include all files in Group1 plus the files where *manual* was found in files in Group1. **Total search hits: 1952**
+x-ways +manual	Logical AND. Include files containing both search term. **Total search hits: 96**
x-ways −manual	Let Group1 be the set of files where *x-ways* was found. Exclude files from Group1 where *manual* was also found. **Total search hits: 100**

To add the plus or minus operator to a search term, use the +/− keys or the context menu that is shown after right-clicking a search term.

Alternate method

In addition to using the + and − operators on search terms, you can select multiple search terms with the mouse or keyboard. After selecting at least two search terms, a new option will be shown to the left of the **Enter** button that allows you to select the criteria used when combining the search terms. By default, this option shows **Min. 1** along with up and down arrows. Depending on how many search terms you select, this would change to **Min. 2** or **All** *x* where *x* is the number of search terms selected.

XWF TIPS AND TRICKS

One or the Other, but not Both!

To use the alternate method to combine search terms, make sure you clear any +/− operators before the search terms. If you do not do this, the option allowing you to select the minimum number of hits in a file will not be shown. To clear the +/− operators, use the context menu or press the **ESC** key.

Proximity between search terms using the Search Hit List

As discussed, when we covered **GREP syntax**, the preferred way in XWF to find search terms that are near one another is to use the **Search Hit List**. The **Near** option becomes available in two ways: when at least two search terms are selected and at least one search term is prefixed with either + or −, or when two search terms are selected and the minimum is changed to **All 2**.

Enabling the **Near** option results in yet another option being displayed that allows for entering the number of bytes a given search term must be found in relation to the other search term.

XWF TIPS AND TRICKS

Position Manager

In addition to using the powerful search capabilities in XWF, you can manually annotate blocks of data when viewing files in either **Volume/Partition** or **File** mode.

To add a selection of bytes to the **Position Manager**, select a block of data in **Volume/Partition** mode or **File** mode, right-click, and select **Add position**. This will bring up a dialog that allows you to enter a description, select a color for the annotation, etc. The dialog is also displayed by clicking the middle mouse button after selecting a block of data.

To view the **Position Manager**, select **Navigation | Position Manager** or press **CTRL+M**. To get back to the **Directory Browser**, press **CTRL+M** a second time or use the related menu item.

This functionality is rather old and is considered deprecated. It is recommended to create user search hits instead. User search hits will be covered in Chapter 7.

TEXT SEARCH

When in any of the modes (**Volume/Partition**, **File**, **Preview**, etc.), you can search for text strings by using **Search | Find Text** from the main menu or pressing **CTRL+F**. Doing either results in the dialog shown in Figure 6.16.

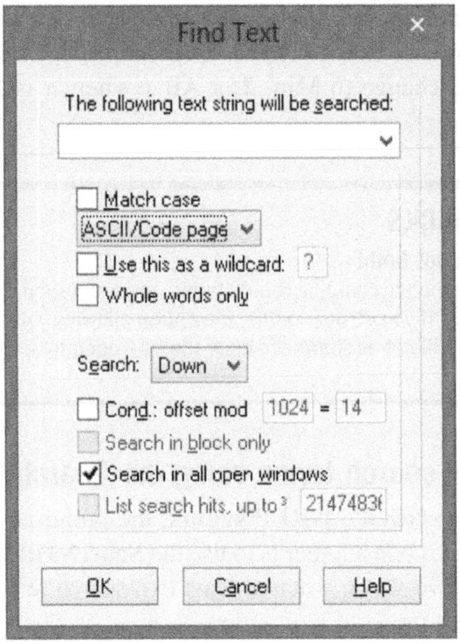

FIGURE 6.16

Find Text dialog.

The dialog has several options, some of which we have seen before. Change the **ASCII/Code page** dropdown to match the encoding of the data for which you wish to search. **Use as wildcard** allows you to enter a character that will be treated as a wildcard when searching for text. For example, if you were searching for *sung* or *song*, enable **Use as wildcard** and search for *s?ng*. Since ? is the wildcard character, you would get hits for both required values (albeit one at a time). This saves time in that you do not need to do two separate searches. **Search in block only** is only available if you search for hex values after selecting a block of data. **Search in open windows** will perform the search in all items that are opened in the **tab control** above the **Directory Browser**. The **List search hits** option is only used in WinHex, not XWF.

Find Text is always a physical, linear search of data. It ignores any selection of files in the **Directory Browser**, any file-wise filters, and any structure such as file systems, path, compression, fragmentation, and special ways of encoding.

In most cases (when in **Volume/Partition**, **Gallery**, **Calendar**, or **Legend** mode), a text search behaves as a physical search starting from sector 0 and continuing until a match is found or the end of an evidence object is reached. The exception to this is when you are in **File** mode. When in **File** mode, the search is limited to the contents of the file *last* selected in the **Directory Browser**.

In all cases, a text search is done against the raw contents of a device or file. No interpretation of the data is done to decode the data and then search the decoded data.

For windows where the content is populated by the viewer component, **Find Text** is a different command with a different dialog box as provided by the viewer component.

HEXADECIMAL SEARCH

When in either **Volume/Partition** or **File** mode, you can search for hexadecimal values by using **Search | Find Hex Values** or pressing **CTRL+ALT+X**. Doing either results in the dialog shown in Figure 6.17.

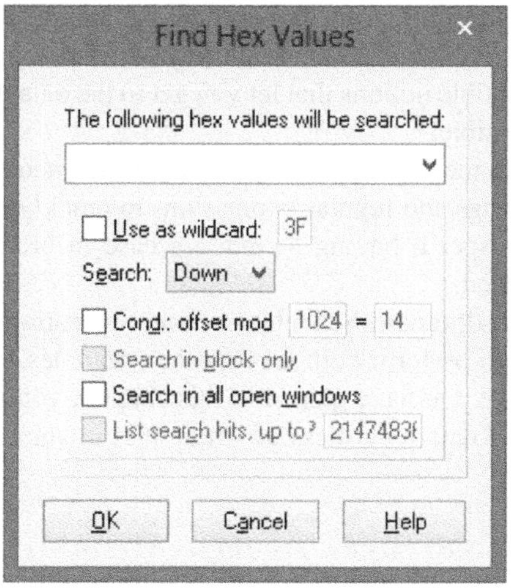

FIGURE 6.17

Find Hex Values dialog.

The dialog has several options, most of which work the same as when finding text. **Use as wildcard** allows you to enter a hex value that will be treated as a wildcard when searching for hexadecimal values. For example, if you were searching for hex *001F2B* or *002F2B*, enable **Use as wildcard** and pick a hex character, for example, 3F. Since 3F is the wildcard hex character, you would get hits for both *001F2B* and *002F2B*.

In most cases, you will want to find the next occurrence of a hexadecimal value, and therefore, you would enter the hex value that you wish to find. In some cases, however, it is useful to be able to continue a search while a certain value is *not* found. For example, if there are thousands of sequential "FF" values in a file and you are interested in finding the position in the file where the "FF" values stop, search for *!FF* which will repeat the search until the first non "FF" value is found.

SHORTCUTS

ALT+F10: Bring up **Simultaneous Search** dialog.
CTRL+F: Bring up **Find Text Values** search dialog.
CTRL+ALT+X: Bring up **Find Hex Values** search dialog.
CTRL+ALT+F: Bring up **the Search in Index** dialog.
CTRL+ALT+I: Bring up the **Indexing** dialog.
CTRL+M: Toggles between the **Directory Browser** and the **Position Manager**.

SUMMARY

XWF's search capabilities are unrivaled and unique among digital forensic tools.

In this chapter, we have covered all of the ways to search for information in XWF using powerful and flexible options that let you get to the data that is relevant to your case as quickly as possible.

The primary search mechanism in XWF, the **Simultaneous Search**, allows you to use both simple strings and regular expressions to quickly and easily find search terms. Because of its speed, having to index a case in order to perform various searches is rarely needed.

After covering **Simultaneous Search**, we covered creating and using an index as well as various ways to perform both text and hex searches.

With the knowledge you have gained in this chapter, you are equipped with the skills necessary to find data regardless of where it is in your evidence.

Advanced Use of X-Ways Forensics

INTRODUCTION

The topics covered in this chapter are advanced not in the sense that they are harder to use than other areas of X-Ways Forensics (XWF), but rather that they cover areas that some users may not use regularly. The intention of this chapter is to lay bare some of the more difficult to understand or esoteric features of XWF in such a way that the widest possible audience can benefit from them.

XWF comes with an extensive collection of file signatures and types, so many in fact that you may never have to add your own. Should you find yourself in a position where the defaults do not include a signature for your particular requirements, this chapter details how to add and preserve your customizations. Users are encouraged to send their customizations to the XWF developers for possible inclusion in a future release of XWF.

After covering file customization options, we will discuss several other unique features of XWF such as various options for interacting with raw data, timeline analysis, collecting ambient data such as free or slack space, and RAM analysis. This chapter concludes with a discussion of the different ways to automate XWF through scripts or the application programming interface (API).

CUSTOMIZING X-WAYS FORENSICS CONFIGURATION FILES

XWF comes with several text-based configuration files that let you add to the already robust number of file types and file signatures provided with the program. These files are updated regularly by the XWF developers and are included in the XWF zip file.

There are two locations where these configuration files can be stored: in the XWF program directory or in a directory in a user's profile.

Each of the configuration files discussed below are tab delimited. Using a program such as Microsoft Excel makes customizing these files much easier as it will create separate columns for each section of the configuration files. Since the files are plain text, any text editor will work as well, but we recommend using a text editor that allows for visualizing TAB characters so the file layout remains consistent. UltraEdit (http://www.ultraedit.com/) and Edit Pad Pro (http://www.editpadpro.com/) are two very capable text editors that have this capability (among many others).

XWF directory-based configuration files

This configuration is used by default in a new installation of XWF. Recall in Chapter 1 that XWF is a portable application and as such does not require a traditional installation. *Directory based* means the configuration files live in the same directory as the XWF executables.

User profile-based configuration files

This configuration type is used in two scenarios: when a user runs XWF from a directory where the user does not have write permission or when the behavior is forced. To force XWF to store its configuration files under the user's profile, create an empty file named *winhex.user* in the XWF directory.

It can be necessary to store this configuration in the user profile tree "necessarily" if no write permission exist to the program folder or "forced" by the user (if *winhex. user* is present). The reason why XWF stored its configuration files in the user profile directory can be seen in the About dialog via **Help | About X-Ways Forensics**.

The default location for XWF to store its configuration files when in user profile mode is *%USERPROFILE%\AppData\Local\X-Ways*<directory from which XWF was executed>. For example, if you execute *C:\xwf\xwforensics64.exe*, the complete path to the user profile configurations would be *%USERPROFILE% \AppData\Local\X-Ways\xwf*.

XWF will automatically create several files in the user profile directory to keep track of such things as the **Name** column filter as well as the last used search terms. It will also create a *WinHex.cfg* file in the same folder.

When in user profile mode, XWF will load certain configuration files from this location by default. When this is the case, it will be indicated in each configuration file's section below.

File Type Categories.txt

This configuration file is used for several purposes including creating categories of file types, assigning ranks to file types, and assigning groups to file types. The layout of the file is straightforward, but for complete details, see the XWF manual.

Assigning ranks

Ranks range from 0 to 9 with 0 being the default if a file is not given an explicit rank. Higher ranks denote more important file types across a wider variety of cases. To assign a file type a rank, insert a TAB character at the end of the file's type description and then enter a number from 0 to 9. Only one rank can be assigned to a file type at a time.

Assigning groups

Groups are used to bundle several file types together. They serve as a way to select one or more file extensions as a whole as opposed to selecting several individual file extensions from different categories. Groups also let you assign a meaningful name to them such as "Hacking related" or "Encryption stuff."

Group names can optionally be specified at the bottom of *File Type Categories .txt* (*FTC*) and take the form

```
=Group designator=Group description
```

where Group designator is a single alpha character. For example, the two groups above would be defined as:

```
=E=Encryption stuff
=H=Hacking related
```

A group can be assigned to one or more file types by appending the group designator to a file type in the same way you did for a rank. Ranks and groups are not dependent on each other, so an extension does not need a rank in order to assign it to a group (recall however that an extension without an explicit rank is considered Rank 0). Figure 7.1 illustrates several groups as well as file types assigned ranks and groups.

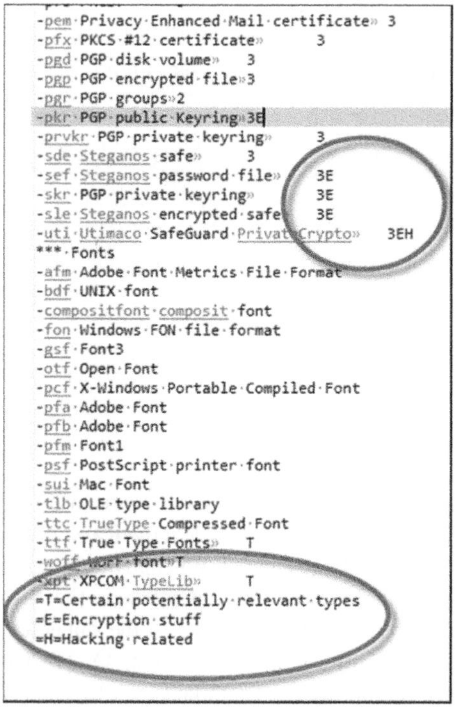

FIGURE 7.1

File Type Categories.txt groups and ranks.

While creating groups is optional, if you do create your own groups, they must be added at the bottom of *FTC*.

The effects of FTC customization

Every time the **Type** filter in the **Directory Browser** is changed, *FTC* is saved to disk. If you open the file in an editor, any items that are checked in the **Type** filter dialog will be prefixed with a plus sign. Unchecked items are prefixed with a minus sign.

Two options exist for loading customizations to *FTC*.

- Copy the default *FTC* to a different name, customize it as needed, and load it via the **Directory Browser**'s **Type** column filter dialog. For example, you can check BMP, JPG, and JPEG in the **Type** filter box and then, from the dialog, save your filter as a file named *Graphics Filter*.
- Copy the *FTC* to your user profile folder and XWF will load it by default. When using this method, be aware any updates by the developers of XWF will not be present unless the copy of *FTC* in the user profile directory is updated manually.

By saving your customizations to a different filename or keeping your customizations under your user profile, you guarantee your changes won't get overwritten when upgrading XWF.

The contents of *FTC* affect what is shown in the **Type**, **Type status**, **Type descr.**, and **Category** columns of the **Directory Browser**.

Once you have customized *FTC*, you can filter by rank and group via the **Type status** column filter in the **Directory Browser**. Figure 7.2 shows the **Type status** filter dialog.

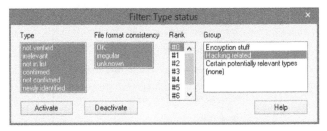

FIGURE 7.2

Type status filter dialog.

To filter the **Directory Browser** by group, select one or more **Groups** from the list and click **Activate**. Note that you must also select the **Rank** of the files (files without a rank inherit rank 0) for them to be displayed. When in doubt, select all ranks. The same is true of the **Type** and **File format consistency** lists in that accurate values must be selected in those lists for files to be displayed in the **Directory Browser**. In other words, all four of the options are combined via logical *AND* to determine the final filter while the items in each option list are combined with logical *OR*.

File Type Signatures Check Only.txt

This configuration file is used when the **Refine Volume Snapshot** (RVS) option **Verify file types with signatures and algorithms** is selected. It too is a plain text, tab-separated file. The layout for this file is more complex than *FTC*. See the XWF manual for complete details.

Additional signatures can be added to this file by using the **Signatures** button in the RVS dialog next to **Verify file types with signatures and algorithms**. You can also edit the file directly.

Any signatures added to this file will be used for file type verification only.

XWF TIPS AND TRICKS

Don't Lose Your Customizations!

If you customize either of the File Type Signatures files, be sure to save it as a new file and do not overwrite the default file. The reason for this is that when upgrading to a new version of XWF, your changes will be overwritten as a results of the upgrade. To avoid this, create a file with file mask *File Type Signatures *.txt*.

For example, if you wish to customize *File Type Signatures Check Only.txt*, create a file named *File Type Signatures Check Only Custom.txt* and add your customizations to that file. If you wish to customize *File Type Signatures Search.txt*, create a file named *File Type Signatures Search Custom.txt* and add your customizations to that file.

If the file name contains the word *search*, the entries in the file will be used for RVS option **File header signature search**. Without the word *search* in the file name, the File Type Signatures will only be used for file type verification and not carving. This distinction can be important, so choose wisely. Up to 4096 signatures are supported, so there is plenty of room for customizations.

File Type Signatures Search.txt

This configuration file is used when the RVS option **File header signature search** is used. It too is a plain text, tab-separated file. The layout for this file is identical to *File Type Signatures Check Only.txt* file. One additional possibility for this file is the inclusion of categories. The categories work in the same way as *FTC* in that they group a related set of file types.

Additional signatures can be added to this file by using the **Signatures** button in the RVS dialog next to **File header signature search**. You can also edit the file directly. As covered in Chapter 4, if you choose to edit the file via the **File Header Search** dialog as part of an RVS operation, you must close this dialog and reopen it for the changes to take effect.

Any signatures added to this file will be used for file carving.

MANEUVERING IN HEX

In Chapter 3, we covered the mode buttons, such as **Volume/Partition** and **File** modes. In either of these modes, data are displayed in hexadecimal/text.

When in either of these modes, you can interact with data in several ways, from manually carving files by selecting blocks of data to interpreting data directly by converting it to different formats.

XWF TIPS AND TRICKS

Hex, Text, or Both!

When viewing data in **Volume/Partition** or **File** mode, the default view includes both a hex display and a text display. You can use **View I Text Display Only** and **View I Hex Display Only** to toggle the corresponding view depending on your needs.

Data Interpreter

To reiterate, when in **Volume/Partition** or **File** mode, data are displayed in hex/text. Clicking different values when in these modes changes which hex character is active. The active hex character will, by default, be highlighted with a blue rectangle.

Data often are stored in binary as opposed to ASCII (text), and it may be necessary to decode blocks of binary data into an easy-to-understand format. XWF automatically decodes many of the most popular formats and displays them in the **Data Interpreter** as shown in Figure 7.3. If you do not see the **Data Interpreter** window, click **View | Show | Data Interpreter**.

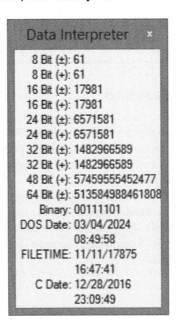

FIGURE 7.3

Data Interpreter.

The most important thing to know about the **Data Interpreter** is that XWF interprets the data *from the position of the cursor regardless of any block of data that are* *selected.* In other words, if you select eight bytes (16 hex characters from left to right) that make up a timestamp, the data will not be interpreted as a block. Rather, simply click the *first* byte/hex character in the timestamp and XWF will do the rest. By default, the **Data Interpreter** employs little-endian order, but it can be changed to big-endian by right clicking within the box (see below).

XWF TIPS AND TRICKS

52 65 66 65 72 65 6e 63 65 20 74 61 62 6c 65 73 21

Should you need them, several cross-reference tables are available via the **View I Tables** menu including decimal to hexadecimal, hex to ASCII, and hex to a user-selected code page. In addition to these tables, XWF also includes a hexadecimal converter that can be accessed via **Tools I Hex converter**.

To change what is displayed (or the format the data are displayed in) in the **Data Interpreter**, right click the left side of the window and a context menu will appear. Selecting **Options** will bring up a dialog where you can add or remove various formats as shown in Figure 7.4.

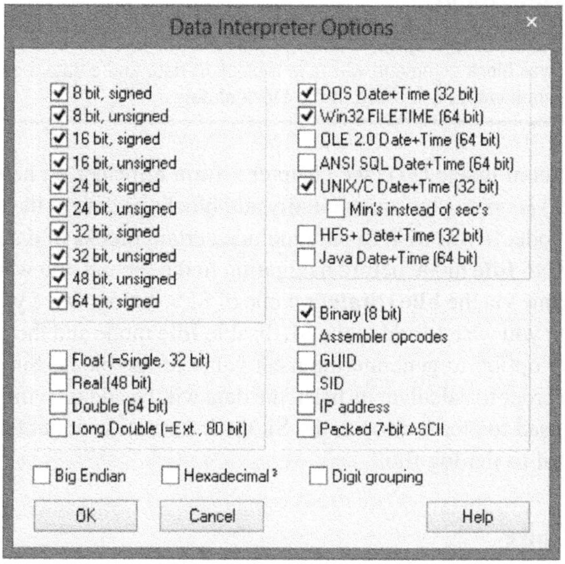

FIGURE 7.4

Data Interpreter options.

If you close the **Data Interpreter** window while changing options as shown in Figure 7.4, it can be displayed again by clicking **View | Show | Data Interpreter**.

The **Hexadecimal** option toggles between three numeric systems:

Fully checked: Hexadecimal
Half-checked: Octal
Unchecked: Decimal

Digit grouping, when checked, will add separators when the data are using the decimal numeric system (i.e., 6000000 vs. 6,000,000).

Defining blocks of data

Before you can interact with data beyond a single byte, the data have to be selected and, as with other areas in XWF, there are several ways to do so.

The simplest way is to use the mouse to select a block of data. To do so, left click and hold the button down and then drag the mouse to the end of the block to highlight the data in which you are interested. In XWF terms, this is a "block" of data. Alternatively, you can right click and use the relevant block commands from the context menu: *Beginning of block* and *End of block*.

Keyboard warriors can set the start of a block with **ALT+1** and the end of the block with **ALT+2**. The **ESC** key will clear any selected block.

XWF TIPS AND TRICKS
Block Statistics the Easy Way
The **Tools | Analyze block** command will take a block of data and create a bar graph for all unique hexadecimal values contained in the block of data.

When a skeleton image (SI) (see Chapter 2 for a refresher on how to work with skeleton images) is open, you can manually add blocks of data to the skeleton image when in **Disk** mode. If you wish to only include certain blocks of data in your SI, be sure to set the SI to **Idle** mode before navigating to the sectors you want to include in the SI. This is done via the **File | State**/<name of SI> dialog. Once you have defined the block of data you wish to add to the SI, disable **Idle** mode and then use the **Tools | Compute Hash** option to generate the hash value of the block. Since XWF has to read the data in order to calculate its hash, the data will be added to the SI. Depending on the options used to create or open the SI, the information about the block of data will be appended to the log file.

User search hits

You can arbitrarily add data to "search hits" regardless of whether the "hit" was found by traditional methods. A user search hit can be created on a given block of data when in **Volume/Partition** or **File** mode. To create a user search hit, simply select a range of bytes, right click, and choose **Add to User search hits** as shown in Figure 7.5. A dialog will be display allowing you to name the search hit.

```
30 31 20 4A 61  6E 20 31 39 38 30 20 3
3A 30 30 20
41 20 48 54
61 67 6D 61
6F 2D 63 61
41 20 4E   1
45 52 2D 55
22 68 74 74
```

Beginning of block	Alt+1
End of block	Alt+2
Add to User search hits...	
Add Block as Virtual File...	
Add Position...	
Edit	

FIGURE 7.5

Adding a user search hit.

Once a block is added as a user search hit, it will be available in the **Search Term List**. User search hits are distinguished from other search hits by appending an asterisk to the name given to the user search hit as seen in Figure 7.6.

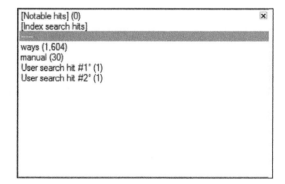

```
[Notable hits] (0)                                    ⊠
[Index search hits]

ways (1,604)
manual (30)
User search hit #1° (1)
User search hit #2° (1)
```

FIGURE 7.6

Search Term List with two user search hits.

Add Block as Virtual File will be covered below, and **Add Position** allows you to add the block of data to the **Position Manager** as discussed in Chapter 6.

Other options

In addition to adding a block of data as a user search hit, several other options are available after selecting **Edit** from the context menu as shown in Figure 7.7.

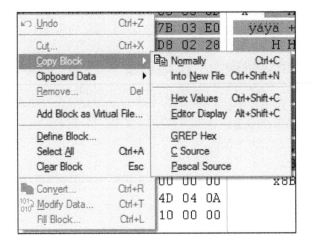

FIGURE 7.7

Edit context menu.

In addition to the options that behave like most Windows programs (Undo, Cut, Select All, etc.), several options of note exist under **Copy Block**.

Hex Values: The selected data are copied to the clipboard without any separators. For example, if *FF FA A1 10* is selected, *FFFAA110* will be copied to the clipboard.

Editor Display: The selected data, along with corresponding offsets and column headers, are copied to the clipboard, much like a screenshot.

GREP Hex: The selected data are copied to the clipboard in GREP format (\xDE\x2F\xA9...). This is useful because it can be used in a **Simultaneous Search** without any additional formatting.

Add Block as Virtual File allows for adding the block of data to the case as a virtual file as opposed to simply listing it as a search hit. This is useful because it also allows you to add the virtual file to report tables. When a report is generated, the virtual file containing the block of data is exported (assuming the relevant reporting option to do so is active) and linked to in the report. Without this capability, you would have to add a comment indicating where the data are and what they are, or take a screenshot and then manually incorporate it into your report.

The location at which the virtual file will be created depends on the mode. When in **Volume/Partition** mode, the virtual file will be created under the virtual directory *Path unknown**Carved files*. When in **File** mode, the virtual file will be created as a child object of the file selected in the **Directory Browser**.

Once the virtual file is added to the volume snapshot, the full range of XWF capabilities can be brought to bear against it, including a RVS operation, adding the file to a report table or simply adding a comment.

Sector superimposition

Consider the case where a disk is recovered and certain key sectors are damaged. In most cases, XWF will still be able to determine the file system and display its contents automatically, but in some cases even XWF will be unable to do so.

By taking a closer look at the data in **Volume/Partition** mode, it may be obvious as to what the problem is, but how can you fix the error without altering your evidence?

XWF solves this problem with the unique ability to superimpose data on top of data in an image. In our example above, if the sectors containing the master boot record (MBR) were damaged and you knew which bits were damaged, you could select the sectors that comprise the MBR and copy them to a new file outside of XWF.

After correcting the errors in the newly created file, use the **Edit | Superimpose sectors** menu item and select the corrected file. XWF will then virtually "replace" the damaged sectors with the sectors in the selected file and the changes will be reflected in **Volume/Partition** or **File** mode. The same menu item removes the superimposition as well.

Once the superimposition is in place, refresh the view and XWF will use the new data when interpreting the superimposed sector(s). Depending on the kind of damage that was repaired, XWF may create an initial volume snapshot. Once XWF finishes creating the initial volume snapshot, a new image can be created that incorporates the fixed data permanently. If you choose to create a new forensic image, be sure to document it accordingly.

Sector superimposition is a powerful option that can make working with damaged media a lot easier. As its name implies, sector superimposition only works on complete and not on partial sectors.

Templates

When in **Volume/Partition** mode, an extra button (a down arrow) is available to the right of the hex column headers as shown in Figure 7.8. This button allows you to

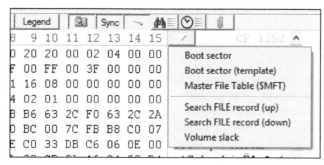

FIGURE 7.8

Template button.

quickly jump to key areas of the Volume/Partition such as the boot sector, master file table, etc. Another function of the button is to view certain critical areas of the Volume/Partition in a way that is easier to understand as key sections of the data are broken down into individual pieces.

For example, it is possible to manually determine the different parameters present in the boot sector of a given volume by selecting the bytes that make up each parameter and making note of their values. For more common operations, XWF comes with prebuilt templates that automate this manual process. Figure 7.9 shows the boot sector template for the active volume.

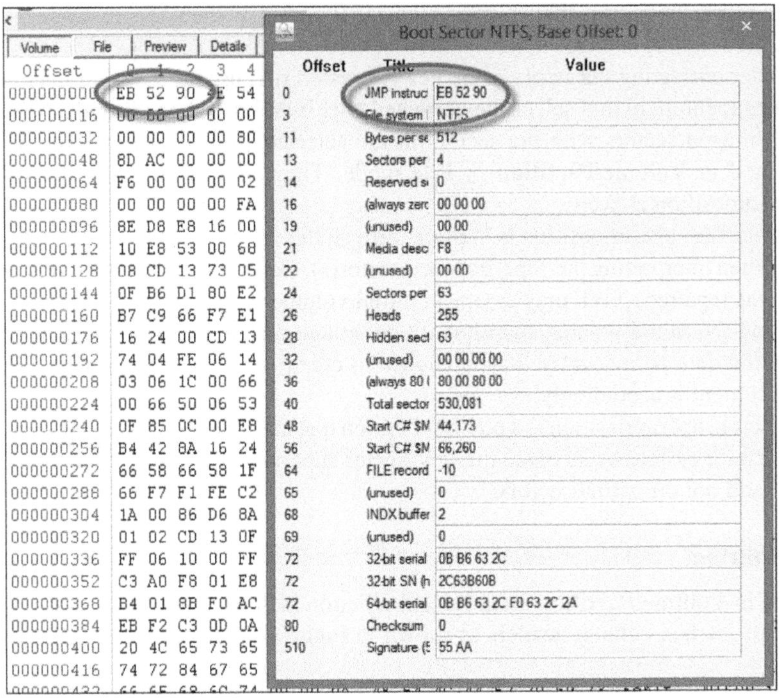

FIGURE 7.9

Boot sector template next to raw data.

XWF ships with no fewer than 13 templates that can decode such things as boot sectors, Inodes, directory entries, and volume headers for various file systems.

Templates are plain text files that contain rules for how to parse certain data structures. A list of available templates can be seen in the **Template Manager** (TM) that is accessed via **View | Template Manager** or **ALT+F12**. The TM can be used to create, edit, or delete templates.

The NTFS FILE record template is particularly useful in that it will decode all of the pieces of the FILE record into human readable form (such as all the timestamps, etc.). Figure 7.10 shows a partial view of an NTFS FILE record.

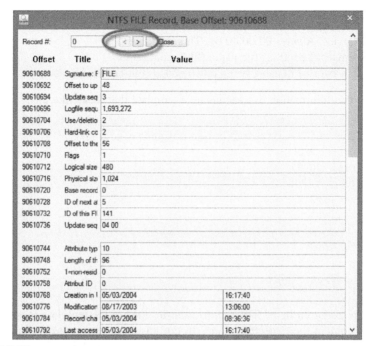

FIGURE 7.10

NTFS FILE record template.

Notice the navigation arrows (circled) at the top of the template. These allow you to quickly navigate to the next FILE record in the MFT.

To create a template, you must understand the binary layout of a file. Once you have the layout, you can begin building a template to decode the file.

You can create and edit templates directly from XWF with the **Template Manager** or, since the templates are plain text, you can use any text editor.

Once you have your file-based template defined, switch to **File** mode, bring up the **Template Manager**, select your template, and click **Apply**.

As an example, consider the binary file shown in Figure 7.11.

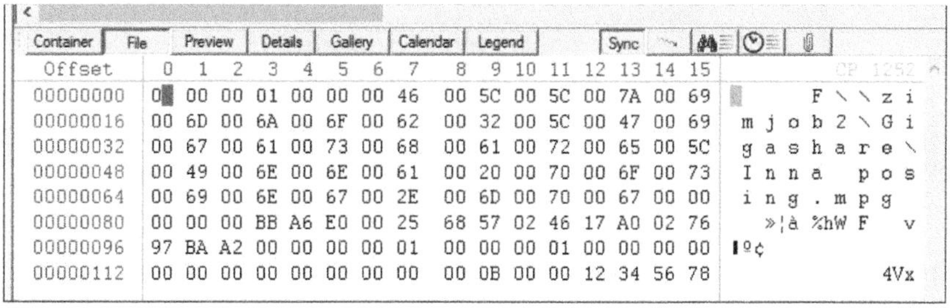

```
<
 Container | File | Preview | Details | Gallery | Calendar | Legend |        Sync          |
 Offset      0  1  2  3  4  5  6  7    8  9 10 11 12 13 14 15              CP 1252
00000000     0  00 00 01 00 00 00 46   00 5C 00 5C 00 7A 00 69                   F \ \ z i
00000016     00 6D 00 6A 00 6F 00 62   00 32 00 5C 00 47 00 69      m j o b 2 \ G i
00000032     00 67 00 61 00 73 00 68   00 61 00 72 00 65 00 5C      g a s h a r e \
00000048     00 49 00 6E 00 6E 00 61   00 20 00 70 00 6F 00 73      I n n a   p o s
00000064     00 69 00 6E 00 67 00 2E   00 6D 00 70 00 67 00 00      i n g . m p g
00000080     00 00 00 BB A6 E0 00 25   68 57 02 46 17 A0 02 76      »¦à %hW F   v
00000096     97 BA A2 00 00 00 00 01   00 00 00 01 00 00 00 00      |º¢
00000112     00 00 00 00 00 00 00 00   00 0B 00 00 12 34 56 78                   4Vx
```

FIGURE 7.11

Binary file.

This is a Gigatribe .state file and the first three sections of this file are defined as:

- First 4 bytes: Always 00 00 00 01. This is the header
- Next 4 bytes: Length of file name (little-endian)
- Next XX bytes: Filename being downloaded (big-endian Unicode)

Based on this information, we can create a template that looks like this:

```
template "Gigatribe 3 .state"
description "Demonstrate template for part of a .state file"
fixed_start 0x00
requires 0x00 "00"
requires 0x01 "00"
requires 0x02 "00"
requires 0x03 "01"
begin
hex 4 "Header"
big-endian int32 "Filename length"
big-endian zstring16 "Filename"
end
```

So what is going on here? The *requires* entries ensure the template is applied to files that contain the expected values. In our case, the four *requires* lines check for 0 values in the first three bytes of the file and a value of 1 in the fourth byte. If the template is applied to a file where these four things are not true, XWF will display a warning. We grab the first 4 bytes in hexadecimal and name the field *Header*. The next 4 bytes (in big-endian) are the *Filename length* field. Finally, we tell XWF to look for a big-endian null-terminated Unicode string and this is the *Filename* field.

If we apply the template to a .state file, XWF displays the information broken down as shown in Figure 7.12.

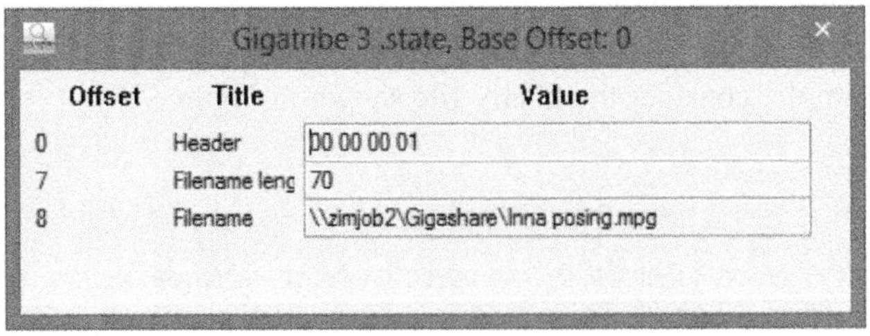

Offset	Title	Value
0	Header	00 00 00 01
7	Filename leng	70
8	Filename	\\zimjob2\Gigashare\Inna posing.mpg

Gigatribe 3 .state, Base Offset: 0

FIGURE 7.12

.state template example.

Appendix A in the XWF manual contains the syntax for creating or editing templates, including all of the data types available.

TIMELINE AND EVENT ANALYSIS

XWF contains several mechanisms to allow for viewing data contextually as it relates to last modified, last accessed, and created (MAC) dates. XWF also can provide a more comprehensive timeline based on timestamps retrieved from object metadata. Both have their uses depending on the needs of your investigation and both complement each other's abilities to paint a complete timeline of the activity in a given case.

Calendar mode

Calendar mode works by building a graph that visually displays the MAC dates of one or more files selected in the **Directory Browser**. When in **Calendar** mode, a spreadsheet-like graph is displayed where the numbers across the top represent the month of the year and the numbers down the left represent the days of the month.

Figure 7.13 shows the results of selecting one file in the **Directory Browser** and switching to **Calendar** mode.

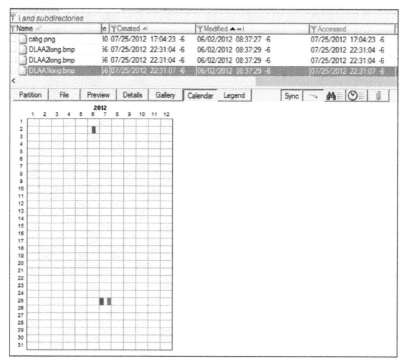

FIGURE 7.13

Calendar mode with a single file selected.

While you cannot tell from the screenshot, XWF uses different colors to represent modified (green), accessed (blue), and created (red) dates. These colors are reflected in both the graph and in the **Directory Browser** window. In Figure 7.13, the topmost block represents the modified date, the bottom left block represents the created on date, and the right block represents the last accessed date (the created and accessed dates are the same). Hovering over any of the blocks displays the full timestamp for the calendar entry.

Calendar mode is useful when you already have a general timeframe of interest and want to visually depict file activity. By filtering the **Directory Browser** on one of the MAC date columns, selecting one or more files in the **Directory Browser**, and switching to **Calendar** mode, you can easily see the time of day where files were changed. Figure 7.14 is an example of **Calendar** mode with several thousand files selected.

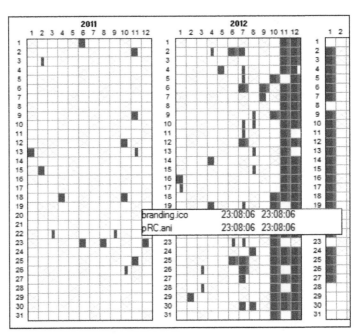

FIGURE 7.14

Calendar mode with tooltip.

When a graph that is pertinent to your case is found, it can be added as a log entry by right clicking the graph, selecting **Add log entry**, and entering a narrative to associate with the graph. This log entry will be added to the case's activity log that can later be included in an XWF report as shown in Figure 7.15.

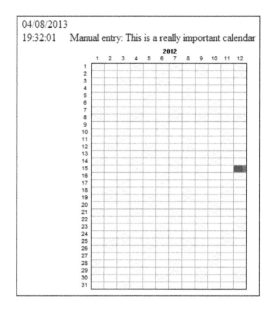

FIGURE 7.15

Log entry for calendar graph.

Events view

Switching to **Events** view is similar to switching to the **Search Hit List** view. Figure 7.16 shows the **Events** view button.

FIGURE 7.16

Events view button.

An initial volume snapshot will contain no events, and as such, switching to **Events** view prior to performing a RVS will result in an empty list.

To populate the **Events** list, you must run a RVS. Specifically, the **Extract internal metadata, browser history, and events** option must be enabled in the RVS for events to be generated. Recall from Chapter 4 that this option is responsible for extracting things like internal file timestamps, browser history, e-mail, file system journals, shortcut (.lnk) file data, etc. Because XWF is enhanced so frequently, we cannot provide a complete list of all the objects from which events are extracted. If we try, our list will be outdated by the time you read this. For a complete list of the types of files XWF extracts events from, see the most current XWF manual.

Before we populate events, let's take a look at the additional columns available in the **Directory Browser** when in **Events** view: **Timestamp**, (event) **Type**, (event) **Category**, and **Description**.

The **Timestamp** column contains the date and time extracted from metadata. As with other date-based columns, a filter is available for this column.

The (event) **Type** column describes where the data in the **Timestamp** column were found and, at the time of this writing, contains more than 40 different event types. Do not confuse this column with the (file) **Type** filter that we have studied earlier. The (event) **Type** column is related to the **Category** column in that it describes a more granular event inside the more general **Category** column. A filter is also available for this column and allows for selecting only the types of events you are interested in seeing (*Registry: Key changed* for example).

The (event) **Category** is a higher level group than the **Type** column. Examples of categories include *Registry*, *File system*, *internal file metadata*, *Internet*, etc.

The **Description** column is populated for certain events, but not others. The **Description** column is used to convey more specific information about what is in the **Category** and **Type** columns.

For example, in the case of a *Registry* event, the **Description** column would contain such things as the key that the **Timestamp** column corresponds with, whereas in the case of an *Internet* event, it would contain the URL with which that **Timestamp** and **Type** correspond.

As mentioned earlier, to populate the list, perform an RVS on one or more evidence objects using the necessary options.

Once events have been generated, click on the **Events** view button. Some of the columns in the **Directory Browser** will be the same as in **Calendar** mode including the MAC dates, size, etc.

After selecting one or more events from the **Events** list, XWF will generate graphs exactly as we saw in **Calendar** mode.

The power of **Events** view is that it incorporates many, many more sources of time-stamps than just the file system's MAC dates which traditionally serve as the basis for timeline analysis. The weakness to the traditional approach is that timestamps can be altered with little effort. XWF has pioneered a new approach to timeline analysis that removes this pitfall and provides insights into the activities on a system that is not possible with other tools.

Another benefit of **Events** view is that it allows you correlate and cross-reference data in a similar context that simply is not possible with traditional timeline analysis. By digging into the internals of files and extracting metadata that are difficult to change, XWF provides a new and powerful way to interpret data as they relate to a wide range of activities on a computer.

Be sure to read the XWF release notes closely as many new events are sure to be added regularly to this unique feature.

GATHERING FREE AND SLACK SPACE

The **Specialist** menu contains several options that allow you to export certain data to files that can then be further analyzed or used for such things as brute-forcing pass-words. XWF can gather four different kinds of data as seen in Figure 7.17.

FIGURE 7.17

Specialist menu highlighting Gather options.

Gather Free Space will collect all unused clusters from the active logical drive and save this data into a file. You can split the files into chunks depending on how much free space is present.

Gather Slack Space will gather the slack space of every file in the active logical drive. The resulting file will contain a reference to the cluster where the slack data were found. After selecting this menu item, several other options are presented. The **Strip initial zero bytes from all occurrences of slack space** option removes all instances of 0x00 from the beginning of slack space. Using this option can reduce the amount of data contained in the file because a cluster's slack space leading zero-byte values will be removed. **Mask non-printable characters** replaces all non-printable hexadecimal characters with a space character (hex 20). Using this option makes it easier to pick out strings.

Gather Inter-Partition Space collects data from all sectors on a hard disk that is not allocated to a partition.

Gather Text is similar to running the UNIX *strings* command on the active logical drive in that XWF will only gather printable strings and save them to a file. Invoking this option results in a dialog box being displayed that allows you to adjust the type of strings XWF will gather. The resulting file will contain one string per line.

Regardless of the gather command you choose, the file containing the data will be opened and displayed in XWF's **tab control**.

RAM ANALYSIS

RAM analysis is an advanced discipline that requires a degree of experience and technical knowledge. This section will not explain how data are stored in RAM or techniques to discover rootkits or the like. Rather, it will focus on XWF's ability to view memory dumps.

XWF primarily supports memory analysis on 32-bit versions of Windows for memory dumps up to 4 GB in size. XWF also contains limited support for certain 64-bit versions of Windows.

XWF is capable of imaging memory when executed on 32-bit Windows 2000 or Windows XP systems. For all other systems, we recommend using Moonsols DumpIt, winpmem, or similar. For other operating systems, memory can be imaged when XWF is used in conjunction with F-Response as discussed in Chapter 2. XWF can also decompress *hiberfil.sys* files that it finds as part of a RVS and add the decompressed version to the case as a memory dump automatically.

After capturing memory, you can add it to XWF like any other evidence object by right clicking the case root folder and selecting **Add Memory Dump**. As we saw when opening a disk, XWF will traverse the memory object and generate an initial volume snapshot.

Navigating a memory dump in XWF is very similar to navigating any other evidence object. XWF will create folders for such things as modules and objects. Figure 7.18 shows a RAM dump after the initial volume snapshot.

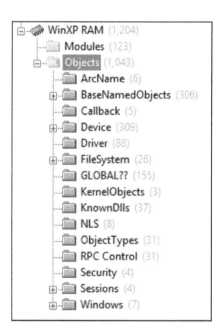

FIGURE 7.18

Initial RAM presentation.

As seen at the top of Figure 7.18, there are currently 1204 items in the evidence object. Like any other evidence object, the RVS process can be used on a memory capture in order to find additional items. When performing an RVS, we recommend using the following options:

- Particularly thorough file system data structure search
- File header signature search
- Extract internal metadata, browser history, and events
- Extract embedded data in miscellaneous file types

Using these options will recover additional items from RAM dumps and extract information from those items. Select the file header signatures that are relevant to your investigation.

After performing an RVS using the above options, there are 2849 items in the volume snapshot as shown in Figure 7.19.

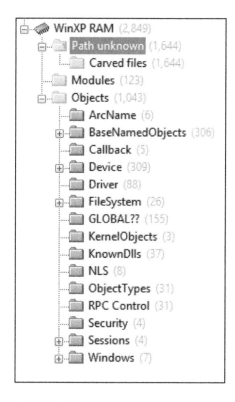

FIGURE 7.19

RAM after RVS.

After RVS, we see a new virtual folder named *Path unknown* that contains a *Carved files* folder. *Carved files* is where XWF adds any items it recovered during the RVS process. Artifacts XWF can recover from memory include pictures, registry hives, programs, videos, documents, IP packets (both TCP and UDP), Windows event files, Windows shortcut (.lnk) files, Prefetch files, etc. Figure 7.20 shows the **Category** filter in the **Directory Browser**, which breaks down each type of artifact found in the memory dump.

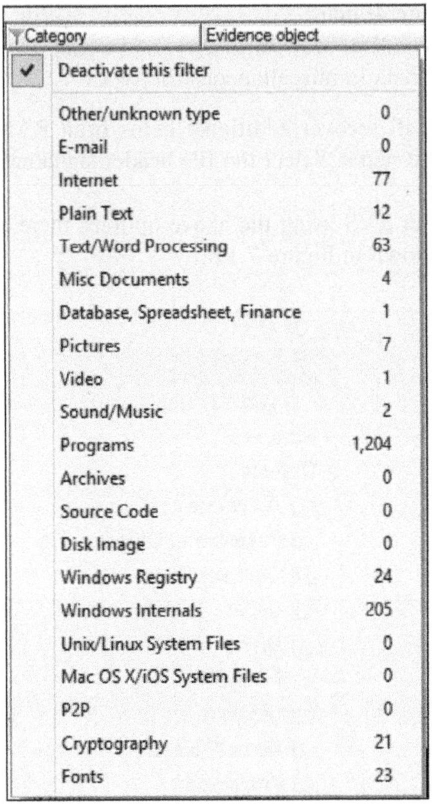

Category	Evidence object	
✔	Deactivate this filter	
Other/unknown type		0
E-mail		0
Internet		77
Plain Text		12
Text/Word Processing		63
Misc Documents		4
Database, Spreadsheet, Finance		1
Pictures		7
Video		1
Sound/Music		2
Programs		1,204
Archives		0
Source Code		0
Disk Image		0
Windows Registry		24
Windows Internals		205
Unix/Linux System Files		0
Mac OS X/iOS System Files		0
P2P		0
Cryptography		21
Fonts		23

FIGURE 7.20

RAM category breakdown.

We now can interact with these artifacts exactly as we have seen in previous chapters. When using **Simultaneous Search** (SS) against memory dumps, be sure to conduct a *physical* search versus a *logical* search. By default, a physical SS will stop after it finds first search hit. To list all search hits, check the **List search hits** option. When this option is checked, XWF will search the entire RAM dump and list any search hits in the **Search Term List** window at the bottom of the **directory tree**.

When analyzing memory, the mode buttons will be different, as shown in Figure 7.21.

FIGURE 7.21

Mode buttons when working with memory.

RAM mode is the equivalent of **Volume/Partition** mode when working with a disk-based image.

When in **Process** mode, XWF will gather and display memory on a per process basis in a contiguous fashion, much as it does when displaying a fragmented file.

The remaining buttons behave exactly as we have seen in previous chapters.

Finally, **Specialist | Technical Details Report** contains a wealth of information about the memory dump including the size of the memory dump, percentage of free memory, and the location in memory of key processes and data structures.

Opening memory from within XWF

When XWF is running, you can view the contents of process memory by using the **Tools | Open RAM** menu. Figure 7.22 shows the **View Main Memory** dialog.

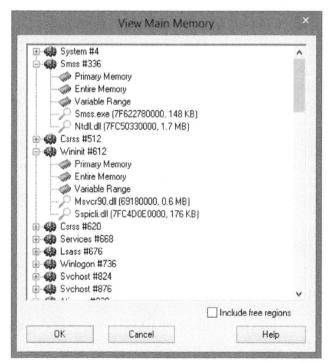

FIGURE 7.22

Open RAM dialog.

SCRIPTING, X-TENSIONS API, AND EXTERNAL ANALYSIS INTERFACE

While it is possible to automate certain tasks in XWF or extend the capabilities of XWF programmatically, doing so has less to do with using XWF and more to do with your ability to program. With that in mind, extensive coverage of these topics will not be presented.

Several example scripts are included in the default distribution and Appendix B in the XWF manual outlines the various commands that can be used in scripts.

Scripting

Since XWF and WinHex allow you to automate many common functions performed in the graphical user interface, we put together a demonstration script as seen below. Its functionality is commented throughout.

```
// The Practitioner's guide to X-Ways Forensics scripting demo
// Chapter 7
// Written by Eric Zimmerman
//Uncomment the next line to enable Debug mode
//Debug
// get things to a known state by closing all open windows
CloseAll
// Welcome the user
MessageBox "Hello and welcome to the scripting demo!"
// ask them to open a drive
MessageBox "After clicking OK, select a LOGICAL volume and not physical
media"
Open :?
//Display a simple menu
GetUserInputI WhatOperation "Init which? 1=Free space,2=MFT,3=Both"
IfEqual WhatOperation 1 //Clear out free space
JumpTo ClearFreeSpace
EndIf
IfEqual WhatOperation 2 //Clear out unused MFT records
JumpTo ClearMFT
EndIf
IfEqual WhatOperation 3 //Clear out both
JumpTo All
EndIf
// This is here in case the user does not enter one of our item #s
JumpTo AllDone
// These are not necessarily needed, but are here to demonstrate how to
reuse blocks of functionality
Label ClearFreeSpace
InitFreeSpace
```

```
JumpTo AllDone
Label ClearMFT
InitMFTRecords
JumpTo AllDone
Label All
InitFreeSpace
InitMFTRecords
JumpTo AllDone
// By creating a label for this, we can add additional stuff to it and it will
be used everywhere "JumpTo AllDone" is called from
Label AllDone
MessageBox "All done! OK to exit, Cancel to stay in WinHex"
// all done, so exit
Exit
```

X-Tensions

The X-Tensions API allows programmers to write programs that use XWF function-ality in an automated fashion. The complete X-Tensions reference is available at http://www.x-ways.net/forensics/x-tensions/api.html.

External analysis interface

The external analysis interface is another mechanism that can be implemented by pro-grammers to allow for the exporting of data from XWF to a third-party program for such things as categorization, etc. Once the external program has finished its proces-sing, the results can either be automatically or manually imported back into XWF.

In the **Case Data** window, select **Edit | Export Files for Analysis** as shown in Figure 7.23.

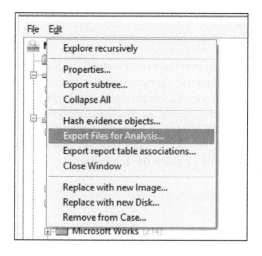

FIGURE 7.23

Export Files for Analysis menu.

As with using the **Recover/Copy** context menu in the **Directory Browser**, an entry is also created in the activity log when exporting files via **Export Files for Analysis**.

The options in the **Export Files for Analysis** dialog, shown in Figure 7.24, are straightforward and are similar to those we have seen in other places. After selecting **OK**, XWF exports the files to a subdirectory of the **Output folder**. The subdirectory's name is a unique CRC value that XWF and programs written to use the IEA will use at various stages of the process. In addition to the files exported from the case, XWF also creates an additional file named *Checksum* that contains additional information used in the IEA process. Once all of the files have been copied, the external analysis program is automatically executed against the files.

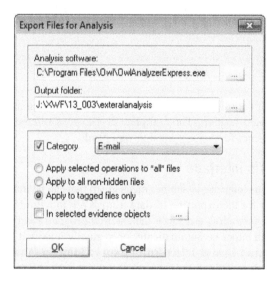

FIGURE 7.24

Export Files for Analysis.

In some cases, external programs can create files that XWF can use to import the results of this process back into the case. DoublePics (http://www.dotnetfabrik.de/de/doublepics) is an example of a program that is capable of doing this. In cases where programs do not have this capability, using **Export Files for Analysis** is useful in that it automatically starts the external software. Of course setting up an external viewer via the **Directory Browser**'s **Viewer Programs** context menu allows for the same thing, but in this case, files are exported to XWF's temporary directory (**General Options | Folder for temporary files**).

SHORTCUTS

ALT+1: Set the beginning of a data block
ALT+2: Set the end of a data block
ESC: Deselects all bytes in a block of data
ALT+F12: Display Template Manager

SUMMARY

In this chapter, we covered file customization, maneuvering in hex, and timeline analysis. We also touched on the different ways to automate and extend XWF via scripting and API.

We began by adding ranks and groups that allowed us to review a set of files that are pertinent to a particular type of investigation. From there, we moved on to cover various ways to interact with raw data, including selecting blocks of data and adding those blocks of data to the volume snapshot as virtual files.

We also saw how the **Data Interpreter** can be used to convert hexadecimal data into different human readable formats. In addition to being able to interpret hexadecimal values via the **Data Interpreter**, we explored how XWF employs the concept of templates that allow for automatically parsing and displaying chunks of data in a way that removes the risk of misinterpreting data since the template will always be applied to a block of data in a consistent way.

We then moved on to two ways that XWF allows for timeline analysis, **Calendar** mode and **Events** view. While both contain common aspects in how they present data, the data used to generate the timelines come from radically different sources.

We concluded this chapter with a reference to RAM analysis and the various ways to extend XWF programmatically via scripting or the XWF API.

X-Ways Forensics Reporting

INTRODUCTION

It is critical for examiners to have a means to convey the information they have found in an easy-to-generate and easy-to-understand format.

XWF's reporting capabilities center on the use of report tables (RTs) that can be thought of as bookmarks or categories of sorts. X-Ways Forensics (XWF) allows examiners to create up to 256 different RTs that can be assigned to one or more items in a case.

RTs allow examiners to logically organize their findings for review by their customers, be it prosecutors, peers, clients, etc. In addition to RTs, you can assign freeform comments to items to convey any information you desire.

At any point in the review process, XWF can generate a report of not only items that have been assigned to RTs but also, if enabled, the audit trail of the case.

XWF generates HTML-based reports that contain the contents of each selected RT in your case. Because the reports are HTML based, they are easy to edit using a simple text editor or even Microsoft Word.

ADDING ITEMS TO A REPORT TABLE

This chapter assumes you are working with a case that contains at least one evidence object. Once the case is open, locate some files of interest by whatever means you wish, such as a filter in the **Directory Browser** or simply selecting a directory from the **directory tree**.

To add the selected items to a RT, select **Report table associations** from the context menu as shown in Figure 8.1.

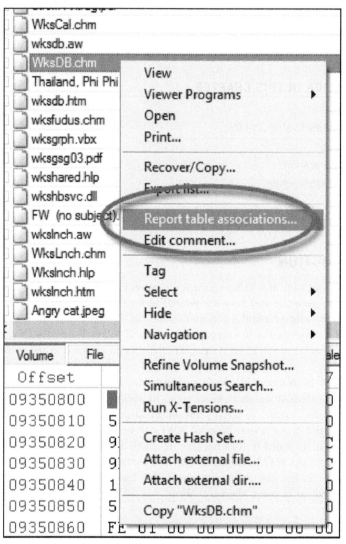

FIGURE 8.1

Adding an item to a report table.

The **Report table associations** dialog box will then be displayed as shown in Figure 8.2.

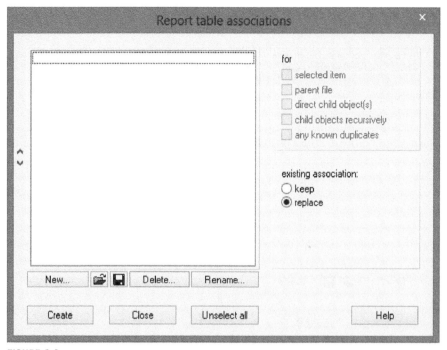

FIGURE 8.2

Report table associations dialog.

RT associations options

On the far left are two arrows that allow you to move RTs up and down in the list. Of course, you must have at least two RTs for this to be functional.

The large list box to the right of the arrows will contain RTs. When a new case is created, XWF initially contains no RTs, but as XWF performs various options such as a Refine Volume Snapshot (RVS), XWF may create one or more RTs that it assigns to certain files in the volume snapshot.

For example, if, during a RVS process, XWF finds an animated GIF graphic, it will create a RT named *animated GIF* and then assign the GIF to that RT. In addition, a message will be added to the **Messages** window informing you to manually review the file to determine if it is relevant to your case. A manual review is suggested because XWF cannot render the GIF in an animated fashion.

Any RTs created by XWF will be differentiated in two ways from user-created RTs (shown in black and are left justified): they will be indented and be light gray. Figure 8.3 shows an example of two user-created RTs and several XWF-created RTs.

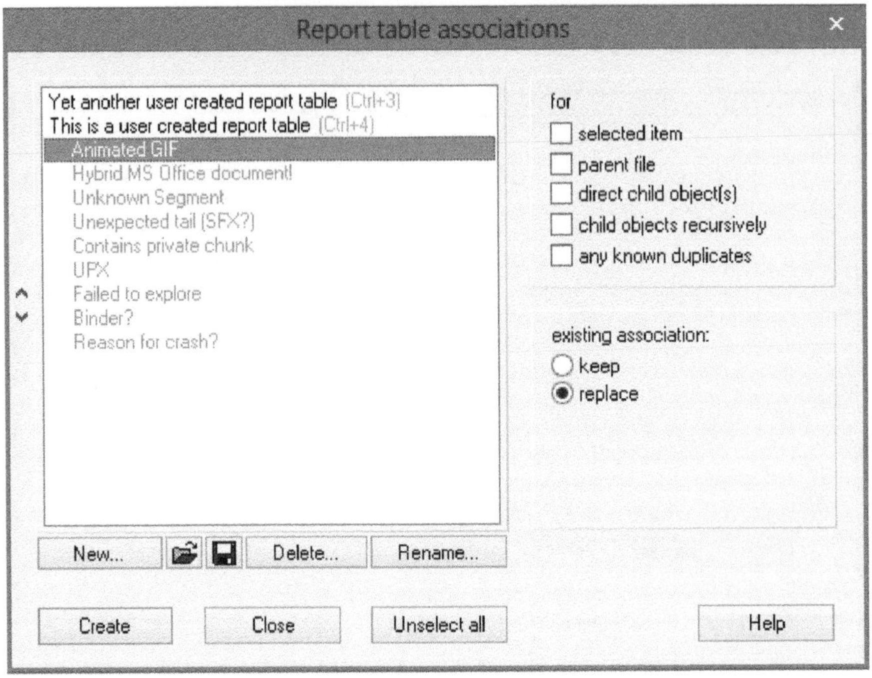

FIGURE 8.3

XWF- and user-created report tables.

Below the RT list are several buttons that allow you to create new RTs, open previously saved RTs, save selected RTs to a text file, delete the selected RTs, or rename the selected RTs.

XWF TIPS AND TRICKS

Save Time Creating RT Associations

When saving RTs, XWF will save each selected item on a separate line in a text file. This allows you to use any text editor to create RT templates for different kind of cases and then load the template file to quickly create RTs in a given case. This also allows multiple examiners to share templates which results in more standard reporting should the templates be stored in a shared directory.

On the right side of the dialog are two sets of options. The top option, **for**, controls the scope of what will be added to the selected RTs. Notice the use of checkboxes that allow you to select one or more of the options at once.

selected item: Adds only the items selected in the **Directory Browser** to the selected RTs.

parent file: Adds the parent file of the item selected in the **Directory Browser** to the chosen RTs. This is useful when exploring items with one or more child objects. If you decide one of the child objects is relevant and want to add the parent file to a RT, check this option.

direct child object(s): Adds a single generation of child objects of the highlighted items in the **Directory Browser** to the selected RTs. For example, if a zip file contained five PDF files that each contained three JPG images, only the five PDF files would be added to the selected RTs.

child objects recursively: Adds all generations of child objects of the highlighted items in the **Directory Browser** to the selected RTs. Reusing our example from above, this option would add the PDF files and all JPG images to the selected RTs.

any known duplicates: Adds all items with a hash value identical to one of the selected files in the **Directory Browser** to the selected RTs as well as any hard links. When a single file is selected and this option is used, the selected file will NOT be added to the RTs (even though the hash is the same) unless the **selected item** option is also checked. If more than one item with the same hash is highlighted, all identical items will be added to the selected RTs.

The bottom option, **existing association**, has two options:

keep: Adds the selected RTs to the items selected in the **Directory Browser**.

replace: Any existing RTs are removed and replaced with the selected RT associations.

At the very bottom of the dialog is a row of buttons that work as follows: The **Create** button will assign the selected RTs to any selected items in the **Directory Browser**, the **Close** button dismisses the dialog without associating any RTs, and **Unselect all** deselects all selected RTs.

Adding a new RT association

To add a new RT association, click the **New** button and enter a name for the RT. RT names must be unique, and if you enter a value that already exists, XWF will append a number to the end of the name.

As you add new RTs, notice a shortcut appears in parenthesis at the end of the RT's name as shown in Figure 8.4.

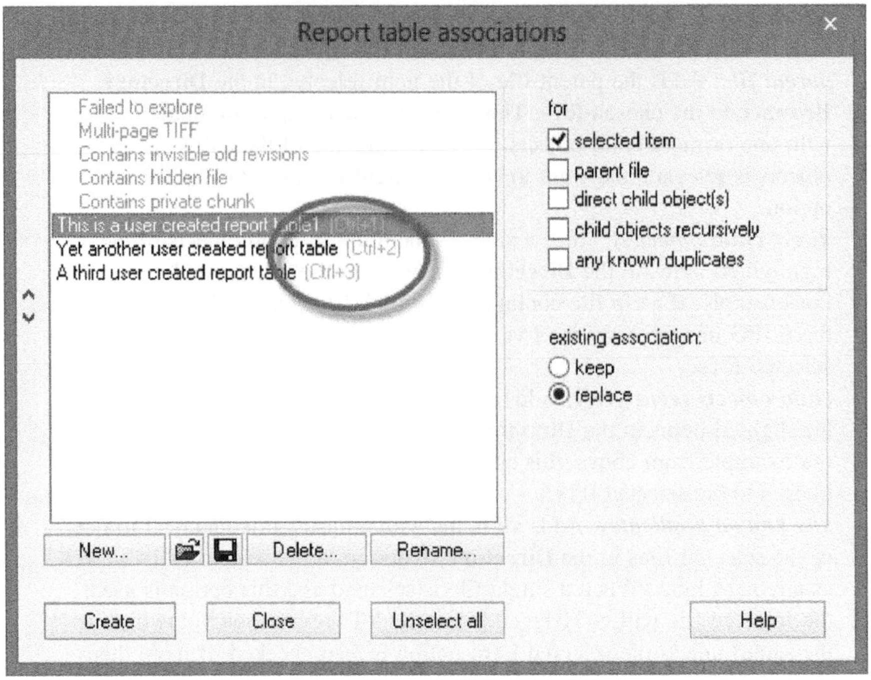

FIGURE 8.4

Report table association shortcuts.

These shortcuts can be used to quickly assign highlighted items in the **Directory Browser** to a given RT. If an item is already associated with one or more RTs, using the shortcut will add to or replace the existing RTs (depending on the value of **existing association**).

As an alternative to using a CTRL-based shortcut, on most computers you can use the numeric keypad and simply press a number without the need to hold CTRL.

If you create more than nine RTs in a single case, you will run out of automatically created RT shortcuts. To reassign a shortcut to a new RT, select the new RT and press the shortcut key combination you wish to use for a given RT. You can use either the CTRL-based or numeric-keypad-based approach to reassign shortcuts.

XWF TIPS AND TRICKS

Easy Come, Easy Go!

Not only it is very easy to add RT associations to items, but it is just as easy to remove associations from items by pressing either **CTRL+0** or simply 0 on the numeric keypad.

To actually assign items to a RT, select one or more RTs and click the **Create** button. This will assign the RTs to the items selected in the **Directory Browser**.

Meanwhile, back in the Directory Browser

Now that you have added items to one or more RTs, several options become available. If you do not have the **Report table** column visible in the **Directory Browser**, use the **Directory Browser Options**, **Filter** dialog to add it. The **Report table** column has a filter that allows for selecting one or more RTs along with the logic to be used to combine them as shown in Figure 8.5.

FIGURE 8.5

Report table filter options.

The +**siblings** option, when checked, will filter the items in the **Directory Browser** to also include any items that exist in the same directory as the items that are part of the selected RTs. This is useful to quickly find items that may be related to items already added to RTs to determine whether any additional items should be added to the RT.

For example, assume you find an item based on a hash value and you have added it to a RT. You then filter on the **Report table** column. With +**siblings** checked, all items in the same directory as the item you found via the hash match will be shown in the **Directory Browser**. You can then quickly look at these items and, if warranted, add these additional items to the hashed file's RT.

Another use for the **Report table** filter is to limit what is shown in the **Directory Browser** to a certain RT in order for those files to be **Recover/Copy'ed** to a directory without commingling files from other RTs. This allows for more flexibility when used in conjunction with the options we have already covered in Chapter 3 in relation to the **Recover/Copy** command.

Sharing RT associations

When splitting up the workload across multiple examiners (who work with copies of the same case or receive evidence file containers with selected files from the same case), there may be a need to share findings (both the RTs and their associated files) with other examiners. To allow for this, all RT associations can be exported or imported by using the options available by right clicking the case title as shown in Figure 8.6.

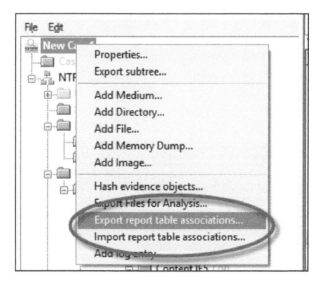

FIGURE 8.6

Export and import report table association options.

When exporting RT associations, you will be prompted to select a directory in which to save the .rtd files. Any existing .rtd files will be deleted, so take care not to lose any previously exported RT associations. To avoid this, we recommend exporting RT associations to a unique directory for the case.

When importing RT associations, select the directory containing the .rtd files. XWF will then import the files and add any files contained in the case to the relevant RTs.

COMMENTS

Comments serve as a way to add free-form information to one or more items that cannot be conveyed via some other means in XWF.

To add a comment, highlight one or more items in the **Directory Browser**, right click, and choose **Edit Comment** from the context menu. If more than one item is highlighted, XWF will ask whether to apply the comment to all of the highlighted items. Selecting **No** will apply the comment to the *first* item you highlighted, not the last one. Selecting **Yes** will apply the comment to all highlighted items.

To remove a comment, select an item with an existing comment, right click, and again choose **Edit Comment** from the context menu. Delete anything in the comment window and click **OK**. XWF will then ask whether you want to remove the comment. If more than one item with a comment is highlighted, XWF will ask whether you want to remove the comment from all highlighted items.

REPORT GENERATION

Now that you have added items to various RTs, it is time to generate a report of your findings. XWF reports contain up to three different sections: main, RT, and the case activity log/audit trail.

The main report (also referred to as the basic report) includes information about a case such as when the case was created, the path to the case file, the examiner, etc. It also contains information about each evidence object including the path to the image file, the date the item was added to the case, the item's hash value, physical descriptors such as the number of sectors, total capacity, image hash verification information, etc.

The RT section includes things such as file metadata, thumbnails of pictures, HTML representation of various artifacts like e-mail messages or shortcut (.lnk) files, and any other information concerning files that are in your RTs. The files themselves can be exported and accessed through links in the XWF report. Reports can be generated for any combination of RTs at various levels of detail depending on your requirements. File metadata can optionally be included as well as the information contained in any or all of the columns available in the **Directory Browser**.

To initiate the report generation process, select **File | Create Report** from the **Case Data** window as shown in Figure 8.7.

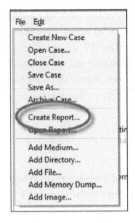

FIGURE 8.7

Create Report option.

After selecting **Create Report**, the Report options dialog is shown as in Figure 8.8.

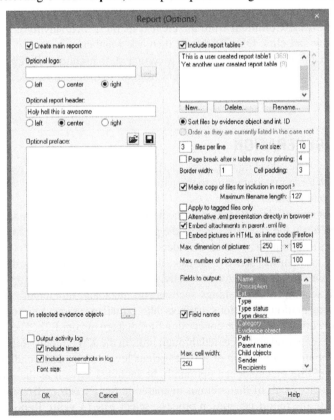

FIGURE 8.8

Report options dialog.

By default, the selected report sections will be generated across all evidence objects in a case. You can optionally include only a subset of evidence objects in a report by first checking **In selected evidence objects** and then clicking the button to the right of the option to select one or more evidence objects to include in the report.

Main report options

The main report options are found on the top two thirds of the left side of the dialog starting with **Create main report** and ending with **Optional preface**.

If **Create main report** is checked, XWF will generate and include in the report information about the case and each evidence object in the case. The main report can be customized with the remaining options.

Optional logo allows you to choose an image to be included at the very top of the report. The image will be inserted into the report without resizing the image, so ensure the selected image is appropriately sized before inserting it in your report.

The contents of **Optional report header** will be added to the report directly below the logo (if selected) using the alignment indicated.

The contents of **Optional preface** will be inserted below the report header (if a header was entered). You can optionally use HTML in the preface to customize the look of the information in the preface.

Audit trail options

Below the main report options are the options to include the case activity log in the report. The case activity log is an audit trail in that it includes all the steps you have taken in XWF related to processing evidence objects.

When **Output activity log** is checked, XWF adds a new section to the report titled *Log* that contains both text and images outlining all activities related to the operations against evidence objects as performed by a user. If the main report section is also selected, the audit trail section will be generated after the main report section. A hyperlink will be added to the top of the report that allows for quickly navigating to the *Log* section of the report. This is a handy way to later review the exact steps that were taken during the course of a review. This option also includes suboptions to allow for including or excluding timestamps and screenshots in the report.

By default, XWF will want to save the report to the case directory. If you change the path where the report will be saved and have included the activity log, you will have to manually copy the _log directory (found in the case directory) to wherever you saved the report to. If you do not do this, none of the images will show up properly in the report.

RT options

The **Include report tables** option has three values:

Fully checked: All selected RTs are included in the report.

Half-checked: Only the total number of items in each of the selected RTs is included in the report.

Unchecked: No RTs are included in the report.

In the upper right of the list containing RTs are two arrows that can be used to rearrange the order that the RTs will be added to the report. These arrows and the **New**, **Delete**, and **Rename** buttons work exactly as we saw earlier in the **Report table associations** dialog.

If **Sort files by evidence object and Int. ID** is selected, the report will be ordered first by the evidence object where each item in a RT was found and then by the value in the **Int. ID** column in the **Directory Browser**.

The **Order as they are currently listed in the case root** option is available if you first select the **Case Root** folder in the **directory tree** and recursively list one or more evidence objects. Once the recursive listing is generated, you can sort the **Directory Browser** columns on up to three different columns (refer to Chapter 3 for a refresher on how this type of sorting works).

XWF TIPS AND TRICKS

Active Directory Browser Filters Matter!

When using this option, be aware any items that are not visible in the **Directory Browser** because one or more filters are active will NOT be included in the report even if the nonvisible items are included in one or more RT associations.

Do not worry about this though as XWF will detect this situation and inform you of the number of items that were omitted from the report. If you did not mean to exclude the items from the report, adjust the active filters and regenerate the report.

The **files per line** option determines how many columns a given RT will contain. This option can be adjusted depending on the kinds of files associated with RTs. Increasing this option (up to a maximum of nine) allows you to make the report more "dense" in that each row will contain more items.

If **Page break after x table rows for printing** is checked, XWF will add explicit page breaks to the generated HTML code. This is useful to prevent RT rows from being chopped in half when a report is printed. Adjust the number of rows up or down depending on the type of items in your RTs if you need to print your reports.

The **Make copy of files for inclusion in report** has three options:

Fully checked: All files in selected RTs will be copied and included in the report.

Half-checked: Only pictures in selected RTs will be copied and included in the report.

Unchecked: No files will be copied and included in the report.

The **Maximum filename length** option sets the cutoff point for filenames XWF will use when copying files for inclusion in the report. Any filenames longer than the entered value will be truncated for purposes of linking in the report, but the report itself will reflect the actual filename as it exists in the evidence object.

Certain options below become unavailable depending on the state of **Make copy of files for inclusion in report**.

If **Apply to tagged files only** is checked, XWF will selectively export files for only those items currently tagged in the **Directory Browser**. This is useful to only copy a subset of files in one or more RTs. For example, if you added hundreds of images of child pornography to your case but only wished to include five images in your report (so as to not overwhelm the consumer of the report, the jury, etc.), tag the five images that you want to include in the report and check this option. All of the metadata about all the files in the RT will be included, but only the tagged files will have actual images associated.

The **Alternative .eml presentation directly in browser** has three options:

Fully checked: An HTML version of the e-mail message is generated and linked to in the report. Any attachments contained in the e-mail message are listed, but linked only from the main report (if also part of a RT).
Half-checked: XWF will rename plain text e-mail files to .txt and HTML-formatted e-mails to .html so that they can be viewed directly in the browser. The text file will be able to be viewed directly in the browser.
Unchecked: The e-mail message is treated like a normal file and clicking on it in the report allows you to open the .eml file in an external program such as a text editor or an e-mail client (Thunderbird, for example).

If **Embed attachments in parent .eml file** is checked, XWF will Base64-encode any attachments associated with an e-mail message and embed the encoded attachments inside the e-mail file. When checked, this option disables the **Alternate e-mail presentation directly in browser** option.

If **Embed pictures in HTML as inline code** is checked, XWF will Base64-encode any pictures and embed the encoded data directly in the HTML as opposed to exporting and linking to a physical picture file. This option can generate massive HTML files very quickly and, for this reason (and that it only works for Firefox), we recommend leaving this option unchecked.

Max. dimension of pictures determines the maximum size of thumbnail pictures in the report. If both values are set to zero, XWF will link to pictures in the main report and will not display a thumbnail. The link, when clicked, loads the full-size image. When nonzero values are used, XWF will respect the aspect ratio of pictures so as to not distort them. This option does not resize the pictures in any way. Rather, it adds HTML tags to limit the size of the thumbnail pictures in the report.

Max. number of pictures per HTML file determines how many picture files XWF will include in a single report file before creating a new one. This option prevents huge HTML files from being created that will be slow to load and sluggish to interact with as links are clicked, etc.

The **Fields to output** option allows for selecting one or more columns from the **Directory Browser** to be included in the report. To select multiple fields, hold CTRL and click field names. If **Field names** are unchecked, the name of the selected fields will not be prepended to the associated data for that field. Unless you are including only a few or obvious fields, we recommend keeping **Field names** checked.

XWF TIPS AND TRICKS

Softwares from Dan Mares

Dan Mares has written several programs that work with XWF reports. Dan's programs primarily focus on processing metadata found by XWF. You can find Dan's programs at http://www.dmares.com/maresware/tz.htm#X-WAYS.

After adjusting the reporting options to suit your needs, click the **OK** button to begin report generation. You will be prompted for a location to save your report to (the default location is the directory where the rest of the case information is saved).

A progress bar will be displayed and once the report is generated, XWF will offer to open the report for you. Clicking **OK** will open the report in your default browser. If XWF splits the report into multiple report files, the dialog box asking you to open the report will indicate this as well.

REPORT CUSTOMIZATION

Depending on the options used in the RT options section, XWF may generate more than one report file. For example, if you have RTs that contain 250 images and **Max. number of pictures per HTML file** is set to 100, XWF will generate three report files: *Report 1.html*, *Report 2.html*, and *Report 3.html*.

In this example, the top portion of *Report 1.html* will contain hyperlinks to each of the RTs contained in all of the report files. However, if any of these hyperlinks point to RTs that are contained in either *Report 2.html* or *Report 3.html*, the links will not work.

You can correct this in several ways such as using any text editor to manually edit the HTML code in the report files. You can also use Microsoft Word to edit the files. By using Word, you can visually adjust the layout of the report if you are not comfortable editing HTML directly.

The easiest way to correct this issue is to use XWFRT or X-Ways Forensics Report Tweaker (created by Eric Zimmerman).

XWFRT allows you to easily adjust the reports generated by XWF. After pointing XWFRT at the main report file, XWFRT will generate a set of wrapper HTML files to display the XWF reports in a frame.

XWFRT will then determine which RT associations are in each file and create a menu on the left side of the main index reflecting this. After this is done, opening the main index page (as opposed to one of the *Report x.html* pages) will allow you to browse all of the XWF report files at once without having to open and close separate files in your browser.

XWFRT simplifies adding things like an agency logo, your agency, a list of external files, and report narrative to your final report. Because of this, do not use the logo, report header, or the preface option in XWF when generating your initial report.

You can get XWFRT from the X-Ways Forensics forum or from http://xwaysforensics.wordpress.com/.

Each report file and subsequent RT associations in each report file will be added as menus to the left side of the main report index page that XWFRT generates.

XWFRT uses a cascading style sheet (CSS) for all the HTML files it creates. By editing the CSS, you can easily adjust the entire look and feel of the report.

SHORTCUTS

CTRL+1, . . ., CTRL+9: Associates highlighted files to the RT with the corresponding shortcut key

CTRL+0: Removes all RT associations from highlighted files

Numeric pad digits: Same as above, but without the need to use CTRL key

SUMMARY

Reporting in XWF is straightforward and simple. In this chapter, we covered how to create RTs, associate items to these RTs, and generate a report of our findings.

The reports generated by XWF are universally viewable by anyone with a Web browser and as such are very portable. XWF includes many options that allow you to adjust both the layout and contents of your reports. Because XWF reports use HTML, the reports can be customizable by anyone using various editors.

X-Ways Forensics and Criminal Investigations

INTRODUCTION

This chapter aims to cover the use of X-Ways Forensics (XWF) as it relates to criminal investigations: specifically knock and talks, search warrants, and probationary-type reviews of computers.

This chapter assumes that, prior to any activity, valid legal authority or consent has been given to officers who will examine any device. In most places, "valid legal authority" equates to either a search warrant or some kind of parole or supervised release status. A search warrant is typically authorized by a judge after probable cause has been adequately demonstrated by some law enforcement entity. Once signed, the search warrant gives law enforcement the right to search and seize relevant items as specified in the warrant. While there are exceptions to the search warrant requirement, this chapter will not address those areas of search and seizure law.

A knock and talk involves the owner of a computer consenting to the search by voluntarily waiving his or her rights. Knock and talks are usually undertaken when there is not enough probable cause to justify a search warrant. This waiver gives a government agency the authority to search property. Each jurisdiction has its own policies, procedures, and laws pertaining to consent searches, but generally the citizen must voluntarily give up his or her rights of search protections in order for a consent search to be legally valid.

Since consent searches typically occur on property controlled by the suspect, one of the most important factors in conducting a search for evidence is time. If there is reasonable suspicion that a crime has occurred or will occur and the offense involves a computer, time is of the essence to find that evidence in the event that the suspect revokes consent. XWF provides speed of searching and preview capabilities that can help find evidence quickly and easily in those circumstances. If relevant evidence is found before a subject revokes consent, the computers can be seized and further legal process obtained to continue the search.

XWF can be used in the context of a search warrant to find additional information that traditional triage tools are not capable of finding, such as deleted files or more esoteric operating system artifacts. By initially using triage tools to narrow the focus of the investigation during a search and continuing to examine relevant computers in more detail with XWF, a clear understanding of the information on the computers can be used by investigators while on scene during interviews. Unlike a consent search, time is not as critical when reviewing digital media during the service of a search warrant as the premises are under the control of law enforcement for the duration of the search.

Regarding the supervision of parolees, especially those convicted of crimes involving the use of computers, the rules are usually different. Typically, parolees waive their right to searches while on parole as a condition of their parole. With this waiver in place, parole officers have the legal authority to enter and search property including computer systems. However, the terms of the condition of release govern the scope of the search. Time is not of the essence in these cases as the parolee cannot revoke consent as he or she would be in violation of the terms of the supervised release.

In all cases, the ability to quickly and easily search for evidence is still important as it ensures law enforcement is as minimally intrusive as possible. The following sections pertain to the scenarios described above, with the only difference being the ability of someone to revoke the consent to search.

X-WAYS FORENSICS AND CRIMINAL INVESTIGATIONS

For the purposes of this case study, you have legal authority through a search warrant, consent, or a supervision order to search a computer in the home of a suspect/parolee. There is either probable cause (in the case of a search warrant) or reasonable suspicion that child pornography exists on one or more computers. The goal is to validate either probable cause or reasonable suspicion.

If for no other reason but the sake of time and efficiency, searches of computer systems should not be fishing expeditions but rather should target specific known or suspected evidence. There is simply too much data on a hard drive to justify spending time hunting and poking in hopes of finding pertinent data.

A common technique to determine which computers are more important than others involves triaging computers. The concept of triage is to separate the "wheat from the chaff" as it relates to digital information pertinent to an investigation. By triaging computers, you can quickly focus your efforts on relevant computers. For example, triage tools can quickly determine what files have been opened on a computer, what applications are installed, when applications were last executed, etc. By using this information, you can quickly hone in on the computers relevant to the investigation at hand. This technique also lets you eliminate computers that have nothing to do with your case. In short, triage techniques enable us to be minimally intrusive to both us (in terms of the amount of digital evidence that we have to review) and the subjects of the search (in that we are not taking computers that have no bearing on a particular case).

In all of the scenarios described above, a full forensic exam while on scene is not a practical use of time nor is it feasible in most cases. Although plenty of software applications are available that conduct automated searches of computers for previews, XWF allows for more customization and more granularity when it comes to searching. Additionally, if evidence is discovered during the search, XWF can immediately make note of such evidence through report table associations. In addition, we can create a forensic image of the hard drive being reviewed. As you have seen in previous chapters, all of the activity taken in XWF can be documented in an audit trail that allows you to write accurate reports related to the processing of digital media while on scene.

When a running computer is encountered, the common technique has been to simply "pull the plug" and process the computer later. With the advance in encryption technologies, such as TrueCrypt (available at http://www.truecrypt.org), we do not recommend this approach. Rather, if a suspect's computer is running, it should be examined for such things as encryption, running processes, network connections, etc., as all of this information is volatile and will be lost when power is removed. Finally, with advances in memory analysis frameworks like volatility (https://www.volatilesystems.com/default/volatility), we recommend capturing RAM when a live machine is encountered.

Conversely, if the machine is off when you approach, attempt to boot the system to a forensically sound media such as the Windows Forensics Environment (WinFE) and conduct the search in a forensic environment. Another option is to place the hard drive behind a write blocker and examine it from your laptop.

As previously discussed in the eDiscovery example from Chapter 9, XWF does not care whether it is running within a suspect's operating system or your operating system, such as booting to WinFE or using your laptop.

Prepare XWF

We recommend having XWF available on more than one device. A WinFE CD containing XWF plus an external USB hard drive that also contains XWF gives protection against one point of failure. With searches conducted onsite, an external USB hard drive is necessary to create a forensic image or copy evidence files before shutting down the computer system.

Finding evidence as quickly as possible should be a primary goal with onsite searches. Consent searches can end abruptly if the person retracts his or her consent and, if evidence has not been found, there may be no authority to seize or search further unless other facts are present. Even in the case of parole searches where having the search ended by the parolee is not a concern, time is a factor when your caseload demands searching the computers of multiple offenders over a large geographic area.

For these reasons, we recommend preparing XWF before leaving your office. As seen in Chapter 9, the XWF program files can be copied to an external USB drive and a case created without having to add evidence. Just be sure to use relative paths when

XWF is used on removable storage since you won't know what drive letter will be assigned to your device. Once onsite, evidence can be added to the preexisting case.

Once you are in front of the computer you wish to examine, plug in your external device, insert your dongle, and start XWF. There will be a minimal footprint of the XWF dongle on the system, but drivers are not installed.

XWF TIPS AND TRICKS

Don't Worry About Modifying System Data!

When using XWF on a live system, certain data will change but this is a reasonable compromise for this type of search. If you have probable cause to believe that criminal evidence exists before conducting a live search, consider creating a forensic image with write protection instead of a preview on the live machine. Remember, XWF is not making any changes to files on the system that were created by a computer user. Windows will, of course, create registry entries when USB devices are attached, but such changes can be explained easily in your report.

Adding evidence items

Add your evidence through the **File | Add Medium** menu command. XWF will see all attached storage devices so add each available object to the case. Since this example consists of an onsite preview where the time is generally important, the specific circumstances of your investigation dictate the type of evidence for which you will search. For example, in matters relating to child exploitation, you will generally search for pictures and videos, evidence of peer-to-peer programs, etc. Other crimes will have different types of relevant artifacts such as crimes involving e-mail or Internet use involving stalking.

For our example, we will focus on an investigation related to the possession of child pornography. In this scenario, we will be primarily interested in reviewing pictures and videos found on the computer. We may also be interested in data carving for these file types. Remember that data carving takes time but with XWF, you can data carve with **Refine Volume Snapshot** (RVS) and conduct a preview at the same time by starting the RVS in one instance of XWF and previewing the hard drive in another.

Once your evidence items have been added, open the RVS by pressing F10. As we already know the specific types of files that we are interested in finding, namely pictures and videos, select only these categories in the **File Header Search** options. Other RVS options may be helpful, such as **Compute hash** and **Match hash values against hash database**, if you have a hash set containing known child pornography hash values. For each additional selection in the RVS, the time to complete the process may increase. We suggest using the RVS for pictures and videos in order to quickly find evidence that previously existed.

As the RVS is processing, start a new session of XWF. Within the new session of XWF, **Explore recursively** on an evidence object and then use the **Type** filter in the **Directory Browser** (Chapter 3 covers filtering in more detail). Next, switch to

Gallery mode and XWF will generate thumbnails of the graphic files found in the evidence object. Figure 10.1 shows the gallery view of graphics. If, after reviewing the existing graphics and videos, you have not found evidence, the RVS may be near completion giving you additional files for review.

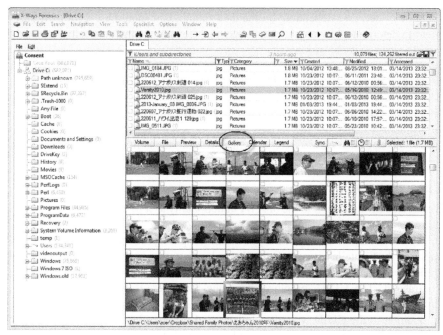

FIGURE 10.1

Gallery view of graphic files.

Depending on your legal authority (consent or search warrant for example), additional options become available once evidence is found, e.g., a probable cause arrest, seizure of digital media, another search warrant, or a violation of parole.

XWF TIPS AND TRICKS

Don't Turn Off the Computer Yet!

Prior to exiting XWF and shutting down the computer, ensure that you adequately document and preserve what you have found by using one or more report table associations and using **Recover/copy** to export any evidence that has been found. As encrypted systems become more common, you may be unable to access it again if the system is shut down and encryption is being used. By exporting relevant files and generating a report before shutdown, you ensure that you at least have the items you found during your initial search.

In the case of *United States of America v Jeffery Feldman*, the court declined an application to compel Feldman to turn over his decryption keys. This resulted in being unable to access the electronic evidence (Order Denying Application to Compel Decryption, 2013).

> Another factor to consider is whether to create an image of the system as it is running (live). For any number of reasons, imaging onsite may be a good option. If you know *or even suspect* encryption is being used, it is critical to image the logical partitions before shutting down the computer.

As a search progresses, the relevancy of the computer being examined will increase or decrease depending on the data found. You should use your own judgment to determine how much time to spend reviewing a computer before deciding whether it is or is not of interest.

If no pictures or videos are found, it may be necessary to examine additional artifacts on the computer, such as the registry, shortcut files, installed applications, etc. The quickest way to hone in on these types of files is to use **Directory Browser** filters (the **Category** filter is particularly useful in this scenario). Once a given type of artifact is located, use the various features of XWF such as **Preview** and **Details** mode, the Registry Viewer, etc., to drill down into those files.

Case scenario

To provide a more concrete use of XWF functionality as it pertains to use in the field, consider the following scenario.

You are assigned a case where you are investigating the trading of child pornography on the Gnutella network. Gnutella is a large peer-to-peer (P2P) network used to trade files. You have observed a LimeWire client with a specific identifier trading contraband. The GUID, or globally unique identifier, is what Gnutella uses to uniquely identify a client on the network. The GUID is also unique to an installation. In addition to the GUID, you also downloaded several files from the subject. You have hashed these files to generate their SHA-1 Base32-encoded hash values. A search warrant has been authorized based on your investigation to date.

After making entry and securing the scene, several computers are located in the residence. You triage each computer and find one that contains activity that pertains to the viewing of child pornography. Specifically, you locate within the registry several entries in *RecentDocs* for jpg files. The file names for these recently viewed pictures contain keywords associated with child pornography.

Having eliminated all other computers in the home based on live response information, you conduct a search for active pictures on the remaining computer, but none are located. During the search, you find indications that LimeWire is installed as well as TrueCrypt.[a]

Because no active pictures were found during triage, you decide to employ XWF to look for evidence of deleted files and other artifacts related to your case. After starting XWF and adding the hard drive to your case, explore recursively and use the **Name** column filter in the **Directory Browser** to look for the files *limewire. props*, *configuration.xml* (the configuration file for TrueCrypt), and *fileurns.cache*

---

[a]An encryption program that can encrypt an entire volume or files within an encrypted container.

(*fileurns.cache* tracks the files that may be available for downloading for a given LimeWire client). Each of the files is found on the computer.

After selecting *limewire.props* in the **Directory Browser** and switching to **Preview** mode, look for the *ClientID* key/value pair. *ClientID* contains the GUID used by the installed instance of LimeWire. You compare the GUID you have to the *ClientID* and note that they match. Right click *limewire.props* and add it to a new report table (*P2P client* for example). At this point, you know this is most likely the computer you observed earlier on the Gnutella network.

While reviewing other keys in *limewire.props*, you notice the *LAST_ FILECHOOSER_DIR* key points to the path *R:\sort* and the key *DIRECTORIES_ TO_SEARCH_FOR_FILES* points to *R:\share*. When you added the hard drive to your XWF case, you did not see an R drive. You can add this information as a comment to *limewire.props* so it can be easily referenced and included in a report later.

Recall that you also found a file named *configuration.xml* on this computer. To view the contents of this file, select it in the **Directory Browser** and make sure you are in **Preview** mode. By default, you will not see the contents of the XML document because the viewer component is rendering it. To see the document in its entirety, click the **Raw** button. As with *limewire.props*, we see several key/value pairs. In reviewing this file, you find a key named *LastSelectedDrive* with a value of *R:*. TrueCrypt uses this key to reselect the last used drive letter when mounting a TrueCrypt container.

With the information from *limewire.props* and *configuration.xml*, you now know the subject is storing his contraband inside one or more encrypted containers on his computer or other device he controls such as a thumb drive. The easiest way to find these containers is to explore recursively and then sort by the **Size** column in the **Directory Browser**. After doing this, you notice a 3 GB file buried several directories beneath the Windows directory. You add this file to a report table as well.

Now that you know encryption is being used to hide child pornography, how can you determine what is inside the encrypted container? If it was currently mounted, we can simply image the drive like we would any other partition, but in this case, the container is not mounted. Recall that you also found *fileurns.cache* during your initial search.

As mentioned above, *fileurns.cache* tracks the files made available for downloading by a Gnutella client. This file contains several pieces of information such as the full file names and hash values of files being shared. Another aspect of *fileurns.cache* is that, when LimeWire shuts down, it verifies whether each of the files listed in *fileurns.cache* exists in its entirety. If a file listed no longer exists, the entry for that file is removed from *fileurns.cache*.

After selecting *fileurns.cache* in the **Directory Browser**, switch to **File** mode. Even though *fileurns.cache* is a binary file, it contains quite a bit of plain text. In reviewing this file, you see all of the files being shared on LimeWire are found in the *R:\share* directory. You also see all of the SHA-1 values that correspond with the files that you downloaded. You observe that several of the filenames listed in *fileurns.cache* correspond with the file names you saw earlier in *RecentDocs* keys in the registry. These findings can be annotated in a comment or report table association.

Based on this information, you now know that the files that are contained inside the encrypted container as of the last time LimeWire was shut down (at least based upon the entries in *fileurns.cache*). You know when LimeWire was last shut down because the second line of *limewire.props* provides a timestamp indicating this.

To further peer inside the encryption without knowing the password, you can use the XWF Registry Viewer to open the user's *NTUSER.dat* file, generate a registry report, and look for *Shell Bag* entries. Among other things, *Shell Bags* track the file names found in directories as they are viewed in Windows Explorer. These file listings persist in the registry even when a directory is deleted or not available (as in the case with drive R). By looking at the *Shell Bags* in the registry, you will be able to see not only a complete listing of folder names but also every file contained in those folders. In addition to the file name, *Shell Bags* also track the size of the files.

Since you downloaded several files from the subject, you know the file names as well as the size of those files. You can now look through the entries for both the file names and the file sizes. By combining the information from *Shell Bags* with the information from *fileurns.cache*, you can determine exactly which files are contained inside the encrypted container.

Remember to this point we haven't even conducted a Refine Volume Snapshot operation that may reveal even more pertinent information about the case.

With this information at hand, you are better prepared for not only the initial interview with the subject but also for future legal proceedings.

The above example illustrates the power you have at your fingertips in the field when using XWF. By exploiting computers as much as possible while on scene, you greatly increase your chances of a successful initial interview. Since we typically only get one opportunity to interview a subject, it is best to make it count.

SUMMARY

XWF brings powerful triage and full forensics capabilities to the field. As data storage capacities continue to increase, it will become more and more critical to triage computers in order to determine, as quickly as possible, the computers that are relevant to your case. By leveraging XWF in the field, you will be able to find more information than traditional techniques allow.

Perhaps the most important benefit of using XWF for these types of searches is the seamless transition from field triage to a more formal forensic examination in the lab. When examining evidence objects in the field in XWF, you can add relevant items to report tables, recover files, etc. In addition, any files reviewed on scene will be remembered by XWF so you will not duplicate work in reviewing the same files more than once.

Reference

Order Denying Application to Compel Decryption, 13-M-449 (United States District Court Eastern District of Wisconsin April 19, 2013). Retrieved April 30, 2013, from http://ia601700.us.archive.org/6/items/gov.uscourts.wied.63043/gov.uscourts.wied.63043.3.0.pdf.

X-Ways Forensics Additional Information

INFORMATION IN THIS CHAPTER

- Introduction
- Online resources
- Keyboard shortcuts

INTRODUCTION

Over the past several years, there have been more resources created to support X-Ways Forensics (XWF). This book is one such example. To further the understanding and use of XWF, this appendix gives additional references for the reader to access. As the Internet is constantly changing, you may need to use a search engine to find a resource that may have had its URL changed since the printing of this book.

The second part of the appendix is a listing of keyboard shortcuts found throughout this book as well as others not mentioned. Depending upon your specific use of XWF, there may be shortcuts that you will use regularly to save time during your analysis. While you may not use all the keyboard shortcuts, we hope that at least a few will become favorites.

ONLINE RESOURCES

The number of digital forensics blogs increases regularly, but few are specific to XWF. Two of the strongest supporters of XWF, insofar as spending lots of their time maintaining blogs with updated XWF information, are Ted Smith and Jimmy Weg. For the XWF user, these two blogs should be bookmarked and consulted regularly.

X-Ways forensics video clips—http://xwaysclips.blogspot.com/

A fantastic blog dedicated to XWF using a multitude of online videos is Ted Smith's blog. Ted creates valuable videos showing specific functionality of XWF. Many of these videos complement or illustrate the information found in this book. A listing of the current videos is shown below:

- Adjusting column layout and re-ordering columns in XWF
- Hashing files of live Windows or Linux systems using a GUI

- Classifying large volumes of picture files
- Physical or Logical Disk Initialization Using WinHex
- Imaging Backwards and Selective Sector Captures.avi
- Conditional Offset Searches of Sectors
- Pausing and Reviewing the Partial Results of an XWF Simultaneous Search
- Conducting E-Mail Client Analysis Using XWF
- Reporting with XWF
- Retrieving files by file header searching (aka Carving) using XWF
- Navigating an image or disk using LBA sector numbers
- Utilizing the Hash Database Functionality of XWF
- Finding and reading Microsoft Windows Link files (LNK) using XWF
- Indexing a Case Using XWF
- Using XWF to Examine NTFS MFT Entries... with auto highlighting!
- Capturing selective files and directories using XWF and Evidence Containers
- Find, filter out, and then exclude known files using NSRL Hash Sets and XWF
- Finding Large Volumes of Black & White Files from Multiple Forensic Images
- Refining the Volume Snapshot
- Performing basic disk imaging using the E01 format
- Running multiple instances on the same workstation using the same dongle
- Setting Up Your Environment Using General Options

JustAskWeg—http://justaskweg.com/

Jimmy Weg's blog is another popular digital forensics blog that covers many topics on forensics with a strong focus on using virtual machines. However, Jimmy is one of those great examiners that use XWF on a regular basis as his primary tool. Therefore, his topics on digital forensics problems and obstacles are generally solved using his favorite tool, XWF.

Third-party software

The XWF development team provides superb support. Few companies are as quick to respond to requests, problems, or questions as X-Ways. No other forensic suite is updated as regularly as XWF when it comes to new features and improvements.

Third-party developers have begun to share their supporting software, and most are shared freely. In support of XWF and this book, two software programs have been developed: XWF Installation Manager (available through the XWF Support forum at http://www.winhex.com) and XWF Report Tweaker (available at http://xwaysforensics.wordpress.com/).

Dan Mares has created applications to support XWF as well, namely, his X-Ways Meta Processing tool (available at http://www.dmares.com/maresware/html/X-Ways_meta_processing.htm). Dan's tools process the XWF metadata fields into delimited fields to import into spreadsheets. Dan also has developed a free tool named VSS (download at http://www.dmares.com/pub/nt_32/vss.exe), which you can use within a virtual machine to examine shadow volumes (among other things).

An X-Ways X-Tension, found at http://www.gaijin.at/en/xtmultifilefinder.php, was developed to automatically find and export files of choice and add them to a report table along with a few other nice options.

KEYBOARD SHORTCUTS

Menu commands that affect individual, selected items in the **Directory Browser** or in a search hit or bookmark list can be found in the context menu that opens when you right-click such items. You will not find such commands in the main menu.

Double-clicking left	Sets the block beginning
Single-clicking right	Sets the block end
Double-clicking the right button	Clears the block
SHIFT+arrow keys or ALT+1 and ALT+2	Define the block
TAB	Switches between hexadecimal and text mode
INS	Switches between insert and overwrite mode
ENTER	Displays the Start Center
ESC	Aborts the current operation
PAUSE	Stops or continues the current operation
F11	Repeats the last Go To Offset command
CTRL+F11	Works in the opposite direction (goes back from the current position)
ALT++	Variant of Go To Offset command to jump a certain number of sectors *down*
ALT+−	Variant specifically to jump a certain number of sectors *up*
SHIFT+F7	Switches between three character sets
(SHIFT+)ALT+F11	Repeats the last Move Block command
CTRL+SHIFT+M	Invokes an open evidence object's annotations
ALT+F2	Recalculates the auto-hash after a file was modified
ALT+LEFT ALT+RIGHT	Switches between records within a template
ALT+HOME and ALT+END	Access the first and the last record, respectively
ALT+G	Moves the cursor in the edit window to the current template position and closes the template window
CTRL+F9	Opens the Access button menu (disk edit windows only)

Shortcuts and commands under "File"

Ctrl+N	Create New file
Ctrl+O	Open Files
Ctrl+S	Save Sectors
Alt+C	Create Disk Image
F12	Backup Manager
Alt+Enter	Properties
Ctrl++	Open Directory
Alt+F4	Exit
Ctrl+E	Execute
Ctrl+P	Print
	Restore Image
	Save Modified Files
	Save All Files
	Save As

Shortcuts under Edit

Ctrl+Z	Undo
Ctrl+X	Cut
Ctrl+A	Select All
Del	Remove
Esc	Clear Block
Ctrl+T	Modify Data
Ctrl+L	Fill Disk Sectors
	Define Block

Shortcuts under Edit | Copy Sector

Ctrl+C	Normally
Ctrl+Shift+N	Into New File
Ctrl+Shift+C	Hex Values
Ctrl+Shift+C	Editor Display
	GREP Hex
	C Source
	Pascal Source

Shortcuts under Edit | Clipboard Data

Ctrl+V	Paste
Ctrl+B	Write
Shift+Ins	Paste Into New File
	Empty Clipboard

[H2] Shortcuts under Search

Alt+F10	Simultaneous Search
Ctrl+Alt+I	Indexing
Ctrl+Alt+F	Search in Index
Ctrl+F	Find Text
Ctrl+Alt+X	Find Hex Values
Ctrl+H	Replace Text
Ctrl+Alt+H	Replace Hex Values
F4	Continue Global Search
F3	Continue Search
	Optimize Index
	Export Word List
	Combined Search
	Integer Value
	Floating-Point Value
	Text Passages

Shortcuts under Navigation

Alt+G	Go To Offset
Ctrl+G	Go To Sector
Alt+F11	Move Block
Ctrl+Left	Back
Ctrl+Right	Forward
Ctrl+I	Mark Position
Ctrl+K	Go To Marker
Ctrl+M	Position Manager
	Delete Marker

Shortcuts under Navigation I Go To

Ctrl+Home	Beginning Of File
Ctrl+End	End Of File
Alt+Ctl+Home	Beginning of Block
Alt+Ctrl+End	End Of Block
Alt+Home	Beginning of Page
Alt+End	End Of Page
Home	Beginning Of Line
End	End Of Line

Shortcuts under View

F7	Text Display Only
Alt+F7	Hex Display Only
Alt+F12	Template Manager

Shortcuts under Tools

F9	Open Disk
Shift+F9	View
Alt+F8	Calculator
F8	Hex Converter
F2	Analyze Disk
Ctrl+F2	Compute Hash
Enter	Start Center
	Run X-Tensions

Shortcuts under Tools I Disk Tools

Ctrl+D	Clone Disk
	Explore recursively
	Take New Volume Snapshot
	Set Disk Parameters

Shortcuts under Tools I File Tools

Alt+K	Concatenate
Alt+Z	Split
	Compare
	Create Hard Link
	Delete Recursively

Shortcuts under Specialist

F10	Refine Volume Snapshot
Ctrl+F10	Gather Text
	Technical Details Report
	Reconstruct RAID System
	Evidence File Container
	External Virus Check
	Bates Number Files
	Trusted Download
	Highlight Free Space

Shortcuts under Specialist | Evidence File Container

	New
	Open
	Close
	Description
	Deactivate hidden items

Shortcuts under Options

F5	General
Ctrl+F5	Directory Browser
Shift+F5	Viewer Programs
Alt+F5	Data Interpreter
F6	Edit Mode
	Volume snapshot
	Undo
	Security

Shortcuts under Window

Ctrl+W	Close
Ctrl+Q	Close All
	Window Manager
	Save Arrangement As Project
	Close All Without Prompting
	Cascade
	Tile Horizontally
	Tile Vertically
	Minimize All
	Arrange Icons

X-Ways Forensics How to's

INFORMATION IN THIS CHAPTER

• Frequently asked questions and more XWF tips

FREQUENTLY ASKED QUESTIONS AND MORE XWF TIPS

This appendix contains small "how-to's" or recipes that can be used in X-Ways Forensics (XWF) to quickly accomplish a task. Although some questions could be related to other questions, they each stand on its own as one question and one answer. These "how-tos" refer to information in this book and give more than a few new methods of using XWF specific to the type of question asked.

How can I find encrypted containers?

The easiest way to find encrypted containers in XWF is to view the case recursively, sort by the **Size** column, and then look for the largest files in the case. While you can create small containers that are only a few megabytes in size, these are of limited use. Using this method, you can quickly find possible encrypted containers in a few minutes.

Can I search slack space while eliminating logical file contents?

This involves two steps. First, use the **Directory Browser** filters to only show the file types you know do not contain your search term (video files, for example). **Explore recursively**, select all the files in the **Directory Browser**, and then hide them via the **Hide** menu item in the **Directory Browser**'s context menu.

Next, press **ALT+F10** to bring up **Simultaneous Search** and enter your search terms. Make sure that **Open and search files incl. slack** is fully checked as this will ensure that the slack space is checked while omitting the logical contents of all hidden files.

Once your search is complete you can unhide the files from step one via the **Directory Browser Options, Filters | Unhide all** button.

I want to list files so that parent files precede its child objects. Is this possible?

Make sure that **Directory Browser Options, Filters | Full path sorting for parent objects** is fully checked and then sort by the **Path** column.

I need to recursively list two directories at once. What is the easiest way?

The easiest way to do this is to use the **Path** filter. Enter the directories you want to look at recursively and then explore recursively against the evidence objects that contain those directories.

You can also add the directories to a container, add the container to your case, and explore the entire thing recursively.

Another method would be to hide all directories you don't want to explore, leaving only the directories of interest to recursively view.

How can I export a recursive file listing?

In the **Case Root** node, right-click and select the evidence objects to include in the listing. If you want to specifically order the items in the list, sort one or more columns in the **Directory Browser**. Select all the files in the **Directory Browser** via **CTRL-A** and right-click and choose **Export list**. Select the fields to include as well as the format and click **OK**.

Is it possible to conduct a keyword search on cell phone evidence?

XWF is not a cell phone analysis tool; however, XWF can open an image of a cell phone. Once the image is opened, searches can be run just as with any electronic media, yet XWF will typically be faster and can search for all phone numbers at once (some tools may only allow one keyword to be searched at a time).

How can I import Base32-encoded SHA-1 hashes?

The process to import Base32-encoded hashes is no different than importing hexadecimal encoded SHA-1 or MD5 values. The first line of the file should be SHA-1 and then enter one Base32-encoded hash per line. As XWF imports the hashes, it will convert them to hexadecimal encoding and then store them. To display the hashes in Base32 format, check **Directory Browser Options, Filters | Display SHA-1 hashes in Base32**.

How can I export a search hit list?

Switch to **Search Hit List** by clicking the appropriate mode button. Select the terms to export in the **Search Term List** in the lower left corner. Select **Export list** from the context menu in the **Search Term List**. You can now copy the search terms with the number of hits from the **Messages** window.

I need to export search hits. Where in XWF can I do this?

Switch to **Search Hit List** by clicking the appropriate mode button. Select the search hits you wish to export, right-click, and select **Export list**. Select the *Search hits* field to include the context where the search hit was found.

Can XWF generate a registry report for every hive in a case?

Explore recursively across the evidence objects you wish to include in the report. Use the **Category** column in the **Directory Browser** and select *Windows Registry* from the list. Select all of the registry hives by pressing **CTRL-A**, right-click, and choose **View** from the context menu. After all of the hives are loaded, right-click anywhere on the left side of the Registry Viewer, select **Create Report**, and finally, choose all of the Reg Report files you want to include. A single HTML file will be produced containing all of the data from every hive open in the Registry Viewer.

What if I need to reprocess items from an evidence object? How can I do this in XWF?

As new versions of XWF are released you may wish to reprocess certain files with the latest version that contains added functionality for a particular file. Rather than taking a new volume snapshot, select the files you wish to reprocess and then press **CTRL+DEL** to effectively "reset" the selected files. Finally, right-click the selected files and choose **Refine Volume Snapshot** from the **Directory Browser**'s context menu.

How do I verify the hash of an image?

Right-click the evidence object in the **Case Data** window and select **Properties**, then click **Verify Hash**. Once the hash is calculated, it will be appended to the bottom of the **Description** property.

How can I find which volume shadow copy a file came from?

The **Find related file** option found in the context menu of the **Directory Browser** causes the **Directory Browser** to jump to any files that XWF has determined are related to the selected file. Examples where you will see this option are when looking at files with hard links or for files found in volume shadow copies (VSC). In the case of a file found inside of a VSC, using this option causes the VSC host file to be selected (i.e., where the new file was found). When working with VSCs you can find the corresponding snapshot properties file by repeating the process with the VSC file selected. Rather than using the context menu item, you can also use the **SHIFT+Backspace** shortcut to achieve the same thing.

I want to tag every item in an evidence object. How can I do this and how can I untag if needed?

Middle click the **Case Root** node in the **Case Data** window.

I can't find files that I know I tagged! What happened to the files?

It is possible that the files are hidden from view. Open the **Directory Browser Options, Filters** (CTRL+F5) to see if you have **List tagged items** unchecked. You should also check if you have filtered the files through the **Type** or other filtering criteria in the **Directory Browser**. You may have also hidden these files, so be sure to check **List hidden items** in the **Directory Browser Options, Filters** to determine if you hid the files.

There are so many files I see that I know are duplicates, but I can't find how to hide them. How can I hide all duplicates?

Use the **Hide | Duplicates in directory browser based on hash** command to hide the duplicates. Only one file will be shown for each identical hash value.

How can I find and export all e-mail addresses from an image?

You can write a GREP expression (or use one from the manual) to search for all e-mail addresses. After the search has completed, export the search hits.

I just need to copy active files from a custodian's machine and don't need a forensic analysis. Do I have to take a refined snapshot?

Not at all. If the goal is copying active files, once you add evidence to XWF, select the files for export. However, taking a refined snapshot of only the files to be copied will give you more information (metadata) that may be useful in your case. And of course, consider creating an X-Ways container to preserve the files first.

I want to use XWF as a consent search application. Should I run it from an external device on a live machine or should I use a traditional method like using a physical write blocker?

It depends. If the evidence machine is already on, it is probably more reasonable to execute XWF from an external drive in case encryption is present. If the machine is off, it is probably more reasonable to protect the drive through a write blocker or a forensic boot system like Windows FE.

There are some things XWF does not do that I would like it to do. Will XWF update to what my needs are?

There is good news and better news. A month hardly goes by before there are several updates and improvements to XWF. Any of these might be the improvements you want. If not, at any time you can submit features as a wish list through the XWF support forum at http://www.winhex.net. All requests are considered and you never know your request could be one of the best ideas!

There are a lot of features and options available in XWF. Am I expected to know where everything is?

You are right; there are many features available in XWF and getting to know most of them will take time. As you gain experience using XWF, you will start using many features and functions on a regular basis. For other options you use less frequently you can refer to this guide, the manual, or the XWF support forum. There are some functions that you may use constantly in cases and we suggest learning the shortcuts for those functions. This is a great time saving feature.

I have been using so many filters and hiding files that I don't remember which files I am hiding or able to view. Can I just reset everything?

The filtering feature of XWF is extremely powerful and may be overwhelming at first. If you ever feel lost and don't know what files have been hidden from view, simply deactivate all filters and unhide all files. You can start fresh and filter/hide files again as needed. You can remove all filters at once by clicking the filter icon in the caption line of the **Directory Browser** and unhide files in the **Directory Browser Options, Filters** dialog.

I want to use WinHex and XWF but I want to be sure that I do not edit evidence by mistake. Since the two programs look the same, how can I tell them apart?

Easy. The application title bar (very top left corner of the application) will show the program's name.

Index

Note: Page numbers followed by *f* indicate figures and *t* indicate tables.

Printed and bound by CPI Group (UK) Ltd, Croydon, CR0 4YY

03/10/2024

01040324-0011